polka

happiness

In the Visual Studies series, edited by Douglas Harper

Ronald Silvers, *A Pause on the Path* (1988)

Builder Levy, *Images of Appalachian Coalfields* (1989)

Richard Quinney, *Journey to a Far Place: Autobiographical Reflections* (1991)

Glenn Busch, *You Are My Darling Zita* (1991)

Melody D. Davis, *The Male Nude in Contemporary Photography* (1991)

David Heiden, *Dust to Dust: A Doctor's View of Famine in Africa* (1992)

Charles Keil and Angeliki V. Keil
With photographs by Dick Blau

polka
happiness

Temple University Press
Philadelphia

Temple University Press, Philadelphia 19122
Copyright © 1992 by Charles Keil, Angeliki V. Keil, and Dick Blau
All rights reserved
Published 1992
Printed in the United States of America

The paper used in this publication meets the minimum
requirements of American National Standard for Information
Sciences—Permanence of Paper for Printed Library Materials,
ANSI Z39.48-1984 ∞

Library of Congress Cataloging-in-Publication Data

Keil, Charles.
    Polka happiness / Charles Keil and Angeliki V. Keil:
with photographs by Dick Blau.
        p.   cm. — (Visual studies)
    Includes bibliographical references and index.
    ISBN 0-87722-819-1 (alk. paper)
    1. Polka (Dance)—History.   2. Dancing—Social aspects—
United States—History.   3. United States—Popular culture—
History.   I. Keil, Angeliki V., 1936–   .   II. Title.   III. Series.
GV1796.P55K45   1992
793.3′3—dc20   91-45224

Photo on pp. iv–v: Alan Krupski and friend, Milwaukee, 1976.

Contents

Preface

We began this book some twenty years ago. Charlie, Angie, and I were neighbors and colleagues at the time, living in Buffalo, where we had gone to help start the Program in American Studies at the State University of New York.

I remember Charlie coming back one night after having gone to his first polka dance. An ethnomusicologist with an interest in music as a means of cultural survival, Charlie had worked in black America (*Urban Blues*) and black Africa (*Tiv Song*), and he had been saying for some time that he wanted to study polka music, but no one had thought he was serious. While black culture was thought to be cool, the culture of the white ethnic working class was thought to be corny. Fancy our surprise, then, when Charlie came back with tales of a "honky" music that wailed out its own hot version of what African-Americans call soul. It suddenly seemed like a good idea to learn a little more about the people of Buffalo among whom we lived.

Angie was also a music lover; she had compiled a life of Markos Vamvakaris, founder of the Greek "laika" tradition.[1] Angie and I went with Charlie to a polka dance the very next week. It couldn't have been a better introduction. Finding our way to a church hall behind Saint Michael's in Lackawanna, New York, we stumbled upon the very soul of honky or Chicago-style polka: Li'l Wally Jagiello himself, playing his heart out, with five hundred people in transports of joy.

I was a photographer with an interest in theater, making psychological portraits in the intimate, modernist style of Chekhov, Strindberg, and Beckett. Here I found another kind of theater—popular, participatory—that clearly demanded a different kind of photography, one that could enjoy the boisterous carnival Charlie had come upon just a mile down Fillmore Avenue from where we lived.

So we joined up. There were two fan clubs in Buffalo at the time: the Eddie Blazonczyk Fan Club and the Buffalo Polka Boosters. We'd go to meetings and dances, ask dumb questions (there was nothing to read on the subject), and follow the music wherever it led. We scoured the Rust Belt: New York, Pennsylvania, Connecticut, Ohio, Michigan, Illinois, and Wisconsin, with stops in Florida and Poland for good measure. It took us twenty years.

You will hear our different voices in this book. Charlie, who is himself a musician, had particular interest in the development of polka styles and the actual making of the music; he wrote the history and the bulk of the Milwaukee and Buffalo chapters. Angie, whose concerns ranged from the organizational impulse behind the scene to the dynamics of the polka event itself, wrote the IPA chapters as well as the piece on the Assumption Community Hall dance.

I edited the Li'l Wally section (based on a twenty-seven-hour interview by Charlie) and wrote the story of the Julida Boys, but my real contribution is not the writing. The majority of the photographs are mine, my picture of the party and its performers, musicians and fans alike. Wanting to include views from within the culture, I also gathered historical and contextual imagery as a kind of visual equivalent to the oral histories and interviews. Yet I still consider this a book of my photographs, shown not in isolation but amid the swirl of images produced by polka culture.

Charlie, Angie, and I; history, stories, analysis, talk; engravings, snapshots, album covers, portraits: all these voices, words, and pictures to tell of the polka that can't be here.

Dick Blau

Acknowledgments

The three of us have talked and polka-partied with so many people over the years that it is hard to know where to begin to say thanks for help, inspiration, and hospitality. We are grateful to all the people we talk about or whose words are used in this book, but there are many others not named who shaped our understanding in countless ways.

A remarkable student, Lynn Kreuzer, got us started by reporting on Roman and Richard, the tango-playing duo from Toronto at the Polish Village in Buffalo. We met the encyclopedic disc jockey Stan Sluberski there, and it was the beginning of his unceasing efforts to orient and educate us. In the 1970s the live polka bands at the Warsaw Inn across the street from the Village and at Chopin's Singing Society headquarters around the corner on Kosciuszko Street were a revelation. In their music and in conversations between sets the Dyna-Tones, Krew Brothers, G-Notes, Happy Richie and the Royalaires, Modernaires, Polecats, Silvertones—all the bands and their fans shared their feelings, opinions, and facts of life, pleasantly bemused that some "university professors" had finally had the good sense to show some interest in their world.

The couples who promoted dances and led booster clubs in the mid-1970s soon became our informal teachers. The late Carrie and Stan Lewandowski were at the center of a group of dedicated polka lovers who kept the Eddie Blazonczyk and the Versatones Fan Club of Greater Buffalo going; Shirley and Wally Czaska promoted the polka independently with the help of their large family; Emily and the late Ray Boruszewski presided over the Polka Boosters; and they all gave us every possible sort of cooperation and support.

Polka Joe Polakiewicz and his wife Rose, Donna Loomis and her mother Rose Loomis, Estelle Orzechowski and Mr. and Mrs. Joseph Trojak spent time talking to us about their love of the polka, its place in their lives, and their memories of the Buffalo Polonia of their youth. Bill and Josie Barnas invited Charlie Keil to their wedding and permitted him to photograph it. As we joined the polka clubs, our fellow members shared their scrapbooks and their memories with us. Although we cannot list all their names, we want to say that these are the very people we have had on our minds as we worked toward our goal of producing the first polka book.

Daniel Kij of the Polish Union of America helped us locate literature, photographs, and people to interview, and he was a storehouse of Polonia knowledge himself. Joe Macielag lent us his scrapbooks and was always ready with information on the "Eastern style."

The whole Grzankowski family—Greg, Jimmy, Doreen, Victoria, and Mr. Edwin himself—at Edwin's Music Store connected us to a tradition of providing more musical empowerment to people, especially children, than could ever be paid for in mere money.

For decades Henry C. "Skippy" Spychaj, with the cheerful support of his wife, Alicia M., has been making, repairing, and recycling drums for everyone in Buffalo; playing in bands and giving lessons; and demonstrating daily what can be done with patience, skill, and spare parts. He stands for the many craftspeople who are part of the hidden polka infrastructure.

To the new generation of Polonian scholars such as Bill Falkowski (a.k.a. Dziki Bill), Kate Koperski, Kyle and Mark Kohan, who understood our interest and carried their own studies of Polonia to levels from which we can learn, we owe thanks for intellectual companionship and inspiration.

Connecticut bandleader Johnny Prytko sent us outlines of an early polka seminar he conducted and copies of interviews with Ray Henry and Joe Lazarz that helped shape our view of polka history. Johnny Huber in Bristol, Connecticut, had a basement full of 78 records and a machine to play them on.

Drummer Nick Timko from the Binghamton, New York, area sent in a thorough analysis of polka tempo measurements proving that major differences in Eastern and Chicago styles are matters of phrasing and articulation more than of speed or tempo. One of these days his findings and those of Larry Trojak may become the basis of a theoretical article on tempo.

When Michael Nowak was at the Rockefeller Foundation, we received a grant for research during the summer of 1975. His good advice was to do a little book quickly, but we were already lost in the many polka places, times, and movements that had never been studied and needed to be understood. This Rockefeller Foundation support was the only financial aid we received for our research, and we are very grateful.

Early in our study Dick Wentworth and Judith McCulloh at the University of Illinois Press gave us encouragement when it was needed.

Paul Buhle took the time to piece together the Keils' early writings and presentations to make up an article for his journal, *Cultural Correspondence*. And R. Crumb's response to that article inspired some happy, snappy polka correspondence with R. over the years.

Richard Spottswood gave an earlier (and much larger) manuscript a very loving and careful reading that helped clear up a number of errors, as did Leon Kozicki's and Chet Schafer's careful readings of early drafts of the IPA chapters.

Jim Griffiths in Tucson was a great help during various phases of our historical and comparative work; later he helped get the Joaquin Brothers to Buffalo for a Polka Pow-wow.

We thank the Krolikowski family of Bridgeport, Connecticut, especially Gloria, for supplying photographs and information as needed.

We thank the Ciesielski sisters of Buffalo, New York, for providing pictures and access to their father's great collection of musical scores and magazines.

Special thanks go to Les Blank, Maureen Gosling, and their associates at Flower Films for responding to polka generosity with their film on the polka, *In Heaven There Is No Beer*, a great audiovisual introduction to the world of the polka.

A particular debt of thanks goes to Jerry Halkoski, musician, DJ, and historian, whose Pod Nogi Polka Hour on Milwaukee's excellent WYMS is a constant source of pleasure. Jerry's own deep interest in the field and his selfless generosity and encouragement have been very important to us. The knowledgeable Jim Ebner, who hosts the Blue Chip Polka Show, also on WYMS, has been another great source of help.

In Chicago, bandleaders George Stevens, Lenny Gomulka, and Al Jelinek, along with promoter Johnny Hyzny, were instrumental in our learning firsthand about the Chicago polka scene. Gene Wozniak of the IPA was particularly kind, and Dominic Pacyga, historian of Chicago's Polonia, showed Dick Blau the North and South Sides one sunny cold day, turning up hot leads everywhere.

Among Milwaukee musicians, thanks are due to Jimmy Maupin, Louie Bashell, Jeff Winard, and especially Loren Kohel; they, along with the inspirational Frank Yankovic, provided entry into the world of Slovenian-style polka.

At the University of Wisconsin, Milwaukee, Dick's colleague Michael J. Mikos threw open his extensive library to us, and Donald Pienkos, another colleague, drew not only on his understanding of Polish-American history but on his own youth as a polka musician to help us understand polka styles and scenes.

Among many persons of great help in our research and manuscript preparation, there is first and foremost Mary Yelanjian, whose work in picture research for the book was of the highest order. Dot Conrad must have typed the manuscript five times over, juggling versions with great skill and endless good humor. Char Johnson proved to be a fine and gentle reader of the manuscript. Without Marge Bjornstad of the University of Wisconsin, Milwaukee, Graduate School, who found space on a crowded campus for the darkroom in which many of these pictures were made, the task would have been much more difficult.

For further assistance in graphic matters, we thank Tom Bamberger and Steve Foster for the inspiration of their own work and the insight they brought to these pictures; Ken Hanson for generously offering his immense facility—and facilities—as a graphic designer when we worked through the early versions of the project; Milton Rogovin, who early on allowed Dick to sit in while he worked his magic in the darkroom; and Jane Gallop for friendship and more.

The photographic work of *Polka Happiness* was funded by the Wisconsin Arts Board, the Milwaukee Artist's Foundation, the University of Wisconsin System Committee on Ethnic Studies, and the Focus/Infinity Fund. Their help is greatly appreciated.

Finally, for permission to publish material under copyright, we thank all those listed in the credit lines shown in the Permissions section of this book.

polka
happiness

Trumpeter, Buffalo, c. 1972.

Introduction

What happiness can compare with the shared joy of dancing to music that at every instant announces its unique community of feeling?[1] This is our music and our dance. We are in and of it. The whole world spins around this moment.

Polka aficionados have cultivated a ritual sense of present time in which individual freedom of expression and maximum sociability reinforce each other. The polka dancer steps outside daily routine and everyday cares to move in complicated communion with music, a partner, and a revolving group of dancers, all at the center of a long and evolving tradition that has been sustained by generations of polka dancers in a specific community. Probably all dancing "in the tradition" delivers such happiness, but in the middle of the twentieth century it has taken extraordinary efforts to keep polka alive, and even greater energies will be required to sustain it in the future.

The documentation of polka in North America, long overdue, might contribute something important to the effort to sustain polka happiness. Slavic polkas (Polish-American and Slovenian-American), Germanic polkas (German-American and Czech-Bohemian-American), and southwestern polkas (Mexican-American and Papago-Pima) have all existed in the Americas for over a century. Since the late 1920s these six styles—and we may have missed some—have come to define a certain persistent quality of ethnic working-class identity. People who still polka in the 1990s must not care much about what fashionable people think of them because in the wider society "polka" has long been a symbol of the "corny, dated, two-beat, and square." So these six styles of hyphenated American expression within three broad polka streams represent at least a hundred years of resistance to the melting pot, a refusal to disappear into mediated entertainment, a "no" to monoculture, and an ongoing vernacular alternative to the sorts of fun manufactured and sold by the culture industry.

Of course, polka people partake of the assortment of commercial entertainments available to society at large, but they also insist on something more. Back in 1971, when we first asked Scrubby Seweryniak, singer and concertina player with Buffalo's Dyna-Tones, what

made the 500 to 1,000 polka fans who often come out to dance different from the other 300,000 Polish-Americans in western New York, he replied quickly, "We're crazier!" Twenty years later Scrubby gives the same answer, and we still don't know exactly what he means. Why do some people want to stomp and spin together on weekends in an ethnic working-class idiom while most don't? What does a polka party do that a rock concert or discotheque cannot? Why do some people prefer live music to recorded music? There are no easy answers to these related questions, but the people who make a continuation of polka happiness possible and who have talked with us as we developed this book have given us a lot to think about.

This book traces our explorations of the Slavic stream of polka happiness, concentrating on Polish-American polkas in Buffalo and Chicago but including a comparative chapter on Slovenian-American style in Milwaukee. Over the years we have attended dances, gone to booster club meetings, and traveled to national and regional conventions. We've interviewed musicians, promoters, disc jockeys, and fans and consulted community publications and leaders to learn about Polonia, as Polish-Americans call their community.

There was no polka scholarship to draw on when we started. What we have assembled here is just a beginning because polka happiness is first and last a local phenomenon, and we don't know what is happening in most Polish-American communities, not to mention all the many contexts for other styles of polka. Every urban Polonia and every Polish-American polka belt (such as the Connecticut River valley or the Pennsylvania-Ohio border area) evolves a different music in response to local history, personalities, economic conditions, and the particular mosaic of ethnic working-class neighborhoods that promotes some kinds of cultural borrowings and antagonisms but not others. Each polka locality could be the subject of volumes of reporting and analysis; we have concentrated on the communities we know best and hope others will do likewise.

Dancers at IPA Festival, Rosemont, Illinois, 1991.

Wanda and Stephanie, "America's Polka Sweethearts," Erie, Pennsylvania, c. 1973.

The Polka Party

Festive release in a social whirl of music-dance-drink-food-humor-conversation is a residue from societies in which social class distinctions were not made and is probably part of our human nature. Where else does the "will to party" come from? And the best news is that, given the concept of "ritual happiness" successfully maintained and honored over the centuries in the practices of a particular group, this need is easily satisfied. In some communities a family and a few friends with a small budget can rent a storefront, find someone willing to preach, and open a "Church of the Living God." Similarly, the secular rite of polka requires simply a designated time and place, a group of people working toward making it a success, and a live band that performs above a certain minimum level of expertise in order to set people dancing, drinking, partying without any big fights or conflicts. The result is some measure of "polka happiness."

Whatever the style, every polka event is built by polka people.[2] The wedding is perhaps the prototype: find and rent a hall; buy booze; pick the band or bands and set a day when they are available; send out invitations (or, for a dance, put up posters, pass out slingers, sell tickets); and make sure that all the tasks of preparation are spread evenly yet done so well that everyone can be equally happy on that happy day. Similarly, the time, energy, and volunteer labor required to produce

a parish dance or a lawn fete or a booster club monthly "meeting" are considerable, and the return on this investment is carefully measured by everyone in terms of the number of people who come and how good a time they have.

In fact, this calculation is as aesthetic as it is economic. Since the highest goal is happiness for the greatest number, and not profit, anything that contributes to keeping the cost of tickets low and the price of drinks down is a plus. Big summer events under a tent when a dozen of the better bands agree to donate their services or play for small fees are the high point of the season, pointed to with pride by everyone because so many people attend and pay so little for so much fun. These criteria are applied to all polka events.

Other values linked to this ideal are explicit or implicit in the many features that make a polka fest such a joy. For brevity's sake, we'll list some of these features:

All ages participate.

Everyone dances.

Although the spinning and stomping can become very intense and although the floor is full, people rarely bump into each other.

Coupling is not at a premium.

A new partner for every dance is the ideal.

Women dance with women a lot.

Festival of bands, Glendora House, Chicago Ridge, Illinois, 1988.

Some of the best musicians are also some of the best dancers.

All the younger musicians enjoy dancing. Many musicians can play two or three different instruments, and a few can play all the instruments in the band.

All musicians hold jobs in addition to their polka work.

Songs for the band repertoire are often suggested by fans, and in most bands all members contribute to the composing and arranging process.

Dancing feet, Johnny Hyzny's Personality Lounge, Chicago, 1987.

Each band has an "English book" with a mix of popular hits that emphasize "country and western" or "soul" or "50s rock" or "Glenn Miller songs," depending on the band.

Bands try to answer every request.

Almost every song is dedicated to someone or to whole families or "tables," "going out" either from the band or from one participant to another via the band.

Sexual teasing and joking and open flirting at polka dances have a "fun for the whole family" feeling.

There is wide tolerance for different styles of clothing, hair, demeanor.

Individual dancing styles and distinctive dancing couples are very much appreciated.

Birthdays are always announced by the band and the song is sung. Anniversaries, weddings, engagements are also noted. No one's life cycle event is neglected.

IPA Festival, Milwaukee, 1976. *Left to right:* Tom Mrozinski, Pete Mrozinski, Jr., Mitch Biskup, Jim Plattes, Jerry Zelazny, Roger Lichwala, Jan Cyman, Doug Sparks.

IPA Festival, Rosemont, Illinois, 1991.

IPA Festival, Milwaukee, 1976.

Musicians are not stars or sex symbols but are expected to be "regular," part of the crowd, to play until they are exhausted.

Everyone should drink a lot (eat some too) to get silly or happy but not to get drunk.

There should be "no fights."

Did everyone have a good time?

Polka Paradoxes

Polka may seem to be a simple pleasure, but polka culture is not simple. The following overlapping, paradoxical statements hint at the complexity of the polka story:

Polka is a global style that can exist only locally.

Polka is a modern urban style that enables traditional cultures to persist.

Polka becomes more important to the community as community support for it declines.

Once the polka became a craze in Paris and London during the spring of 1844, it diffused rapidly to the rest of the world. It is fascinating to discover the ways in which polka has adapted uniquely to each local niche and then evolved successfully for over a century. How does something that starts as a Parisian fashion

Cartoon from *Punch*, 1844.

become a "roots" music, a people's music? Why isn't polka displaced in each locality by the next international fashion or the fashion after that? Cakewalks, foxtrots, tangos, mambos, merengues, and lambadas may come and go, but the Papago-Pima in Tucson and the Celebes Islanders in Indonesia, as well as Polish-Americans in Buffalo, Chicago, and Connecticut, still dance the polka. Why? Perhaps it has something to do with the historical moment at which a particular people takes a stance in relation to the dominating world economy. The polka became the national dance of Paraguay because Paraguay was becoming an independent nation just after the polka fashion arrived from Paris and London in the 1840s. "Polka bands" were invented by

9   Introduction

Polish-Americans toward the end of the economically booming 1920s as second-generation immigrants came of age and decided to stay in America. We speculate that some similar amalgam of historical forces and fashion was formative for all the other polka-partying peoples of the world.

Part of the explanation for the polka's persistence in any locality is that it is an urban dance, a couple dance, and modern in relation to the gender division in dancing that prevailed in most traditional cultures around the world and in Europe until the end of the eighteenth century. Once a community has one basic couple dance, it doesn't need another, or subsequent fashions in couple dancing will be seen as possible supplements but not replacements. It is almost as if having one urban style immunizes a people to the danger of being swept up in the next Paris fashion that comes along. But more important, the polka as a style can be built upon and expanded as necessary, just as any living tradition serves to keep people in tune with one another by including whatever is novel and interesting to that community.

When we first started going to dances in Buffalo's Polonia in the early 1970s, most bands would include a twist number (either by itself or as part of a 1950s rock medley), just as they would do at least one rhinelander (borrowed from nineteenth-century German neighbors) during the evening. It wasn't part of a twist revival but rather part of a collection, one of the dances that the people in this community had experienced and were maintaining. We also saw people doing what is called "polka-twist," a polka with a hip-shimmy in it. This exemplifies the power of the polka as an urban style to feed on other urban styles—as well as rural music and dance resources that came before it—and to take in new influences as they come along. Polka persists as a modern, urban couple dance because it embodies a style that is not too esoteric and can be understood by other urbanites as an identity marker, a presentation of cultural self—even if that presentation is often used by outsiders as a caricature or exaggeration of what it means to be Polish-American.

Because having a polka style and being polka people is understood by both insiders and outsiders as stand-ing for "ethnicity" or "working-class ethnicity," the symbolic weight of the polka within a community increases even as the community itself disperses to the suburbs and takes up normative middle-class American lifestyles, even as the per capita energy put into polka parties declines. Polish-Americans who are opposed to the rites of polka happiness as "bad for our image," "part of the beer and bowling stereotype," "causing the Polish jokes," are giving energy and importance to the polka as they attack it. As attendance at an annual parish dance declines year by year, those who do come out for it can see and hear more clearly what it is that they might lose. Every loss in the struggle for polka happiness makes the remaining polka party delights more precious, more symbolic, a distillation that stands for all the bigger parties of the past. The steady decline and dispersal of once tightly integrated face-to-face neighborhood communities empowers the polka as a living echo of that social coherence. And any polka heard on the radio today has great resonance for those who danced it through the roaring twenties, the depression thirties, the war years, and the postwar boom and who associate that special sound with the whole historical sweep of American Polonia. The big question central to polka's survival is this: can the echo of that social coherence, the resonance with all eras of Polish-American history, be transmitted to youth raised on television?

Polka Origins and Diffusion

Do a little research in the library reference shelves on the origins of the polka, and soon you will come upon one version or another of the story that a Czech servant girl invented the polka back in the 1830s: a local schoolmaster is said to have observed her song and dance; he wrote down the tune, and the first polka was born. From one encyclopedia to another, the name of the servant girl changes and the name of the town also. What originally appeared a historical account of a true beginning enters the realm of myth. In this origin myth we may also have a charter for later polka developments. The story fits well the major outline

"Montesquieu. A Lively Polka." After a lithograph by Vernier.

Cartoon from *Punch*, 1845.

of what we know. No specific peasant dance is a polka antecedent; from the very beginning the polka has been an urban style. Women play a prominent role in polka dancing, often dancing together (*Polka* is the Polish word for "Polish woman," as *Polak* is the word for "Polish man"). The polka tends to be working-class music wherever you find it in the world. And the schoolmaster's transcription serves to remind us that even so powerful an activity as the polka becomes part of the historical record only when there is someone to write it down!

There are early references to a dancing master who was teaching something like a polka to pupils in a German city circa 1839; entertainers who were seen doing it in Baden-Baden; a Czech bandmaster who introduced it in Prague. But whatever "the polka" was before March 1844 (our best guess is that it began as a simplified and stereotyped Czech version of how Polish women danced a regional style called the *krakowiak*), it was an international, urban, and primarily proletarian couple dance thereafter. In March of 1844, polka-mania took Paris: common people, servants, workers and, one assumes, anyone else who wasn't too stuffy were dancing the polka in the streets of the capital and soon in Bordeaux and other French cities as well. A week or so later it took London by storm. And from

these two great centers of fashion, empire, and influence, the polka diffused rapidly upward into the rest of French and English society and outward to the rest of the world.

Why Paris in the spring of 1844? And how did the polka claim and sustain a central position in working-class recreation the world over? A one-word answer to both questions is *Zeitgeist*, German for "the spirit of the times." By 1844, Polish aristocrats were scattered all over France, refugees from desperate and failed

"Le Bal Mabille." From *Paris Guide*, 1867.

THE FOURTH POLKA BY JULLIEN.

Composed on National Bohemian and Hungarian Melodies.

From *Illustrated London News*, 1844.

"The Waltz." After Gavarni.

battles to unify and liberate Poland; they were heroes to the French people. The American and French revolutions of the late eighteenth century had settled down into business as usual, while the conditions of life for working people under the growing discipline of industrial capitalism were getting worse and worse. It was in 1844 that Karl Marx wrote what came to be known as "The Philosophical and Economic Manuscripts of 1844," Friedrich Engels wrote "The Condition of the English Working Class in 1844," and the two revolutionaries joined forces in Paris to work on the Communist Manifesto for the revolutions of 1848. Oppressed

workers, revolutionary intellectuals, Polish "freedom fighters," and "image revolutionaries" captured the popular imagination. There was ferment, frustration, a glimpse of a better world to come. And the polka burst loose, expressing this moment much as the waltz had expressed the spirit of the bourgeois revolutions sixty years earlier.

The waltz was the couple dance of romance and individualism that tolled the death knell for feudal choral or group dancing by aristocrats and peasants everywhere. From our late twentieth-century vantage point, it is easy to forget that in the early 1800s for a man and a woman to hold each other in public and spin around looking into each other's eyes was an amazing break with centuries of feudal tradition. Yet in the 1980s Scrubby Seweryniak was still introducing a Dyna-Tones waltz medley as "sex music."[3]

There remains a sense in which the waltz is the residue or spirit of the failed revolutions of the late eighteenth century, and the polka the residue or spirit of the failed revolutions of the mid-nineteenth century. We call them failed because neither set of revolutions freed people from the formation of the social classes and nation-states that still block full liberation today. In fact, both revolutionary eras solidified nation-states and enabled the owning class to control a process that spawned the murderous world wars of the twentieth century. At least part of the explanation for the deep commitment people feel for these dances, and their amazing persistence over two centuries, must be the way they embody in movements of tune, limb, and fancy the unkept promise, the vision, the utopian moment of liberation.

In any case, once the polka was all the rage in Paris and London, streets were named after it, clothing fashions like "polka dots" derived from it, high society opened its doors and tried to smooth it out,[4] dancing masters took their versions of it to the provinces and to the capitals of emerging nations all over the world. But wherever the polka persisted beyond the phase of fad and fashion, wherever it sank roots in a community and built a tradition, it did so as people's music, "proletarian" in the sense that working-class people consciously maintained a process, a party, keeping a sense of festival alive even when they knew that other sectors of society were no longer interested in it.

The polka's diffusion all over the globe often gives ironic and unexpected testimony to the convoluted dynamics of spreading European culture. At a pre-Lenten party in 1978 on Sifnos, a small Greek island in the Aegean, we watched in amazement as the village baker, a great dancer, stood up from his table and shouted, "Porka! porka!" to the local violin and lute duo that was waiting for the music tapes from Athens to stop playing. The young Sifnian men were dancing urban contemporary styles to the recordings, and the baker was saying, in effect, "Let's get back to live music and the heaviest traditional dance this island knows—the polka." That the polka could be, even to one Sifnian, a symbol of deep local identity—not mainland, not mainstream, not Athens—is the sort of fact that appears stranger than any historical fiction.

In 1984 an Indonesian graduate student, from a town in the Celebes Islands, came to our door. He took a tape from his suitcase to illustrate traditional music from home: there were some waltzes, some "marz" too, played on bamboo flutes and locally blacksmithed brass instruments—but mostly polkas! Describing a traditional wedding, he also said they have "always"

done the polonaise as the first dance of the evening. What the Dutch got as a fashionable dance complex from Paris in the 1840s had become deeply traditional in the Celebes by the 1980s.

Not only were the Papago-Pima people immersed in polkas by the 1860s and playing them for mostly Mexican crowds in Tucson, Arizona, but you can still find mazurkas, redowas, and "chotis" (schottisches, a German term for a Scottish dance) on their LP records today. Mazurkas and redowas had their moments in Paris after the polkamania, so the data from the Celebes and Tucson confirm that a whole complex of "Polish" or "Polish-Parisian" dances diffused to the world. Finns, Swedes, and Norwegians all have a special place for polkas in their tavern dancing, we're told. North and south, east and west, polkas everywhere have stood the test of time. As the national dance of Paraguay, the polka is played with a looping 6/8 rhythm like nothing we have up north.

It is only from a distance that the six (or more) U.S. polka traditions can be seen as forming three ethnic-geographic streams: southwestern Chicano and Papago-Pima polkas; midwestern to western German-American and Czech-Bohemian-American polkas; eastern to midwestern Polish-American and Slovenian-American polkas. A closer view shows that the musicians and dancers within each of the six traditions think of themselves as quite autonomous: the Slovenes don't pay much attention to what the Poles are doing; the Papago-Pima tend to their own events, and even though the musicians may also play in mariachi bands for Mexican-American audiences, the two southwestern polka traditions stay quite separate. Perhaps the German and Czech-Bohemian traditions have mixed somewhat over the years, but it's doubtful because most polka bands are rooted in family-community-neighborhood-locality.

After a century of developments in all six traditions, however, and thousands of students working their way through college by playing in polka bands, the polka shelf at the library is still almost empty. Manuel Peña's fine account, *The Texas-Mexican Conjunto*, documents the largest of the six traditions.[5] This book treats the Polish-American tradition with a look

The Papago Express at Tumacacori National Monument, Arizona, 1981.

at Slovenian style. There is Robert Dolgan's biography of Slovenian-American polka king Frankie Yankovic, and two excellent but as yet unpublished dissertations by Janice Kleeman and Charles Emmons.[6] But from the 1870s to the early 1970s, universities did not encourage a single person to write about any of these ethnic working-class musics for a scholarly journal.

There is an especially large gap in our knowledge of popular music in immigrant communities between the polkamanias of 1844 and the emergence of distinctive polka bands on American records and radio in the late 1920s. What music did the Polish immigrants of 1870 to 1900 carry with them in their heads and hearts and dancing feet? As a group, they brought an incredible variety of rural styles, most likely, and a big mix of musics and dances from diverse urban experiences as well.[7] Many, probably most, immigrants had already left rural "echological" niches and acquired years of experience in cities—Polish and other European, even North African—before they booked passage for the New World.[8] Did they dance the waltz and polka with accordion or concertina accompaniment as symbols of their urban sophistication? Probably. Did they want to put any peasant past behind them and use the break of a sea voyage to invent more dignified identities? All those new "-ski" last names proclaiming links to the nobility suggest that they did. Did they try to assuage

their pain, no matter how old-fashioned they might appear?

We know that they did, at weddings and family get-togethers, taverns and parish dances. Listening to Max Ciesielski and Alvin Sajewski, both in their eighties, talk about their fathers' music, looking over the old sheet music and pictures of brass bands, we can envision a turn-of-the-century Polonia with a great many semiprofessional musicians who worked day jobs but often played both a brass and a string instrument in various ensembles on evenings and weekends, at wedding parties, dances, and picnics. There were many amateur muscians playing concertina behind the bar or guitar on the front porch and a few influential professionals who gave lessons, conducted parish choirs, worked in the orchestra pits at theaters, and so forth. If we could go back to Buffalo's Polonia of 1900, we would be surprised by the number of musicians, the sophistication and variety of the live music we would hear, and the degree to which that music was integrated with family, neighborhood, and parish life. Li'l Wally Jagiello's descriptions of the Polish picnics in the Caldwell Woods outside Chicago testify that a great deal of regional music was played by a variety of bands sponsored by the village associations. Yet we also know that these same immigrants, as soon as they found one another and settled where there was work and a wage in the cities of the New World, set themselves to building communities that cradled both who they were and what they hoped to become.

On Buffalo's East Side we can see that Polonia was built quickly and built to last: seven large churches and a number of imposing organization buildings were all put up before the First World War.[9] Elders can still tell us about the extraordinary vitality of their neighborhoods, but a great deal of research remains to be done. Fortunately, young scholars are coming along in all the American Polonias, documenting this past with loving care and ever greater skill.[10]

What *Polka Happiness* adds to this growing documentation is a discussion of two polka communities within the context of an emerging national scene. Chapters 1 and 2 focus on the invention of Polish-American polkas in the 1920s and their great stylistic transformation from "Eastern" to "Chicago" style during and after the 1950s. Chapters 3 and 4 describe the International Polka Association in Chicago and its national festival, which for many fans is the year's most important event. Chapter 5 discusses the dominance of the Slovenian-American tradition in Milwaukee and the Julida Boys' contributions to polka happiness there. Chapter 6 examines the Buffalo polka scene, centering on the evolution of the Dyna-Tones, a popular local band. Our account of the band's role in the community and its particular approach to polka performance draws on our years of visiting the taverns and parish dances where the group played: observing a rehearsal, listening to recordings, and interviewing the musicians. We discuss the Dyna-Tones and their history in order to spotlight some of the key issues in the polka's ability to survive.

It is our hope that this is just the beginning of a long shelf of books on Polish-American polka localities and personalities. The full stories of Walt Solek, Frank Wojnarowski, Li'l Wally, Happy Louie, and Eddie Blazonczyk: the histories of dozens of bands, great polka disc jockeys, and polka booster clubs in, for example, Pittsburgh, Chicago, and the Connecticut valley; the evolution of Polish-American weddings over time and across regions—all these are waiting to be written. The other North American styles too need to be studied in their own localities, and there is much more to be learned about the worldwide polka phenomenon. Eventually, polka will be seen as a marker of a rich and complex ethnic experience, and "the polka party" will take its rightful place alongside "the jam session" as one of humanity's crowning achievements.

polka
time

Part I:
A History of
Polish-American Polkas

Patriotic saxophone band, Milwaukee, n.d.

1. Made in America

We do not know very much about the polka before it became all the rage in Paris and London during the spring of 1844.[1] Probably it was a Czech idea about how Polish women dance, and most likely it was taken to Paris by traveling entertainers and dancing teachers. Certainly it was danced in the streets and popular dance halls by working people, rather quickly taken into polite society as a fad, and then disseminated as an international fashion.

There is no evidence that before or after 1844 the polka was ever popular in Poland. As the fashion spread from Paris and London, the Polish aristocracy may have resented the stereotype, and Polish peasants probably had no time to be amused by any possible resemblance to their own regional dance traditions. Polish-Americans returning to Poland are often frustrated to find that the music and dance they know and love as "Polish" does not really exist there in the cities or in the villages or even in the folkloric ensembles unless a special effort is being made to please Polish-American tourists.

Jan Kleeman, in her doctoral thesis research, made a great effort to find polkas in Poland, yet in the sixty-six-volume Kolberg collection of 25,000 melodies, she found only thirty-two that were labeled "polka." "These transcriptions," she writes, "are valuable as the only examples of the 19th-century Polish folk polka which my extensive research has uncovered."[2] But was there ever a "Polish folk polka"? Or did Kolberg perhaps collect only a few examples of residual Paris fashion?

The Poles who migrated to America between 1870 and 1920 came from a variety of worker and peasant backgrounds that were shaped by important regional differences. Immigrants from northern and western Poland, where a resistance to German expansion had been a part of life for centuries, tended to have more respect for written music, arrangements, brass band and string orchestra traditions. Those from southern and eastern Poland brought their village ensemble traditions to the New World. Probably most of these immigrants were familiar with one form or another of the urban couple dance called the polka, but it was only one dance among dozens. The Poles certainly did not think of it as "identity music" or "our national dance"; quite to the contrary, they encountered it only once in a while as an internationally popular dance in cosmopolitan centers.

How, then, did the polka become an identity music, a "soul" or "roots" music, for Polish-Americans? The full story will take more research to develop, but thanks to Jan Kleeman's careful musicological treatment of early recordings and Richard Spottswood's important social, technical, and discographic information, we can sketch a general picture of the Polish-American polka's emergence and crystallization as something made in America.[3] Our interviews in the mid-1970s with such founding fathers as Ed Krolikowski and Max Ciesielski begin to fill in some of the details.

Essentially, the early 78-RPM recordings reveal three general streams of music that in time merged into recognizable Polish-American polka styles: a composed and arranged band or orchestra sound, exemplified by the Witkowski family's records in New York City; a more rural-sounding string ensemble or *gorale* (highlanders) style exemplified in many of the first records to come out of Sajewski's music store in Chicago;[4] an experimental or novelty-comedy line of recordings that featured accordion soloists, singers brought in from the street, vaudeville xylophone wizards, and virtually any specialty act with a Polish name on it that might sell more than a few hundred records.

The story of the Witkowski family may be a book in itself someday. We were unable to interview Bernie Witkowski, Jr. (also known as society band leader Bernie Wyte),[5] but Jan Kleeman has pieced together some of his story and recounts his Uncle Leon's early career: "The most professional of the early Polish orchestras was Orkiestra Witkowskiego, as Leon Witkowski's orchestra was called. As a young man Leon and his brother emigrated from Poznan and settled in Brooklyn. In addition to his Polish orchestra, Leon conducted a 45-piece American orchestra that performed at Luna Park, Coney Island."[6] Kleeman elaborates on the qualities that made the Polish orchestra so successful:

A musically educated man, Leon always demanded the highest standards of musicianship from his players, and this

Folk ensemble of the Tatra region, Poland, n.d.

is reflected in his polka recordings. His version of the still popular "Dziaduniu" ("Grandfather Polka," later known as "Clarinet Polka") and "Sokolica" ("Falconer Polka") are careful arrangements and excellent performances. Although they are acoustic rather than electric recordings, the parts are clearly distinguishable and the renditions are as enjoyable to hear today as they must have been sixty years ago.

His ensemble varied from record to record, but Witkowski usually used eight players. The lead clarinet, played with technical brilliance as well as a beautiful tone, is joined on the melody by a flute, a second clarinet, or both. The additional melody instrument(s) play in unison with the lead or double at the octave or in thirds. (The trumpet attempts this feat, but lacking the expertise of the clarinet player he fails to execute the many triplets and grace notes with the same finesse.) The piano bass plays a bouncy vamp and is occasionally doubled by the trombone. At other times, the trombone plays a slow harmony in quarter and half notes, often at a sixth below the melody. One or two fast-moving trumpets fill out the inner harmony and a woodblock and/or cymbals provide color and rhythmic emphasis. The vibraphone adds a shimmering note here and there on some pieces.[7]

The sound and repertoire of the early 1920s is certainly one foundation stone of the Eastern style in polka tradition. But is it really Polish? Or American? Or obviously Polish-American? Kleeman has determined that the early Orkiestra Warszawska (1913–17) was composed of studio musicians at Victor Records

who favored a clarinet and piccolo lead with tuba bass, and that "the studio musicians who performed Polish-American music for Columbia Records were unabashedly called Polska Orkiestra Columbia (Columbia Polish Orchestra)." According to Kleeman, after Leon died in 1923 (at age fifty-five), his orchestra was taken over by his brother Bernard and then by his brother's son, Bernard Junior.[8] The name was changed to Orkiestra Srebrne Dzwony, or the Silver Bells Orchestra.

The three Witkowskis were intimately involved with this "studio polka," a composed, arranged, instrumentally experimental, lyricless, and essentially drummerless sound. They were thoroughly professional and therefore culturally marginal in the emergence of a recognizable Polish-American style circa 1929. We don't know whether Leon's work as conductor of the Coney Island orchestra brought him more money or emotional satisfaction than his role as leader of Orkiestra Witkowskiego, and perhaps Bernie Witkowski, Jr., would have more to say about his role as an innovative Polish-American musician than about his bread-and-butter career as Bernie Wyte, leader of a "society band" at New York hotels for three decades. The point is that from Poznan to New York City, and for most of this century, the Witkowskis led lives that were musically and culturally much more sharply divided than those of most other hyphenated Americans. A Poznan family tradition of professionalism and cultural marginality accounts (better than the notion of

Alvin Sajewski in his Chicago store, 1974.

Prussian perfectionism) for the extraordinary, perhaps excessive, achievements of the Silver Bells Orchestra and the smaller groups it spawned during the polka boom just before, during, and after World War II.

One would have to talk with those who danced to his music to know whether Bernie Junior's fantastic orchestrations really gave more bounce to the ounce on the dance floor or were primarily effective in impressing listeners at a safe distance. Perhaps his highly arranged polka fit in with a peak of Harvest Moon Festival polka choreography in cosmopolitan New York City. The other New York setting where Wyte and Witkowski could be happily united would have been the Polish-American debutante balls. Imagine costumed couples, arms held high, executing impossible routines designed to disguise any possible link to a peasant-worker two-step.

Chicago did not have any major record company

The Old Country Village Musicians, Chicago, 1966. *Left to right:* Mel Nocek, Walter Papciak, Frank Berends, John Zurawski (leader), Vince Dapkus, Steve Jankowski.

studios at the time, but it did have two huge Polish neighborhoods that knew what they wanted in music. The Sajewski Music Store tried to meet that demand from its founding in 1897 until the 1980s, and Alvin Sajewski and his sister Jania Sajewski-Terley are extraordinarily knowledgeable about changing Polish-American tastes and Chicago Polonia's music and entertainment history.[9] But the full stories of the early immigrations and the evolution of the neighborhoods, of the dozens of associations based on common origins in specific Polish villages or small cities, and of the kinds of musical events each was able to support earlier in the century exist today only in the memories of individuals. No one has systematically traced southern Polish Podhale string band continuities from the 1870s to the present, or the "village sound" of eastern Poland—again, a continuous stream of music in Chicago from the arrival of the first Polish immigrants through the recording of John Zurawski's "Old Country Village Musicians," which was released in the 1960s on Chet Schafer's Chicago Polkas label.[10] We

could learn a great deal about the development of Chicago style by listening closely to the bands that evolved from these southern and eastern Polish village band roots—as vocalists were added and concertinas, accordions, clarinets, and trumpets replaced violins in both lead and harmony parts.

Kleeman correctly identifies the Frank Dukla ensemble (its members already old-timers when they recorded in 1926) as a precursor of Chicago style: a position analogous to that of the early Witkowski sound in relation to Eastern style. As Alvin Sajewski put it:

In all the records before 1919 there was very little polka music. . . . If there was any, they were very light. It didn't have that drive. That started with Dukla and Piwowarczyk. Before that it was light, with the violin taking the lead and melody. So around 1925, 1926 is when it all started. Dukla's 1927 record is in a heavy Chicago style, but at the same time the records wouldn't sell that well. . . . We sold them from the very first day they put them out, but . . . we'd order twenty-five at a time and sell a few hundred over a year. . . . On the other hand, any of Dukla's sold regularly up until they were discontinued during the war or just after, a twenty-year span. When "Beer Barrel" was in its prime, around '39, we were selling over fifty a week; couldn't get as many as we wanted.[11]

Kleeman's description of the Dukla band adds some important specifics:

Perhaps the most popular of the early rural orchestras in America was that of Franciszek Dukla, who recorded forty-four selections (twenty of them are designated "polka") for Victor Records between 1926 and 1929. Dukla's lead instruments, violin and clarinet, generally share the melody in unison or with the clarinet at the lower octave; only occasionally does it break into harmonization with the violin. On some selections, such as "Icek Rekrut Polka" ("Isaac the Recruit Polka"), the violin and clarinet are more or less heterophonic, i.e., playing similar but not identical versions of the melody.[12]

Dukla's ensemble was filled out by two "second fiddles," adding "fill-in harmony on the up-beats" and a heavy, bowed string bass, so the echoes of the Pod-hale or *gorale* tradition are strong. Kleeman observes:

The sound of this string ensemble is nothing like that of a classical string quartet. The bowed harmonizations of the violins and bass are abruptly detached and not always precisely on pitch. The lead violin, generally accurate in pitch, has a straightforward folk style which is devoid of vibrato.
The vocalist with Dukla's band, Stefan J. Zielinski (a talented musician, playwright, and set designer) performs his part competently and in the same folk style as that of the instrumentalists. His voice is clear and on pitch, each note is articulated without slurring to the next, phrases are clipped off without sustaining the last note, and there is a noticeable absence of vibrato. This simple vocal style persists throughout the history of Polka. The vocal talents of a singer are never very important; he is expected to be audible and on pitch.[13]

More on the "simple vocal style" later, but it is interesting that a well-educated playwright and set designer was one of the first to put it on record.

Alvin Sajewski doesn't recall Zielinski's singing with Dukla but says that when he did sing it was with a straight, untrained voice. So did Jan Kapalka, the violinist and vocalist Sajewski remembers as sitting in with the Dukla group and sometimes adding vocal parts. By the time electric recording came in around 1925, people wanted to hear voices like their own, not operatic stuff, and a village or *wiejska* band was the preferred sound, at least in Chicago.

Spottswood's interviews with Alvin Sajewski show that technical and marketing changes were making possible more accurate assessment of public taste and that a search for *the* Polish-American style was fueled by the struggle between two corporations over shares of the ethnic market:

By the 1910s, the production of Polish-language records was hitting its stride, but the predominance of trained singers and more-or-less formally arranged orchestrations was beginning to leave some record buyers wanting more. Most of the Sajewskis' customers were not from the wealthy or educated classes, and Victor and Columbia were not producing the music they could hear casually in their neighborhoods, or the music they remembered from the rural villages and countryside of their homeland. . . . As Alvin Sajewski describes the problem:

The companies didn't know what to make. That was their big problem. They had the material and they had the money. We had the people with money in their hand and they wanted to buy a phonograph, but only if they could have some good records to play. There were a few that were good, but not too many. What we had were some waltzes, some marches and band arrangements, but they wanted folksongs. The records featured people who had been on stage, comedians or singers. Some of the comedians talked too fast, and you couldn't understand, and when the punchline came you couldn't catch it. The records were by people from the city who liked the classical singers, the high-pitched soprano solos. Each singer had to show how loud he could sing or how high he could go. People wanted simple pretty melodies, but they would buy these records because there was at least something in Polish on them. And that went on up to 1917 or 1918.

In 1915, Columbia made its first Chicago recordings, and a group led by Frank Przybylski recorded "Laughing Polka" (Sieszmy Się) (Columbia E-2221); on the other side was "Dziadunio Polka," which was the ancestor of "Clarinet Polka." He also recorded two marches with a big band on Columbia E-2220. . . .

The Przybylski records were a step in the right direction, since they at least were locally produced and were intended to respond to what the Sajewskis and their customers wanted. But Frank Przybylski was a trained musician, and his musicians played from the orchestrations he supplied. Nevertheless, he consciously relied on folk materials, and the quality of his records was such that his orchestras and arrangements were in demand by Columbia for more than thirty years. Along with the Sajewskis, he actively recruited talent for a label that by the 1920s was trying to adjust its foreign-language program more closely to the tastes of local markets.

[ALVIN SAJEWSKI:] The salesman would come in, and phonographs and records—Victor and Columbia—were the two main lines. Each one was watching the other; if one had a hit, the other wanted somebody like that.

We were always interested in folksong records. The company would tell us to find somebody and they would record them. Then you would have to find somebody, and then be able to sell the records. So naturally we were always on the lookout. People would come in and ask for a song they knew on a record. They might sing it, and we would find somebody to write it down; Mr. Przybylski was a capable man. He knew how to arrange these things. We would then find an artist who would be able to sing the song in that type of way that the people wanted—not a concert singer, but a person with an ordinary voice. Often people would come in to the store and would sing a song just in that way that you wanted. Then we would have to get Mr. Przybylski or somebody to accompany him.

[DICK SPOTTSWOOD:] *And you would put that person on a record, somebody who walked into the store?*

[ALVIN SAJEWSKI:] Oh, absolutely. That's how we found a lot of our artists. The record companies didn't care who they were; all they wanted to know was how many we could sell. They didn't care what language it was or how it sounded. They left it up to who was in the control room. As a rule, it would be somebody who was selling those records, because

the company representative didn't know what it was all about. He'd ask you, "What do you think? You think you'll be able to sell 'em?" If you went to a record company and said you had somebody who was good, they'd ask how good was he? You'd say, "Oh, he's good. Everybody likes him." Well, they'd turn around and say, "Well, how many will you be able to sell?" And you'd have to be able to say you could sell 500.[14]

The Sajewskis, the musicians and the record companies were certainly trying to give the public what they wanted, but judging by the variety of musical idioms, comedy sketches, and novelty numbers that continued to sell well enough into the 1930s, the Polish-American public was heterogeneous in its tastes. Jan Wanat's accordion solos, some recorded as early as 1917, were popular for twenty years: "He had a way of getting right up to that horn and getting the bass in there. People liked that bassing."[15] Pawel Faut, a crooner à la Bing Crosby, was very popular, doing songs like "Ramona" in Polish. Polish versions of Irish vaudeville routines, such as "Polski Gallagher and Shean," were recorded. Pawlo Humeniuk and other Ukrainian bandsmen recorded Polish versions of their best-selling numbers; if these sold well, they were sometimes redone and passed on to the Lithuanian and Slovak catalogues. And then there were those guys who walked off the street into Sajewski's music store: Wally Polak, owner of a candy store and composer of the classic "Drunkard's Lament"; Bruno Rudzinski, who hummed and scatted along with his concertina in a crazy way that all Li'l Wally fans would recognize.

One can't help hearing in these early recordings things that sound like Eddie Zima and Li'l Wally. Predecessors and antecedents are everywhere. The more one listens, the clearer it is that Eddie Zima and Wally Jagiello did not invent Chicago style by themselves but simply gave it more of a beat and personified it for the 1950s.[16] In the pressure cooker of "Polish Broadway" on Chicago's Division Street, dozens of bands and gin mills competed for wartime dollars and created the style. Bringing natural vocals and squeezeboxes into the group was one important step in the evolution. As is so often the case the world over, electric amplification initially sustained and rebalanced the older

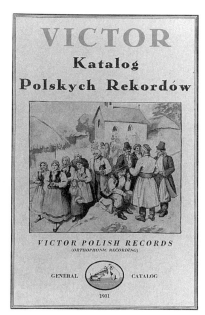

Victor Polish Records General Catalog, 1931.

sounds.[17] By the 1950s the electric bass had picked up the Jan Wanat tradition of standing "right up to that horn and getting the bass in there" as well as the village *wiejska* tradition of bowing the bass for maximum bottom throb. It is clear that electric recording, as well as radio and public address systems, favored natural vocalists such as Stanley Mermel, heard singing with Orkiestra Nadwislanska on a Folklyric collection.[18] From 1926 on, some vocalists sounded more natural than others, but no one was putting on high-culture "airs." The women singing an early version of the familiar oberek "Tam Pod Krakowem" with the Stefan Skrabut Orchestra (actually a Lemko-Ukrainian group) sound a *lot* like Buffalo's mother-daughter team, Wanda and Stephanie.[19] In records of the late 1920s, models for later developments are everywhere.

No one has yet pinpointed the moment when Polish music became truly Polish-American or when Eastern and Chicago styles are certainly themselves and not just foreshadowings of a music to come. Both Kleeman and Spottswood have suggested moments of synthesis, but Kleeman focuses on "rural" and "urban" conti-

nuities, and Spottswood highlights "folk" performers rather than popular successes. Spottswood describes the transition as he analyzes a Victor catalogue:

By 1931, the Victor Polish catalog had changed radically. Only one artist from the 1921 offering, Jan Wanat, was still making records. All acoustical records (those made before May, 1925) were deleted, and the percentage of trained singers is much smaller. In December, 1928, Victor began issuing records intended for minority groups in special numerical series whose numbers were preceded by V-. The V-16000 ten-inch series and V-66001 twelve-inch series were reserved for Polish records; by February, 1931, the series had reached V-16169 and V-66008, respectively. These releases may be divided into a far greater number of categories, many of them interesting as folk music. A rough breakdown reveals the following:

> Village orchestras: 38 (primarily by Frank Dukla)
>
> Popular/standard vocals: 35 (primarily by Paweł Faut, including some skits)
>
> Skits (usually with village music): 14
>
> Singers with village orchestras: 13 (primarily by Stanisław Mermel)
>
> Singers with accordion or concertina: 12 (primarily by Władysław Polak)
>
> "Legitimate" (non-village) orchestras: 12
>
> "New-Wave" polka bands: 12 (primarily by Ignacy Podgórski)
>
> Instrumental duets, trios, quartets: 11 (primarily featuring accordion and violin)
>
> Podhale (Góral): 10 (all by Stanisław Bachleda and Karol Stoch)
>
> Accordion solos: 9
>
> Vocal Quartet or choral: 6

Spottswood goes on to characterize the new music:

I have coined the term "new-wave" polka bands to distinguish the music of Ignacy Podgórski, Edward Królikowski and others from that of their predecessors. Their groups blended brass, accordion, and violin, combining the energy of the village orchestras with a smoother, more emphatic melodic line; their music also had greater speed and a brighter edge. Podgórski from Philadelphia, and Królikowski, from Bridgeport, Connecticut, continued to enjoy great popularity in the 1930s and 1940s.[20]

Kleeman traces the fusion of "rural" and "urban" in three orchestras recording between 1927 and 1929:

Two orchestras about which practically nothing is known combine the sounds of the early rural and urban styles. Orkiestra Hultajska (Roguish Orchestra), which recorded for Columbia, blends clarinet and violin on melody in its version of "Czarny las," circa 1927. . . . This performance is clearly a copy of Dukla's earlier release using brass instead of strings. The brassy sound is louder and brighter and the pace of the performance is snappier. . . .

A similar marriage of rural and urban styles is effected by the Podoszek i Balowa Orkiestra. Władisław Podoszek was an Eastern violinist who performed as a soloist as well as with co-leader Balowa. Their 1929 recording, "Cialy do baksy" ("Charlie in the Box"), is a racy little tune about an old man in a brothel, sung by a female vocalist à la Betty Boop (an example of the ingress of American popular culture). The eight-piece ensemble (violin/trumpet lead, tuba bass, violin/trumpet/trombone harmony, accordion fill-in, and whistle) plays what must have been a formal, written-out arrangement in a loosely jointed style that can only be described as "raucous." The fiddle saws away at the melody while the trombone slides around, the tuba pumps away, and all the while the whistle—it is of the sliding pitch variety—makes weirdly obscene noises. In listening to this piece, we easily imagine that the instrumentalists are having a wonderful time.

A third orchestra which combines the sounds of the old country string band and the brass-oriented urban orchestra is that of the Philadelphian, Ignacy Podgorski. One of the most influential figures in the development of polka, Podgorski was a prolific composer, arranger and music publisher. His series of arrangements of Polish music for dance orchestra, written in the 1930's, were still in print in 1962 and are available in many Polish music stores even today.

From about 1929 until the mid 1930's, Ignacy Podgorski

and His Marvelous Merrymakers (in Polish: *jego nadwyczajna orkiestra*) recorded for Victor Records; in the mid 30's he switched to Columbia, and in the 40's, recorded on the Harmonia label. Podgorski's combination of instruments was unique. . . . He used the string bass and two violins which filled in the harmony on the upbeats, in the usual rural style. In one of his early recordings, "Sokolica" (Falconer 1931), he uses a clarinet and violin in unison in the manner of Dukla and Wyskowski. Yet he also features the trumpet, either as the second lead or, later in his career, with trombone in slow-moving supporting harmony. In all his orchestrations he uses the accordion, the indispensable fill-in instrument of the standard Eastern style orchestrations. Podgorski's imaginative arrangements feature instruments freely exchanging instrumental roles. The accordion is used as a melody instrument, in combination with either violin, clarinet, or muted trumpet. He thus not only spans the gap between the urban and rural styles, but is also a pivotal figure in the development of urban style into the classic Eastern style. He continued to perform, record, and perfect his orchestration techniques right through the 1940's.[21]

Kleeman's musicological line, Spottswood's discographic trajectory, and our pursuit of "ethclass" essence in the first Polish-American polka bands all intersect at Krolikowski-Podgorski-"Ciali do Baksy."[22] One of the remaining questions is whether this intersection occurred just before or just after the stock market crash of 1929. Was "new-wave" polka a swift spiritual response to economic distress? The coincidence of newly linked record and radio media, an economic boom, and perhaps a growing awareness that the possibilities of further substantial immigration were really closed must all have shaped the consciousness of an American Polonia with a destiny, a culture, a sound of its own.

At the moment of its inception, circa 1929, Polish-American polka style was quite coherent. It is hard to guess from the sound alone in which city a number of the early 1930s recordings were made. The dominance of Eastern style in the 1930s and 1940s was only gradually established. What came to be known as the Chicago style needed a gestation period in the Division Street clubs of Polish Broadway, but the prototypes for it were abundant in the 1920s and early 1930s.

The following account of the formation of Polish-American polka style in the earliest years, circa World War I through the early 1930s, relies heavily on interviews with Ed Krolikowski in Bridgeport, Connecticut; Joe Lazarz of Indian Orchard, Massachusetts; Max Ciesielski and Doc Penkson in Buffalo; Walt Solek of Meriden, Connecticut; and Alvin Sajewski in Chicago. The studies by Spottswood and Kleeman have helped to fill some of the gaps between their stories.

Ed Krolikowski was born in Bridgeport in 1892 and was eighty-two at the time of our interview.[23] He and his wife happily pored over the scrapbooks and records, checking each other's recollections of times, places, names, and events, recalling the complex social and musical world from which the distinctive Polish-American polka style emerged in the 1920s.

Like a great many immigrants in the late nineteenth century, Ed's parents decided to return to Poland. The year was 1902 and Ed was ten years old.

I went to school out there, about fifty miles south of Warsaw, Przansnysa was the name of the town, and I went with my brothers and sisters for about three years. Then my father sent me to Warsaw where I took up languages; five languages I took up and I spoke them all fluently, but I've forgotten them since—Polish, German, Russian, French, and Latin. I started to study violin as soon as I got there, with a private teacher. Then when I went to Warsaw I studied with a real good teacher, a concert violinist.

The year I came back to the United States was the year Taft was elected. I remember getting off the boat and everyone was talking about Taft. We lived in New York and in 1916 they [my parents] moved to Bridgeport. I remained in Brooklyn with my aunt and uncle because I figured I had to make a living. I had tried the seminary for a while and that wasn't for me, so I went to an agent and played the violin for him and he said, "That's enough, stop, you're a good violin player but you're not the type we're looking for, we need jazzy music, dance music." So I went to another agent. The same story. I went to a lot of agents before I got a job in a cabaret every night. On Broadway, that was. I had to read music so I didn't mind at first, but the hours were long and I got tired of that. Then I got a job in some hotel with two other guys, Jewish and Italian: violin, piano, and cello. We played a few weeks

together and took a contract for this job in Tennessee at a high class hotel, Signal Mt. Hotel in Chattanooga, I think it was, for four months, June to September. Officers were coming for six-week training nearby, and their families were there. So we had six pieces playing dance music in a hall once a week, and concert music during dinner every night and for one hour at lunch, and after supper for dancing an hour or so. Wasn't too much playing, wealthy people, and we had rooms, food, really royal treatment. We got a notice only three could remain, so we were tired of it and the other three of us decided to go to New Orleans. This was about 1917.

We went to New Orleans and didn't know anybody, so we played in a moving picture theater, continuous playing for three or four hours until we got some money together. Then we went in a cabaret that started at midnight and closed around 4:00 A.M. We stayed there about six weeks. Of course, we heard quite a lot of jazz in those days, and we were influenced by jazz more and more. All kinds of music in the air down there. The next job we got was in a restaurant where they used to like those cowboy songs. All these guys come from Texas and all over, with their girlfriends, and some would even give us music to read. The piano player knew a lot of those songs and we were doing real well. I did have one fight with the manager, never forgot it. He pulled a gun on me. Even in those days, I was always the business man, so I had to face this guy.

The mention of jazz started Rosalie Krolikowski digging into the cabinet for old records and she emerged with 78s by Cow Cow Davenport, Montana Taylor, and Speckled Red! With wonderful old boogie-woogie on the machine and all of us sipping scotch on the rocks, we talked about what the influence of Dixieland and swing had been on Polish-American music and about how Ed's experiences on Broadway, in Tennessee, and in New Orleans had shaped his approach to polka music. There were no clear answers, but Ed's story suggests some connections.

Well, about that time, the three of us were drafted, 1918. The war wasn't quite over, and my mother sent me a card from the draft board. So how to get back was the question, back to Connecticut. We got a job on this boat, playing for our trip home. We played every night, mostly popular songs,

Ed Krolikowski Radio Orchestra, Bridgeport, Connecticut, c. 1928. *Left to right:* Edward Krolikowski, unknown, Chris Hellman, John Motto, unknown, Leo Krolikowski.

some requests, and with no lights on the boat because it was wartime. They had a benefit night for the musicians, and we got home safely with a little cash in our pockets.

I came to Bridgeport and was rejected from the draft because of my eyes, I think. My father had a saloon there for a while, gave it up, and then he wasn't doing anything. So in 1920 my mother suggested I start a music store with $500 of my money and $500 of hers. I ran it for two years. Seemed like it was going OK, so I got married in 1922. I had started my own band in 1921, a five- or six-piece band. Most of our work was small dances and weddings, weddings every second or third week and dances in between. And Polish holidays.

With a band, a music store, and a family started, Ed was laying the foundations for a lot of other activities. His wife and sister did most of the work at the store. Around 1923, Ed began running a nine-piece band in the pit at Park City, a burlesque house, moving from there to the Lyric Theatre in 1925.

Frank Wojnarowski and Orchestra, c. 1954. *Left to right:* Wally Yansick, Lou Puccino, unknown, Mike Vivanti, unknown, unknown, Frankie Chop, unknown, Frank Wojnarowski, unknown, Dorothy Krook, unknown, Joe Slusar, Leo Grabinski, Stanley Smuniewski.

The money wasn't bad there in the theaters. I used to get $50 to $60 a week, strictly burlesque, no movies. I was responsible for keeping the band together. Every show had a big book to be rehearsed and a new leader or director coming in, so we all had to be good readers, versatile musicians. Outside of that I was teaching about sixty or seventy pupils. I used to get a dollar and a half per half-hour. I had my studio across the street so I could keep an eye on the store. In this store we were selling records, sheet music, piano rolls—a big specialty for a while—and then phonographs all through that time. In 1928 I bought a building across the street—four apartments, two stores—and I sold washing machines and stoves and pianos.

Toward the end of the 1920s, just before the crash,

something must have happened to the Polish-American community's idea of itself, because suddenly Ed Krolikowski was on radio and on records as a Polish-American orchestra leader, and not just as an orchestra leader of Polish background.

In 1928, I formed the polka band, and we did our first broadcast in 1929. Dr. Smykowski was a Polonian leader then and he said, "Why not try to round up several Polish merchants to sponsor a show, Ed?" So I went to the station with my nine men and did it, and soon we solicited some more merchants—furniture store, meat market, travel agency, monument maker—and we were doing a broadcast every week. The radio station, WICC, wanted to continue this show but with a smaller orchestra, a six-piece band, so we were there for something like ten years, 1929 to 1939. We were the first ethnics, the first having a polka band—nothing but polkas, waltzes, obereks—the first to have a radio show in the New England states.

As I remember it, my first recordings were for Victor in 1929, six or eight songs, but my real success was with Columbia a couple of years later. The way the Columbia recordings came about was that the Polish people working at the pressing factory in Bridgeport passed the word up, and he got interested—the foreign director at Columbia, Mr. Porges. Originally I recorded eight songs, and those first eight were the best sellers. I must have recorded over fifty 78s, and some did pretty well for Columbia. But those first eight were the big ones. "Helena Polka" must have sold about 250,000 in a short period of time, and "Clarinet Polka" too. I think we used a Sajewski arrangement for one of those. "Marajanka's 1000 Heroes" or "Baruska Polka" was our theme song and one of those first eight songs. Some years later, Arthur Godfrey took it and put English words to it: "She's Too Fat for Me." The local papers said I was thinking of suing him, but it was really a public domain number, and he put the lyric to it. From those first eight songs I used to get royalty checks for $400, $600, $1,500, and even royalties from South America. That was a thrill. There was a time when everyone loved polkas.[24]

Ed went on to describe those times, the boys in the band, their day jobs and various ethnic backgrounds—German bass player, Slovakian drummer and clarinetist, Hungarian piano player—and the variety of dances and weddings they played in different neighborhoods to match the band's diversity:

You see, there were no other bands in those nationalities, so we played the Slovakian neighborhood a lot, the Ukrainian, Russian, Jewish, too. We played a lot of Jewish weddings. An eight-piece band and no one would have to pay more than $25 or $30 in those days, plus the tips we'd get for requests. We'd honor requests for Greek, Syrian, Irish, Italian, German, Hungarian, or any other type of music, some special numbers each place. The drummer could sing in Slovakian and we started adding czardas to the book, but basically we did our regular numbers, arrangements from Sajewski's store in Chicago or Schunke's in Buffalo, and our own original numbers. We were the only ones that could satisfy every nationality.

Ed remembered seeing a very young Ray Henry by the bandstand all night whenever he played Hartford. During the summers he would rent Pleasure Beach Ballroom once each week from the city, charge a fifty-cent admission, and draw over a thousand people, the young Frank Wojnarowski often among them: "Frank said that his only dream was to be a conductor and have a band like mine." Professor Krolikowski and his band certainly helped to design and teach what came to be known as the Eastern style in polkas. But how did this classic Polish-American "radio recording orchestra" come about? Why was an ethnic style suddenly so popular? Why was it Ed Krolikowski in Bridgeport, Connecticut, who set the pattern in 1928–29?

Perhaps 1928 was a good year to start a band of any kind. Fifty-three new musicals premiered on Broadway during the 1927–28 season (an all-time record), and many shows were trying out in Bridgeport and New Haven. Talking pictures with their own soundtracks were only beginning to displace pit orchestras in the movie houses after the success of *The Jazz Singer* in 1927. Vaudeville and burlesque were still going strong. The 1920s were roaring along. But with all of this activity in the musical mainstream, why start a polka band? Why would musicians be interested in forming one when there were so many established opportunities to play for steady wages? Or why not start a jazz band in the jazz age?

In fact, many white ethnics were making their way into the jazz world during the 1920s—Bix Beiderbecke, Frank Teschmaker, Gene Krupa, Benny Goodman, Mez Mezzrow, Wingy Manone, Max Kaminski: the long list contains a great many German, Jewish, Irish, and a few Polish names—but the impulse to form "polka bands" might be considered a parallel response to the jazz wave. Ed Krolikowski was often referred to in his radio and recording days as the Polish Paul Whiteman. Just as Whiteman attempted to legitimize or symphonicize jazz, Krolikowski and his peers can be seen as arrangers of Polish music in an American or jazzed-up form.

I just got tired of playing the theaters, working day and night, teaching in the morning, play a matinee, teach again,

Brunon Kryger, n.d.

back to theater, worrying about the store, not seeing my family. So my wife Rosalie said, "Quit and start a band. Really organize something. There are a lot of good opportunities."

Radio and records were both looking for more material, more music. This new desire to be recognized as Poles in America happily coincided with the media's need for novelty. Organized polka music was something different and interesting for radio to broadcast and record companies to sell. Underline *organized*. The small pickup groups for weddings, the three- and four-piece bands—bass, piano, sax; concertina, trumpet, drums; accordion, clarinet, violin, bass—had been a part of Polish neighborhoods in the eastern and midwestern cities since 1870. But the organized polka band of six or more pieces emerged only in the late 1920s and then everywhere at once.

Let's look for a moment at this simultaneous emergence. Joe Lazarz already knew how to play clarinet, violin, and some string bass when he came over and settled near Springfield, Massachusetts, around 1913.[25] As a youngster he had played clarinet in Jan Sobie-

ski's 38-piece band. After forming his own three-piece group around 1916, he played weddings and local dances ("Strictly Polish—polkas, obereks, and waltzes") for some thirteen years before, as he put it, "people forced me to organize the band" in 1929 or 1930. "I had violin, piano, drums, bass violin, clarinet, trumpet, and banjo. That banjo was very, very good. Then I went from one clarinet to two, one playing clarinet and alto, and the other one clarinet and tenor, eight guys altogether." This band went on to record around 1940 and had its peak years and big hits, "Pizzicato Polka" and "Swinging Elmer," during World War II.

Also in the Springfield area and at about the same time, Jan Robak and Wladyslaw Fronca merged their small groups to form the Robak and Fronca Orchestra. They made many records for both Victor and Columbia between 1931 and 1935 and were on radio regularly after 1935 with station WMAS in Springfield, Massachusetts. In the Buffalo area the legendary concertina player Matt Pajakowski was on radio from 1929 to 1936, so his orchestra must have been established before that time. The Ignacy Podgorski and Brunon Kryger orchestras were formed in the Philadelphia and Shenandoah areas during the same period.

Even if Ed Krolikowski was not the first but only one of the first to be organized in a big way and to be heard on radio and records, the reasons for his early arrival are significant to the larger story of the period. The music store as a base of operations responded to community needs with an inventory of the records and sheet music of all the Bridgeport nationalities, not just the Polish essentials. Rosalie Krolikowski, tending the store, had a sense of what would sell and saw those "good opportunities." Ed's rich experiences in cabarets north and south and in burlesque and vaudeville, plus his knowledge of a multi-ethnic community's tastes and recreational preferences played a big part in the success. The booming 1920s found a solid Polish-American community settled in and a growing second generation; there was no longer so much thought of returning to Poland. (Remember that during the nineteenth century almost as many Poles returned to the old country as came over.) It was a community that wanted to make its mark in America. Ed was successful, and so were some of his neighbors; there were businessmen who wanted to advertise on the hot new medium, radio; and the New York City recording studios were not far. Seen in these terms, the sudden emergence of radio and recording polka bands on the brink of the Great Depression seems almost a logical necessity; it was a happy music and waiting to see people through the hard times ahead.

Ed's early days in New Orleans surely influenced his approach to polka; listening to his early records, one gets the impression of a Polish jazz style taking shape. In his earliest version of "Baruska Polka" (1929), on Victor, the sound is Polish Dixieland: good heavy drum rolls and choked cymbal crashes, plenty of hot breaks by clarinet and woodblocks or tailgate trombone and temple blocks. The trumpet, violin, and clarinet punch out the melodic line of each segment with the trombone an octave below. Even though there is no improvising, the feeling is loose and rowdy. To solve the problem of whether to sing in Polish or in English, one of the refrains features the bandsmen singing a "la la la" chorus in barbershop-style parts with operetta vibratos. Lots of European and American traditions are mixing here, but the drumming textures and slide trombone of Dixieland make the biggest impression.

In a version of the same song just a few years later for Columbia, the arrangement is clearly part of the swing era. There are much mellower harmonies in all segments; a smooth tenor sax playing countermelodies replaces the slide trombone; the tempo has jumped from sixty-one measures per minute to sixty-eight; there are no more breaks; the drummer is in the background; clarinet solo arpeggios over the melody are an added attraction; the leader's violin is inaudible in the neat blend of the horns. This is the way most Eastern polka bands sounded in the 1930s and 1940s. That Dixieland feeling is already a forgotten fling.

At the time of our interview, Max Ciesielski was seventy-eight years old and a meticulous collector of sheet music, old issues of *Variety* and *Metronome*, percussion instruments, newspaper clippings—altogether a precious archive of Buffalo music history.[26] Max's testimony reveals that an enormous amount of live music was being made in Buffalo from the World War I period through the 1920s. When Max joined his father in the Fillmore Band in 1914, it was one of at least a dozen brass bands in the Buffalo area organized by parish (St. Augustine's Band), ethnic neighborhood (East Buffalo Band), institution (Polish Orphanage Band), or organization (Polish National Alliance Band). His memory still sharp, Max compiled a list of forty-two leaders of "Polish orchestras" from the first few decades of his career, all but a few of them deceased. And like Ed Krolikowski, he remembered his years of jobs in movie theaters, vaudeville, burlesque as a great era for musicians.

Max's first organized musical experience was playing at funerals with the Fillmore Band. Looking at an old photo of the Polish Tailors' Organization, Max described the kind of funeral a member could expect: a sixteen-piece brass band like the Fillmore would accompany him "from home on the walk to church and back, to the hearse and maybe play a few selections there at the grave. Sometimes I had to take off from work half a day to play that. They gave you three dollars to play that job. There was no union for us then, till 1919." Since Dobinski, a trumpet player who organized the band along with Max's father, was a tailor by trade, the band had first call on any funerals or weddings connected with the tailors. And, of course, they had sharp tailor-made outfits. Dobinski's son played trombone, and there were other father-son pairs in the group besides Max's father on bass and Max on snare.

When the Fillmore played a wedding, a string group was formed from the brass band personnel.

All these musicians had to double up, for brass band and dance band. See, trumpets would double violin, and clarinets would double violin also. The alto horns do second violin parts, trombone goes to cello, the tuba becomes string bass. Even my father played a little second violin instead of bass drum. If they played a wedding in a house, they brought troughs for washing in, they put these boards on them, and they made a platform, playing against a wall in a room. The minute somebody would be coming in, a few musicians would move to the veranda to welcome them. In those days, weddings were usually on a Monday or Tuesday or some other

The Fillmore Band, Buffalo, c. 1915. *Left to right: (on floor)* Bernard Rydlewski, Max Ciesielski; *(seated)* Thomas Wegrzyn, John A. Dobinski, Sr., Francis Ciesielski, Francis Kucharzewski; *(standing)* John Krzyzanowski, John B. Dobinski, Jr., Francis Kulminski, Francis Petko, A. Ratka, Julius Hichmut, Max Pongorski, August Willert, Francis Bakowski, Walter Grzebinski.

weekday, never on Saturday. You never heard of a Saturday wedding then. Our pastor, when they first started having these Saturday weddings, he wouldn't allow it because he'd say it was stopping people from attending church the next day. That was Alexander Pitas, the second one.

Max was quick to debunk the myth of the three-day wedding: "No, one day. The rest that you hear is only talk, about these weddings going on for days. It was hard enough on the musicians for these weddings, playing from early afternoon till three in the morning most of the time, and they might have to play another wedding the next day." It may have been only one day, but it was a big one. "For my wedding (1922), we

had two different orchestras. One with piano and the Rashayers in one room of this house, playing overtures and selections like that just for listening. Then another eight- or nine-piece orchestra for dancing. That was the band I was playing in at the Rivoli."

Listening to Max talk about all the wedding work over the years, one can feel the "band" and "orchestra" concepts slipping away even before the impact of talking pictures, radio, and recording was felt.

Now this new music [Max meant changes occurring around World War I and after] for weddings, starting with Neubauer, introducing the German style, came about by ordering a piano for the room in the house, and the musicians would sit on the wall side on a platform and play there. Then they would tell the people later just to clear out a bedroom for the piano and have also violin, trumpet, or clarinet, and it was smaller and they could charge less. They would take the wedding for about $10 per man then. And they would get a lot of money in tips playing requests. You would make good money on those jobs. Anyhow, that's what started the trend to pianos and small orchestras at weddings. While I was at the Rivoli, I would sit in with different groups for weddings, and there were a lot of different combinations of instruments with the piano.

Max started work at the Rivoli in 1920 after joining the Musicians' Union on October 19, 1919. He already had his working papers by the age of fifteen and was working steadily as a printer at the biggest Polish newspaper, *Everybody's Daily*. "My mother was against musicians. She'd say, 'I got one at home and I don't want to see more.' So I had to be a printer." But music was Max's passion. He still had his first union book and showed it with pride, since in a union of about five hundred members when he joined, there were fewer than twenty Polish musicians, and most of those were from two or three staunch union families. To get into the union and to land the Rivoli job, Max worked the Fillmore Theater every night for two years with a four- or five-piece improvising "orchestra." "They would give you a cue sheet, 'minute and a half andante.'" So after two years of crashing the cymbals for Chaplin's pratfalls and taking intermissions while the piano player kept pace with cowboy William Hart's chases, Max went with a dance band for a season, then did some more theater work on William Street. Starting with his earliest experiences in the old Fillmore Band—playing at parish stage shows and amateur nights in addition to the weddings and funerals—Max had a long and varied apprenticeship.

Max worked at the Rivoli from 1920 to 1929, printing by day and drumming by night, with piano lessons between shifts. He took one year away to play in the 44-piece pit orchestra (later to become the Buffalo Symphony) at Shea's Hippodrome. He dropped printing for a while but was fortunate to get a good job back just before the Depression. Like Ed Krolikowski, Max broke into radio in 1929, but the show lasted only two years because the musicians were gradually pushed aside by what came to be the most widely listened to and syndicated Polish-American radio show of all time:

You might have heard of Father Justin's *Rosary Hour*. Well, his program took over. At first we were an hour and a half show. Then Kolipinski, the furniture store sponsor, was selling Maytags those days; our mothers never had washing machines, but Kolipinski got affiliated with that firm with the name, that's so funny in Polish, and he sold carloads of the Maytag machines. So Kolipinski started letting Father Justin take time to talk about church and things like that. They were building this college then out in Athol Springs. He would answer questions people sent in during our intermission. We would go out and rest or smoke—though I never smoked in my life—and that's how Father Justin originated that program.

After talking movies, this remarkable talking priest, and the crash of 1929, Max's musical life was never quite the same. Over the years music became less a second job than a hobby. But he continued to play occasional weddings through the 1960s, and in parish bands formed for special events; he often worked with German bands in the 1940s and 1950s; and until the day he died in 1976, Max was active in the Shriners' Band, playing solos on the bells.

Somehow, Max never entered fully into the Polish-American polka style when it emerged with the Depression. He identified himself as a professional, a union man, and his parents were from Poznan—"that was what they called the 'class.' The other ones were from Austria and Russia." An elusive but persistent sense of respecting German standards may have been just enough to keep Max from a deeper commitment to the new polka style. In our interview, one of the first things he was eager to talk about was the wonderful transformation of the German rhinelander into a Polish specialty number. He had kept the sheet music of every rhinelander composed by a local Polish musician; for Max, they apparently symbolized a victory in the *kultur kampf*, demonstrating the ability of Poles to do a German thing better than Germans themselves. The

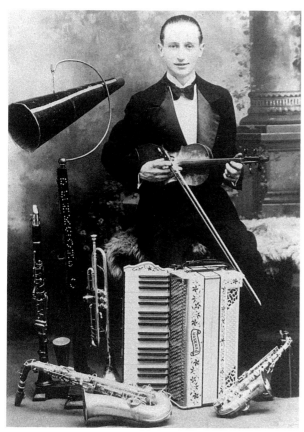

Doc Penkson, Buffalo, c. 1920.

Doc Penkson, however—an old-timer from Buffalo's Black Rock district, a smaller mixed ethnic neighborhood on the other end of town from the huge Polish East Side—led one of the early polka bands in Buffalo and was able to show us his lists of tunes from the early 1930s when singers still used megaphones. He too made a point of putting the polka in the middle of a musical mix that included lots of jazz and dance music. If we had come to Doc with "wedding band" questions, or "dance band" questions, or professional and commercial music questions, or union/non-union issues, he could have contributed to a book about any one of those themes. As it was, we talked about parish dances in the old days and the dangers of working across town or courting a woman from the East Side, since there was a fierce rivalry between the two Polish districts. Doc Penkson's band, like all the Polish-American bands and radio-recording orchestras of the 1930s and 1940s, played what people wanted to hear and dance to from night to night, weekend to weekend, location by location. In all these bands, "polkas, waltzes, and obereks" came to be thought of as "the Polish book"; "the English book" designated all the other music that people might want to hear at a wedding or a dance: jazz-styled foxtrots and lindy-hops, swing standards, crooned ballads, tangos, rumbas, hillbilly songs—you name it.

The emergence of distinctive made-in-America polkas around 1928 coincided with a dual or dialectical recognition that Polish-Americans were both Polish and American, able to make music and to dance in the styles of mainstream America and yet insisting at the same time on maintaining a Polish-American way of singing, dancing, making music. In the years leading up to World War II, this dual identity was carried by Polish-American bands mixing swing and polkas in the manner that came to be known as the Eastern style, once it became clear in the 1950s that "Chicago style" was proposing a very different Polish-American identity. The story of these two polka styles is the subject of the next chapter.

old Fillmore Band had been part of that same German-Polish competition. It was named the "Fillmore" rather than something more Polish so that it might "be used for Italian affairs, German affairs." Because the German community has been almost completely dispersed by the African-American migration from the South, it is easy to forget that the Germans more than any other neighbors helped shape Buffalo Polonia's self-image for three generations, from 1879 to 1940.

For Max Ciesielski, polka remained a part of the musical mix but was not a field in itself, a style alone.

Li'l Wally, Lackawanna, New York, 1972.

2. From Eastern to Chicago Style

Today at Polish-American polka dances anywhere you will hear "push" and "power" variations on Chicago-style polkas pioneered by Eddie Zima and Li'l Wally Jagiello in the early 1950s and developed by Marion Lush, Eddie Blazonczyk and Happy Louie Dusseault in the 1960s.[1] It is easy to forget that for the two decades leading up to and through World War II, when polkas were at their peak of popularity, Eastern-style orchestras dominated all the recordings and were featured at dance halls all over the country.

This chapter celebrates the personalities of band leaders, those individuals with an ability to shape the playing of a group of musicians into a distinctive "sound" that becomes recognizable to polka fans everywhere. Still, we must pause for a moment to praise all the musicians who won't be named here but who added unique shadings, special touches and timings, ideas for arrangements, and promotional energies; without them a particular polka sound might never have emerged or been delivered to the people for their dancing pleasure. In an important sense, however, each band leader's name is a symbol for all the musicians who have passed through that band and all the fans who have danced to its music and inspired the musicians to perfect their way of playing.

Eastern Style and Walt Solek

Just as Li'l Wally Jagiello has always been Mr. Chicago Style, Big Walt Solek personifies the Eastern style. Just eighteen in 1929 when the moment for polka bands arrived, Solek emerged as a leading figure with the World War II polka boom. Choosing Solek as the representative band leader of Eastern-style Polish-American polkas may seem to slight some other wonderful leaders and their bands. Frank Wojnarowski, Bernie Witkowski, Ray Henry, and Gene Wisniewski could each lay legitimate claim to the title of most typical or best Eastern band at different moments during the 1940s and 1950s. In their different ways the Connecticut Twins, Ray Budzilek's band in Cleveland, Bud Hudenski and the Corsairs in Pittsburgh, the G-Notes

Cover of *Polka Guide*, 1964.

and the Krew Brothers in Buffalo all went on to perfect the Eastern style in the 1960s. And Jimmy Sturr's orchestra of excellent musicians, often featuring Walt Solek on vocals, did everything anyone could ask to keep the tradition alive in the 1970s and 1980s. But Solek is the focus here because through all these developments he has been a presence and a reference point, setting standards of both musicianship and showmanship in a relaxed and cheerful way.

The performing Walt Solek—"Jolly Wally," the "Clown Prince of Polkas," the "Polish Spike Jones"—is both a "character" himself and a "character actor," a comedian of many costumes, the spirit of comedy itself. A colorful presence, a figure of high energy and visibility, Walt Solek became the leading clown or jester, the first one, the best one, and perhaps the last one in a musical style where clowning, jesting, controlled craziness in the face of adversity are central to everything. Why does Solek seem bigger than any one—or even the sum—of his parts? All clowns are one and the same clown, but Solek is Solek. Whether he is in butcher's apron and wondering who stole the *kiska* or in drag and complaining about the size of his

Ray Henry Orchestra, n.d. *Left to right:* (saxes) Walter Obzut, Charlie Wojnarowicz, Jimmy Farber; (trumpets) John Janton, Stanley Bajek, Gene Anop; (drums) Billy Krul; (accordion) Ray Henry; (bass) Peter Jenack; (piano) Peter Pantaluk; (vocals) Eddie Kosak.

The Connecticut Twins on record.

boobs—"They're *always* in the way"—you know that the disguise is just an excuse for Solek to be Solek.

Walt is tall, and his face is long and thin; he seems bigger than the parts he plays. And he doesn't make much effort to disguise his voice, so that whatever the sight, the sound doesn't change. Because we've seen him and his routines before, each song and costume shift can be like meeting an old friend again. And again. And again. If one Walt Solek is a lot of fun, many Walt Soleks are even more fun. The fact of many costumes and characters elicits admiring curiosity— what will this guy get into next?!—and a feeling that the party may go on forever. He is a gal with skinny legs and a big bosom; a loaded American veteran of foreign wars with a few too many medals; a berserk backyard chef with a violin on a big rubber band, which he bounces off the floor; a *goral* (mountaineer); a clown with a phallic cigar in one hand and a plastic piglet he calls "my pork" poking out of his drawers, which are themselves covered with the "smiley-face" emblem. He might just go on and on forever and become everybody.

Solek has been an ongoing protean personality for quite some time now, clowning around since the 1940s and performing actively as a musician for a decade before that. One way to think about him is as the eastern performer who defined polka happiness in one of its essential forms in the 1940s, just as the midwestern Li'l Wally defined it in the 1950s. Both are drummers, both performers, both children of parents from the mountainous part of Galicia, both "crazy," though they differ in important ways. The magic that goes with their names inside the polka world has to do with their ability to deliver the crazy essence, the

Walt Solek and fan, 1977.

Walt Solek at the mike, 1977.

spark, the energy of their respective styles. Happy Louie describes them as his two great teachers: Solek taught Louie the importance of "showmanship," but it took Li'l Wally's first tours of the East to drive the point home.

Walt's story begins in Meriden, Connecticut, where he was born in 1911.[2] He remembers cleaning out the spitoons in his father's saloon: "They used to say, 'All the money you can find in the spitoons, you can keep,' when we would go in there to clean up on Sunday mornings. I remember it was a big rosewood bar that cost about $3,000 and that was a lot of money in those days." Walt's father died of influenza at the

age of forty-eight in 1923, leaving Momma with nine kids. Father Solek was a violin player, and Walt has an old picture of his father and six of his brothers playing in an orchestra back in Szymbark, very near the Czechoslovakian border. In the picture you can see three violins and a clarinet, so "orchestra" is probably the right word. As Walt described what the rest of the ensemble was doing, the sound of resonant old *gorale* string sections came to mind:

And then they have a "secondova," a second violin, then a viola that's a little bigger than the violin. You see, they didn't have no accordions out there. Accordions came into being

Walt Solek in performance, 1977.

Walt Solek with the Krakowska Orchestra, n.d. *Left to right: (front)* Pete Krol, Eddie Smith, Walter Grabek, Syl Markowski; *(back)* Joe Mocadlo, Frank Wawroski, Walter Solek, Matty Krawczyk, Henry Solek (leader).

in this country. Some places they may have had concertina or the little accordion, but really all they did was bass, you know, um-pa-pa. They always had a drum too; sometimes the bass took care of it, but see these strings are really the family. They'll always have a drum, no matter what else they got. But the accordion, no, and then the trumpet, you never saw any trumpet either.

It was basically strings (that whining *gorale* string sound with a clarinet added), a bass (or the "big cello" you can see on some of the contemporary *gorale* folk albums that come out of Poland), maybe some drums or percussion (no drumming on those same Polish *gorale* albums, though) that made up the sound Walt's father brought over with him. The uncles seem to have stayed behind.

Music must have been a big part of the family's life before and after Walt's father died. Walt's older brother Henry was a violinist, a bandleader, and co-founder with Walt Grabek of the influential Krakowska Orchestra. A younger brother, John, played sax and clarinet, leading his own band during the 1940s. And

when Walt's mother married a Lithuanian named Mudry, two stepbrothers also became musicians, Joe as a drummer and Tom as a bassist. Cousin Syl (Uncle Benny's boy on Walt's mother's side) played clarinet and sax, and Walt teamed up with Syl in the late 1920s to form a band called Marko's Jazz Pirates. The way Walt tells it, he was pretty good at the drums after just a few lessons, and when his older brother Henry wouldn't hire him, he and Syl decided to get into jazz piracy on the high seas of Meriden.

That jazz was the idiom of the first band he worked in is another measure of the formative influence of black music on Polish-American polka style. It was not just Ed Krolikowski in Bridgeport and Walt Solek in Meriden who listened to and played jazz in the roaring twenties; every second-generation Polish-American kid who grew up then must have been touched by the sound, and young musicians in particular would have been more than attracted to a music that "everyone" was dancing to in those days. The question, as in Ed Krolikowski's story, is why the sudden turn to old country markers of ethnicity at that particular time.

41   From Eastern to Chicago Style

The big shift for Walt Solek seems to have come at the moment the Krakowska Orchestra was formed. Walt had been breaking into the polka field by replacing his brother in a backup band that would take Saturday night jobs when "Henry Solek and His Orchestra" were busy elsewhere. But this practice of sending the second band caused such confusion and frustration— the Falcons or the Eagles would be angry about not having the real Henry Solek alive and in person—that Walt finally refused to take second bands anywhere. Then, about the time this issue was coming to a head, they had the chance to do a broadcast on WTIC in Hartford:

They wanted an auditioning band. So my brother's five-piece band and another band from Middletown, Walt Grabek's, they combined them together and I played drums. I recall we were at this hall in Middletown, rehearsing. "All right, we want to know what we are going to call the band." "Well, how about Henry Solek and His Orchestra?" The other team: "No, Walt Grabek and His Orchestra!" So we headed it off and said we'd call it the Krakowska—Henry Solek, leader; Walt Grabek, Manager. That was about 1937, maybe earlier, 1936.

For about 11 years we were on [WTIC] at eleven o'clock to eleven-thirty. It went all through the war. They stopped all Polish vocals because they thought it was a way to give messages to the enemy or something. So you had to translate from the Polish into English. It was a great show, always live right from the Polish Home in Hartford. That place used to be filled, a thousand people used to be there, up and down, coming from all over, from way out in Newfoundland, you'd get letters from there. Yeah. The people in Pennsylvania would tell us that all the people in a little neighborhood where houses are close together, everybody would put their radio on in the window, tune in, and they'd all dance in the streets. Because out in Pennsylvania, to hear Polish music, you know, I guess I was the first one to sing it in Polish on a big station like WTIC. I was doing the drumming and they'd put a microphone up to your mouth. Couple of times I'd run up to the front.

His vocals with Krakowska established Walt Solek's reputation, and his big hit, "My Girlfriend Julida,"

made him a star attraction, able to tour and do appearances on his own. Like a lot of important American music history of that time, the "Julida" story is somewhat muddled. A number of struggles were coming to a head all at once—not least, of course, a world war. The big record companies, Victor and Columbia, were still competing for the ethnic market, but other labels were already looking for a piece of the action. Because "Beer Barrel Polka" was such a big hit for the Andrews Sisters, the polka was suddenly seen as a source of mainstream popular music. After Walt recorded "Julida" on the small, independent Harmonia label, the big companies responded with cover versions. With the wartime shellac shortage, all competitors were scrambling for pressings, putting out platters of dubious quality in the effort to meet demand (Walt recalls that the first "Julidas" were worn out and turned white after three or four plays). And though its role in the "Julida" confusion is unclear, the musicians' union waged an attack on the record companies and their practices in a desperate effort to keep live music and musicians in business, or at least to have them better paid for allowing their sound to be reproduced thousands and millions of times. In short, although "Julida" was a hit for Walt, we don't know how big it might have been, because the shellac shortage, the covers and competition, the union pressures, the studio closings, and Walt's joining the Navy after Pearl Harbor all contributed to cutting the popularity of the song in general and Solek's original version of it in particular. "Beer Barrel Polka" was a big hit from 1936 to 1939 and on into the war years. "Julida" might well have had a similar three-year run into "evergreen" or "standard" status if the war had not intervened and kept Walt from going out on the road to promote it.

Walt got out of the service after about a year and was on the road again with a nine-piece band. He also recorded for Columbia at that time. He worked steadily enough to keep the same core group of musicians together through the late 1940s and early 1950s. Their best territory was Pennsylvania, Ohio, and West Virginia: "Union Town, Paw Paw, West Virginia, out in Fairmount. All the name bands used to play out there,

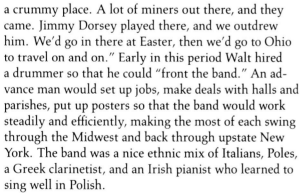

Frank Wojnarowski, n.d.

Walter Dana, n.d.

a crummy place. A lot of miners out there, and they came. Jimmy Dorsey played there, and we outdrew him. We'd go in there at Easter, then we'd go to Ohio to travel on and on." Early in this period Walt hired a drummer so that he could "front the band." An advance man would set up jobs, make deals with halls and parishes, put up posters so that the band would work steadily and efficiently, making the most of each swing through the Midwest and back through upstate New York. The band was a nice ethnic mix of Italians, Poles, a Greek clarinetist, and an Irish pianist who learned to sing well in Polish.

Walt very clearly remembers the moment when he realized that polkas and big-time, big-label, big-band music were in trouble. After the Columbia years, he had a five-year contract with Victor:

But with two years to go, I asked for my release because they weren't promoting. I'd be in the store and a salesman would come in—this is when Eddie Fisher was big—and . . . no mention of polkas. I come up, he doesn't know who I am, I ask about polkas, he says, "Oh, polkas." So I told him who I was, and I said that people are looking for polkas, my polkas. Don't you try to sell any? He says, "Well, the store keepers, they only buy five or ten of them, but when they buy Eddie Fisher, they buy five hundred of them." I said I'd talk to the management when I was in New York. Finally, I asked for a release and they gave it to me. So I went with Dana.

Dana Records was where all the best Eastern-style bands wound up in the early 1950s. By the time we embarked on this study, however, Walter Dana was

Walt Solek's drums, 1977.

Walt and Wanda Solek, 1977.

Walt went to California with the band in 1955:

We got a contract to go out there and do a movie short for Universal. Just ten or fifteen minutes, before the feature. We did it. It came out good. People saw it around at different theaters. We also played this ballroom that was right by the water, Santa Monica. Lawrence Welk was playing in one ballroom. There were three ballrooms. Spade Cooley was in another one and we were on the end. That was when Welk wasn't nationwide yet. He was just in Los Angeles for the Buick people.

Walt tried without success to get Welk to play "My Girlfriend Julida" and "Who Stole the Kiszka." Nevertheless, checking out Hollywood was the right move, because movies, TV, and the rise of rock-and-roll and country-and-western were all taking people away from Eastern-style polka happiness and fast. Li'l Wally was beginning to tour eastward with the Chicago style, winning converts in Ohio and Pennsylvania. And even home base was not safe. By the 1960s the Connecticut Twins, Jas and Stas Przasnyski, with a six-piece band, good amplification, and precision arrangements, were being hired for those big annual parish dances if an "Eastern" sound was wanted. And, finally, Happy Louie and his drummer put together their own Bay State version of Li'l Wally's beat to become the main attraction in the New England area from the late 1960s through the 1970s.

When working full time as a musician-entertainer was no longer possible, Walt settled down to maintaining his apartments in Meriden, working as a carpenter for his contractor son-in-law, and generating polka happiness on the weekends. He remembers the pleasure of taking a band out to the Long Island Polish farm communities near Riverhead where sacks of potatoes and fresh fish were often added to the pay, and the particular joy of playing for the wedding of the daughter or son of a couple at whose wedding he had played twenty-five or thirty years before. Now, at 80, Walt still gets out with his own band or does guest appearances with Jimmy Sturr and other bands. Don't miss him if he comes to town.

in delicate health, and his devoted wife was very protective of his privacy. Bits of information gathered over the years portray a sophisticated Polish emigré, secure in his educated Polish background, for whom Polish-American polka music was almost as exotic and exciting as African-American jazz. In the little anecdotes told about him—that he could fix or fill in a horn part with a few strokes of the pen; that he always wanted "more cymbals" from Wojnarowski's driving drummer, Frankie Chop; that he recognized the essential "dissonance" in Ray Henry's clarinetist and wanted a similar sound from any replacement—it is clear that Dana as a musician, producer, and salesman wanted each band to keep its characteristic sound and be at its zesty best in the studio. The Solek recordings from the Dana era capture Walt and his band, matured by years of touring but still full of zip. The other band leaders would probably agree that their Dana recordings of the early 1950s represent some of their best work and the peak of an era just before its collapse.

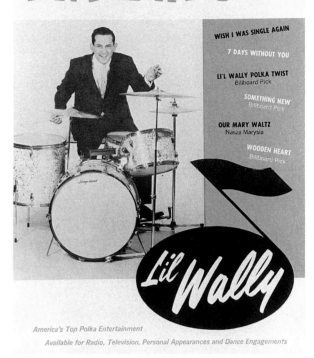

Li'l Wally, 1949.

Li'l Wally flyer, 1958.

Chicago Style and Li'l Wally

In the 1950s Li'l Wally emerged as the crystallizer of Chicago-style polka, which featured a slower beat, clarinet and trumpet, a driving concertina, and Polish lyrics sung "from the heart." Chicago style was improvisational and had both the urgency of expression and the capacity to communicate deeply with an audience that are seldom achieved through composed music. Music with some of these elements had been played in Chicago long before this time, but records and radio persisted in featuring only Eastern-style and Slovenian-style polkas—music that was quick and highly polished but lacked the enthusiasm and abandon of the village-based Chicago style.

Li'l Wally's first records sold astonishingly well de-

spite the fact that local radio shows initially shunned them. Chicago-style polka simply overwhelmed these initial obstacles, flowing out of the gin mills on Division Street, the picnics in Caldwell Woods, and the Polonian halls scattered throughout the city. Rooted in public spaces, the style expressed Polish-American culture in a deeper, more spontaneous manner than anything that had come before; when disc jockeys did begin to play Chicago-style polkas on their programs, they did so in response to their audiences' intense demand. When Wally describes the deep enthusiasm of the fans for his own and other Chicago-style music, he is, if anything, understating the case.

Buoyed by his success in Chicago and sure in his belief that the music was responding to the deeply felt but until then frustrated musical needs of a large community, Wally went on the road, following his records and broadcasts through the polka belts of Ohio, Wisconsin, Michigan, Pennsylvania, and New York. The legend of this appeal was there before he arrived, and Wally succeeded immediately almost everywhere he went. Nearly thirty years later a Polish musician from Minnesota had this to say about the impact of Chicago-style music on small Polish communities that had been, until that time, listening to other musical styles:

I am Polish but I was born into German music in southern Minnesota: Whoopee John Wilfahrt, the Six Fat Dutchmen. These were polished bands. They were recording all arranged music. The musicianship was so good. I love it. The Minnesota Dutchman style was a big influence. There were very few Polish musicians in southern Minnesota. One I know was an excellent concertina player: Eddie Chesny. They played Polish songs, concertina, guitar, violin: the Chesny Brothers. Their recordings are still popular. Their music has a Scandinavian tinge to it. There were no Polish bands there.

I would say that this was about 1959. I was at this dance, the first time Li'l Wally played in the Twin Cities. I was very fortunate. As a musician I had played this ballroom many times with the Minnesota Dutchman–style bands. People would dance, have a good time. It was fine. But when Li'l Wally played, it was another world. People were crying; they were dancing on the tables. Nobody had seen a thing like this before. Northeast Minneapolis is a Polish community. They had records of Eddie Zima and Li'l Wally, but it was the first time a Chicago musician was there in person. And there were people there who had never been to a Polish-style dance before. The old people were crying. They were crying. It was wild. I felt very fortunate that I was there. I do feel this: I speak for the Midwest, south Minnesota and Wisconsin. Every Polish musician in those parts benefited from Li'l Wally. He was the first to bring music out of Chicago. He took it to Wisconsin and Minnesota, and if it wasn't for him the Polish people there would not have their music.

There was a ballroom in Minneapolis. The guy who ran it is called Larson. And he said to me, "It's great when Li'l Wally plays. All the polacks come down when Li'l Wally plays.[3] They don't complain if it is warm; they don't complain if the drinks are warm. As long as he is there, they dance."

Over the decade of the 1950s the Chicago style kept changing, enriching itself as it absorbed new influences and as it captivated fans and young musicians throughout the polka belts. The early 1960s seem to have been a watershed for the development of the polka scene within Polonia. In Buffalo, for example, numerous small neighborhood bands playing polkas in "Li'l Wally," "Chicago," "honky," or "dyno" style began to appear.[4] The Eastern style had been heavily influenced by the big band swing era in American music. The Chicago style was much more in tune with the rhythm and blues and early rock and roll of the 1950s. Furthermore, the abandonment of arrangements and the emphasis on aural learning had a tremendous impact on young third- and fourth-generation Polonian musicians who would probably otherwise have joined the rock-and-roll craze.

Joseph Trojak, an old Buffalo musician and father of Larry, the Dyna-Tones drummer, talks about the facility of these young musicians:

The old bands did not play from the ear like these kids nowadays. This happened because of the Chicago style. It seems to arouse an interest in the kids that's phenomenal. They have greater learning for Polish music. Before, no one could pick up an instrument and just play it like that. Now, they just listen and pick it up. In fact, I know some kids that will switch from one instrument to another without any lessons. In our days it was not done. The kids now have more Polish music in their heads. They are good at it. There is more interest in music. We did not use to have so many Polish bands. Now take a look at Buffalo. Pretty close to nine or ten well-known bands. . . .

Lenny Gomulka has said: "You've got to have it in your heart and in your head, but in your heart, in your soul." You can play any polka in the world—and from memory. I bet you he did not take a bit of a lesson in a lot of those instruments he plays. Many people do not understand that Lenny Gomulka plays trumpet, clarinet, etc. When I took my family to Cobo Hall on one of the first IPA conventions, they all played concertina! Now there is a tough instrument to learn to play, and they played it. . . . Whitey [Ryniec], here in Buffalo, is another case. Here's a guy that plays the trumpet and never took a lesson in his life. He took lessons on clarinet and sax. His

Strand Ballroom, Buffalo, c. 1973. *Left to right:* Joe Swarz, Li'l Wally, Bruno Mikos, Frank Lewandowski (not pictured).

brother Jackie plays the accordion. He plays with the New Brass. He plays the trumpet and he plays the concertina now. He never took a lesson on either. . . . The kids are picking up music by ear and feel. Once you get in your heart Polish music, you just love it.

That's where we break down the Eastern style from the Chicago style. Eastern style you could not improvise even if you wanted to. How could you put in your own riffs or improvise? You hardly had time to play the notes on the score or as you remembered them. Now, the Chicago beat is a lot slower, and you can improvise and put your feeling into it. You can let it come out in the music. . . .

And then there is the language. Most of these kids don't know Polish, but they sing it beautifully. I have a tape from when Larry played for Stan Jasinski's program. "You must have had a good upbringing by your father and mother. You are really good in the language" (Stan said this in Polish). And Larry said, "Whoa, back there! I can't understand a word you're saying!" And Jasinski remarked, surprised: "How can you sing that song better than I even do?"

Larry Trojak explains, "I can read it and write it pretty well. I just don't understand what it means. . . . I can recognize a word here and there, but I have just the sounds. That's all." Larry's music is a family project. His mother transcribes lyrics for him. She says: "You hear it and sing it. He has the gift of a phonetic ear. When I'm copying down the words for him, he'll ask me what does it mean. Then I tell him."

Joseph continues, "Primarily we'll copy the song and he'll follow it. How he does it is a mystery to me because he does not understand a word of Polish. . . . When you love something you can do it. That's the gift the Polish have. They listen to music, and they love it. Period."

The Trojaks' observations point to some basic contradictions in the evolution of this music and in the way the younger generation picks up the older style: they sing the Polish better than their elders but don't understand the lyrics; consciousness of being Polish is increasing even as the community itself diminishes. The most urban Polish-Americans, as well as their sophisticated suburban cousins, are taking up a village-sounding music and crying over the recognition of themselves in the sound.

In this context of versatility and intense feeling, the story of the Chicago style can be told through the history of its major proponent, Walter E. Jagiello— the indefatigable and dynamic composer-singer-instrumentalist-promoter known to his fans as Li'l Wally.[5]

The Li'l Wally story begins in 1930 in Chicago, where his parents (both born in Poland) eventually settled, following a trek that took them from Pennsylvania and through Wisconsin to the Windy City. Settled is hardly the word, for Wally remembers a childhood of bitter poverty, complete with evictions: "In the snow with no blankets. I was three years old." His mother was a houseworker; his father cleaned the streets. Wally remembers his father's frustration well. Jagiello was a smart man who for some reason found it difficult to learn English. He couldn't make money, couldn't speak the language, couldn't "get around; I mean, how downship can you go? You're trying like hell, and you just can't get no place." Wally's mother was very sick: "Thirteen operations. From soup to nuts." A sister, waiting by the tracks for her daddy to come home, was cut down by an oncoming train.

Another, at only three or four years, had died of influenza in Pennsylvania.

Wally never got to high school: "I only went to eighth grade grammar school, and worked in two shifts, three shifts, and enjoyed everything God gave me." He learned his English in school, but "I'm way behind the dictionary. I have to be corrected." At the same time, he is proud of his Polish, recognizing it as in some way the key to his success: "Not good English, but broken English. Good Polish, though. In fact, I was extraordinary because I spoke Polish even though I wasn't born in Poland."

Wally has worked since he was very young. He remembers washing the walls of his apartment when he was four, and he became a junkman at five. "I got a bunch of kids to help me. We would empty a whole garage." For Wally, work was an education in itself.

Since I was a kid, I've always been a hustler, a promoter. You name it, I've done it. Legally, the best way I can. Without no education, just eight years of grade school. They didn't teach me nothing about this. They taught me a little religion, a little history, a little arithmetic, how to be good, how to be bad. But not to make a living. That I had to learn myself.

It's nice to work. I love to work. It's nice to enjoy the better things of life. If you don't have money, it's hard to make money, but make sure you enjoy it at that certain age. Save some money for that rainy day. Always save for that umbrella, 'cause you never know when it's gonna rain.

Wally's musical career began early in the forest preserves outside Chicago where the Polish population of the city went for summer picnics.

I got my start at the picnics in the Caldwell Woods outside of Chicago. I was practically born and raised there with polka music. I'm talking about the bands, not singing. I always sang all my life. When I went to Caldwell Woods, I was five or six years old. It was in Niles, Illinois, right on the borderline. There were thousands of people there. Where else can you go for nothing? With the few pennies you have you want to get away from the city, the smoke, the fog, the smog, and all this bananas.

Polka dance on farm near Getzville, New York, 1927.

In his wanderings through Caldwell Woods, Wally heard an extraordinary generation of Polish-American musicians.

I'd go from one platform to another. That was a beautiful pleasure. There was Stanley Lelito, Matthew Wilk, Joe Kapka, Stanley Pelc, Steve Drwal, Walter Kendzior, Eddie Zima, Walter Mirus. Mirus, he was fantastic. This guy was powerful. He used to rip an accordion in half. He put his whole heart in it. Happy Birthday! He was powerful, a big guy. With music or without it, he was very good. This guy played like very few others. He is on the same order as Eddie Zima. A gift of God. So I used to go to all the stands, stay six feet behind, and sing to myself. From there it felt like I was part of the band. I knew all the songs. I knew them automatically. Nobody taught me. They came to me from old Polish records and from people singing at picnics. Word for word, that's why the dear Lord was very good to me. He gave me a good mind to remember. As fast as they can sing a song, that's how fast I can study it. I remember because I loved what I was doing. Happy Birthday! It penetrated.

Wally's professional entrance into the music came soon afterward. Although Wally describes it as sudden and intuitive, his description of his childhood is evidence that his fervent love for and understanding of urban Polish-American life developed much earlier.

Eddie Zima, n.d.

I only remember the major things before I was five. I remember when I used to play with blocks, play house. My mother and father . . . would come home with their friends and guests, and I would be in the corner as quiet as a bee, no buzz. I would sit there for three or four hours saying nothing, just listening to people talk.

Today's kids run around, they play with toys. Not me. I was a different kind. I sat and just listened because I felt it was their prerogative, and, for one or two, if I had made any noise my mother or father would have slapped me. It wasn't my place to be in the way. I would rather play with my blocks, but still I have to hear what's happening. I learned more by listening about the old times, old country, villages, how times are today, who got hurt.

One day, I suddenly walked into a band. I really liked this guy's concertina. I couldn't go to another platform. The sound came out like a ton of bricks. It hit me like it's the best steak in the world. It got me carried away, and I let loose. I started singing loud. The guy who's playing the squeeze-box says, "Come over here. You know the words to songs?" I said, "Yeah." He says, "Get over here. Sing. Sing for the public. Don't be bashful." I say, "Jesus Christ, I never done this before." He says, "That's all right. Wanna drink?" I say, "Yeah." He says, "What do you want?" I say, "Same thing you're having." I was just a kid–eight years old. Naturally, I had a couple of drinks. He says, "Very good. Keep up the

good work. Where'd you learn all these songs from?" "I don't know," I say, "they just came to me." "Next week," he says, "we're playing at another grove." I say that this is the only grove I know how to go to. He says, "If you want, I'll pick you up and take you there." I say, "I can't. I have some mother and father problems. I'd like to be there. I like the way you play." So we parted. Eight o'clock it was over, it got dark. That was Eddie Zima. He was seventeen, eighteen, nineteen. That's the way I met him.

Anyway, that next Sunday I went from platform to platform. The other musicians had heard me sing with Zima. "Hey, kid, I seen you sing with Zima last week. Belt out a few." So I start singing. There's a couple at a bar who call me over, buy me a drink, and ask me if I'll play at their wedding with the band. I say I'll be happy to come, but I'll have to talk to the musicians. They say they'll give me five dollars and all the drinks I want. "Sing. Make our guests happy." The hall was very close to my house. I could get there in five minutes. . . . I tell them I'll sing at the bar so I won't interfere with the musicians and they'll still have their singing.

He was an instant sensation: a ten-year-old child wonder with a heart-breaking voice and a raunchy wit to match. He did the polka's great "spicy" songs as well as the schmaltzy waltzes. Soon he was doing weddings for pay. Three sets for five dollars, drinks, and food, and he danced with the bride as well: "What the hell, I'm invited." Within two months he was booked solid.

When I sang these do-jiggers, people started to talk to the musicians. Members from different organizations would be at each other's affairs. Musicians started to contact me. When people came to the picnics, they would book me for the winter. I had to mark down dates. That's the way it grew. Weddings were very important to me, even more than organizations' doings. You only get married once, but there are other people going to that wedding, and they're getting married too. They want to entertain their people. If I entertain them at the bar, that's less booze they're gonna drink. They're saving more than what they pay me. The guy is gawking. The woman's gawking. That's wasting time and saving booze. I'm singing seven songs in a row. Multiply that by three minutes. That's twenty-one minutes. You didn't touch that drink. Okay, after that you're gonna have another one, but you might have

Li'l Wally, Division Street, Chicago, 1983.

had three before that because you didn't have nothing else to do.

The next major development in Wally's career came soon after, when he teamed up with Eddie Zima. Wally remembers following Zima, at once an awestruck fan of his musical genius and at the same time a full co-worker in the band.

This was all a big shot in the arm. I like Polish music. I like to sing. Everything's hunky-dory. (By now I'm twelve years old). Shoot the moon! I'm getting a lot of jobs. And as fast as I can find out where Zima's playing, that's where I want to be. Of all the bands, this is my favorite. An idol. That's my idol. When I'd show up, he'd say, "Joe, the kid's here. Put him on a table. Let him sing." That was on a Sunday. We left about 2:30. Then Zima said, "Let's go to another place." I loved it. I thank the dear Lord it happened. I loved the singing. Whatever I did was for the good, even though I wasn't of age. I don't think I was that wrong. So we went to another place. He played the squeezebox, I sang, and we had a few schnupers. He introduced me around. "This kid's gonna sing for my band. Wally, you're gonna sing for me. I'll book you for every job. Five bucks a night." I said, "Okay." He said, "You can only sing with me, cause this is the way I'm gonna book all the jobs." So I sang with him, we were fairly heavily booked, and my parents

wondered what happened. The thing with Zima lasted about a year. It finally broke up over money.

For the next couple of years, Wally went freelance, working both sides of the old Polish Broadway.

I started strolling Division Street. I knew a lot of people there. For example, there was the Gold Star, the Midnight Inn, Phyllis's, Zosia's (that's Winchester and Division), Al's Village Inn, and the Orange Lantern. The Lucky Stop, where I played later, wasn't in existence yet.[6] There were sixty taverns easy, and 90 percent had live music. They either had a concertina player or an accordion player or a two- or three- or four-piece band.

I used to walk in the taverns, sleeves rolled up with a cigarette in my mouth, and pull out four or five dollars and throw it on the bar. Twelve years old: that's a lot of money. "Give me a shot in the beer. Give yourself whatever you want." I never got refused. And when the jukebox was playing, I sang right along with it. If they didn't have too many good Polish songs, I'd just start singing. I'd let loose. I had my shot in the beer. Shoot the moon! Live it up! It was during this time that I started playing the drums.

One night I walked into the Midnight Inn. Mooney, the drummer, wasn't there, and the owner wanted music, so I start banging away. I'd never played drums before in my life, never even been behind them. So I started playing. The concertina player said to just keep the beat with my feet and don't worry about it. I kept the beat and it worked. I been playing them ever since.

The next phase of Wally's career began in 1944, when he formed his own band at the Lucky Stop. That was more than a simple business association: the Lucky Stop's owner, Stanley Korzeniak, had come originally from Poland and was a living repository of the music.

He was a great guy, Stas, a guardian. He loved me and Zima. He loved Polish music, too. We'd work on songs together. Stas knew a lot of songs. He sang, and he was pretty good. We made up the "Lucky Stop Waltz" and the "Break-Up Waltz" together. Then I made up songs. I'd sing them to Stas and say, "Tell me if I'm wrong, Stas. Correct my Polish according to the rhyme." He was right there on the spot. "You just play that son of a bitch!" He was the one who got me started on Jay Jay Records. He borrowed the money to get me into the record business. And I paid him back.

In the next years, Wally's business expanded dramatically. In addition to playing the Lucky Stop, he began to work at the Polish Roman Catholic Union Ballroom. "They got two ballrooms there, one upstairs and one downstairs. They've got a band upstairs, but what are they gonna do downstairs? So they figure, 'This kid on Division Street, he packs 'em in like sardines. Let's get him.' " In a year, he had turned the whole thing around, displacing a more conventional, continental-style dance band in the process. He remembers that triumph with more than a little glee. From early on, Wally was deeply aware of the relation between his own music and the specific community it served.

Lou Breese had been playing upstairs. A big name. Quality musicians. A fourteen- or fifteen-piece band. They played foxtrots, two-steps, a little cha-cha. I was pulling in more people than they were with my four-piece band. I switched to upstairs. I need more dancing space for my people. You need room to dance the polka. I want that, too. I put it in my contract. Some people used to come up and feel that the

modern music should be upstairs and the polka downstairs. They came up and asked, "What's your name?" I say, "If you can't read the poster, then forget about it." They'd say, "Play me this tune," some modern tune. I'd tell them the modern band's downstairs: "Polish polka music. That's all we play." So they'd get the goofs, cut off my speakers and so forth. I just lost $40–$50. The club owners paid for that. Freaky deals, but that's life.

By the age of sixteen, Wally had broken into the South Side. He started playing dances at the Grove Ballroom, and it was then that he met his other idol, Gene Krupa. Krupa, as soulful as Zima, was the premier drummer of his time and a manifest success, a Polish boy who brought sixteen musicians back with him when he returned to Chicago. Wally speaks of Krupa with the profoundest respect.

I've watched him work, watched other guys work, and I still feel they can't compare. It's the way he plays, . . . the feeling behind every song, behind every do-jigger he does with the sticks. He's got the feeling; this is what makes him. The guy is there, and he comes from the olden days. These newcomers, Happy Birthday! I've yet to find anyone who can beat Gene Krupa. Let me explain something. He started out in hard times. Today a drummer can be half decent, and with the right publicity agent and promotion, he can get further ahead than Krupa. Krupa had to walk the hard road while the other guy just slides in. It was just like me and many of the musicians who played with me. There was no expressway to go to different areas. We drove for hours and hours before we got there. We didn't even shave. Just got on the bandstand and performed. Dead tired. You're working for it. That's why I have respect for a guy like Gene. He had to work from nothing. Polish, he came from the South Side of Chicago, from Commercial Avenue, and he worked for everything he got.

In 1952—he was twenty-two—Wally and his brother Joe went into business for themselves: they bought and remodeled the Palace Ballroom, a failing hall with an associated tavern in a Bohemian neighborhood at 31st and Central Park. Success was a little more difficult than the brothers had anticipated. For starters, all the local customers left. "What I didn't

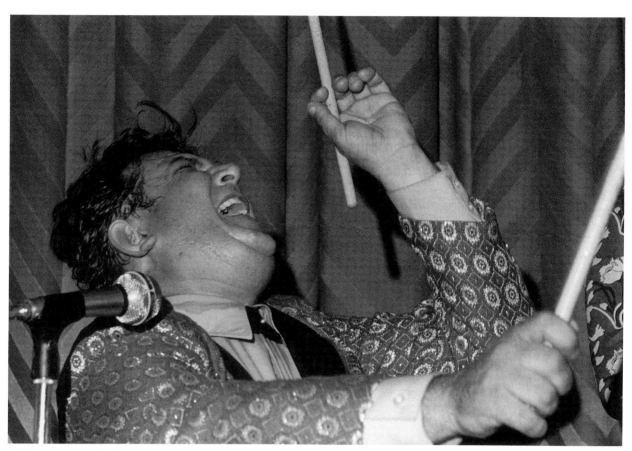

Li'l Wally, Buffalo, c. 1973.

know was that the Bohemian people don't dig the Polish people too well." A new audience had to be drawn to the hall, and this meant doing a different kind of merchandising.

I'm a firm believer in advertising. I bought newspaper ads in the big newspapers, in the *Times*. I advertised a big polka show: "Lucky Polka Show with Li'l Wally! Three Hours on Sunday!" I would blow four hundred, five hundred bucks on an ad. I did bus advertising. I had bumper stickers printed up. Billboard signs, about thirty different ones. You name it, I did it. Every kind of gimmick there is.

Years back, I had other gimmicks too. When I used to play at the Pulaski Ballroom every Halloween I'd advertise "Li'l Wally and His All Girl Band" on the air. People used to come because they thought I'd have all girls playing. I had all the musicians dress up as girls. I dressed up as a sexy broad. In the middle of the dance, around ten or eleven at night, I'd start doing a little strip. On the bottom I had a broad's bathing suit. I also dressed up as an old woman, with a wig and everything. It was novelty for me. And it was a good gimmick for the people. It was a lot of fun. Beautiful. I stopped it when I went on records. Then they were buying me for my music and for what I was, instead of for being a clown.

In two more years Wally had made his next big move: by 1954, he was playing in the biggest ballroom in Chicago, the Aragon. This was a historic moment for Wally. He sees it as a breakthrough, a moment of arrival not only for himself as a musician but also for his music.

They never had polka music before I played there. I got it in myself. I saw all the crowds coming out of the North and South Sides. You put them all together and ask why they're just dancing at a mediocre hall. Why can't all these people be together at the Aragon, the most beautiful ballroom in the world? This is where all the name bands play. It's high class, it's nice. Let's not begrudge the polka. Let's dance the polka at the Aragon.

Wally led his assault on the Aragon with a radio campaign. "Ladies and Gentlemen, wouldn't it be nice to dance the polka in the beautiful Aragon Ball-room, where Harry James, Lawrence Welk, and Glenn Miller have played? Let's dance the polka there! All you've got to do is come out. There's no excuse, not even a wedding." He got his response. Even with tickets at $1.50—Saturdays elsewhere usually cost the polka crowd a dollar or less, and this was only a Thursday night—he packed the place. Four thousand people came. They had to call the bartenders' union for more help.

Wally's experience as a radio entertainer had begun five years earlier when he and Chet Schafer started a weekly half-hour show called *The Lucky Polka Hour* on WCRW. They financed the program—it cost $35 for the half-hour—through a network of sponsors and through their service to the community, passing on information, announcing and celebrating major family events.

Lucky Stop was my first sponsor. Then I got the R and S shoe-store, Little Maxie's, Depend on Refrigeration and Fixture Company, Bill's Tuxedo Rental Shop, Flowers by Ed. People couldn't afford to buy clothes for weddings in those days, so they rented them. I'd tell them to go to Bill's. I had the flowers, the gowns, the whole wedding bit. I'd sell the people the whole package. They got a good deal, the sponsors were happy, and I was happy, too. We made a beautiful family.

Because at first I couldn't get enough sponsors, I'd say to the audience: "Ladies and Gentlemen, I don't have enough sponsors to produce this show, so I need your help. If there's a birthday, anniversary, a communion, whatever it may be, send your dedication with a dollar enclosed and this dollar will go toward producing the program. Also, mention the song you want to hear, and I'll be happy to play it if it is a polka." This is where I pulled in my mail. That helped convince people to sponsor me, that I could draw an audience.

All those special days—especially name days and saint's days—are very important to the Polish. Years ago, we had nothing to eat on the table, but my mother would still scrape up two dollars to buy a shirt and a tie for my brother Joe cause it was his name day, and that was even more important than a birthday. Little things like this mean a lot. You forget your wife's birthday or anniversary and see how fast you get bawled out. She's really down in the dumps: "It only happens once a year and he couldn't remember it!" This is why when

I was on the air I would mention that if your wife, girlfriend, mother, or uncle is gonna celebrate a birthday, make up a list and send it to me. At least two months in advance. This way, I mark it down, and I know I'll do it. Then the day comes, I do it. Right on time. At ten-thirty they have to go to church. They want it done at ten. I sing a few bars. "This is to you. I love you." You put feeling in it. They go bananas. That's the way you win an audience. Okay, we don't get as much attention as other types of music, but the ones that are faithful to you are *very* faithful. You couldn't buy a faithful fan for all the money in the world. You are good to them and they are good to you. You try to make them happy in any way you can.

At the center of a mutually reinforcing relationship, Wally was a primary "toastmaster" in his community as well as an excellent publicist for community business. Once they saw that he could really sell, sponsors stood in line to support his broadcasts. Within nine months, the show moved to WOPA, where he could reach all Chicago. He started with an hour on Sunday and in three months more was playing every morning of the week from seven to ten. Wally sees his ability to sell as a direct parallel to his performance as a musician.

If you give me a name, an address, and some idea of what you're selling, then *I sell.* I'm selling the audience like it was right in front of me. I sell with all my heart, with all my feeling. There is no script. If I screw up, that's all right, nobody's perfect. I do the same thing announcing as I do performing. Whatever comes out of me comes out of me. Nowadays, things are different. Some stations have rules. Thirty-second commercials, sixty-second commercials— sixty-three seconds? You talked too long. It's the FCC rules. There's supposed to be eight one-minute commercials in half an hour. I don't like it. I'm a punch announcer. I don't like to be timed. I talk because I like to talk. This is the way I was born. This is the way I like to perform. When I'm playing on a bandstand, if I want to play five minutes longer I'll just play. If they're happy, give them an extra shot in the arm, an extra kit and caboodle. Make sure they don't forget you.

People really listened. You can sell a lot if people know you. I had fans, people who knew my singing, my records, my radio work. When I asked them to drink Coca-Cola, they drank Coca-Cola. All because they were my fans. A person gets in the limelight, they should know what they're talking about. People listen when you say something. That radio audience was growing all the time. . . . I could talk faster than Carter has Pills, and yet I knew what I was talking about, and I came across to the public.

The same period saw Wally begin his recording career as well. He produced his first disc in 1948. His company was called Amber. The tunes were "Our Break Up" on one side, and "Away from Chicago Waltz" on the flip. Prevented by union rules from playing the record on radio stations, Wally hawked it himself ("I had them underneath my bed") to the taverns. He bought a phonograph for ten dollars and started out: " 'A brand new Polish record. Would you care to buy it? Nobody's got it. You can't buy it anywhere!' I created a demand by going to these taverns. Division Street, Cragin area, St. James, St. Stan's. Around all the Polish churches you had taverns, that's automatic. It worked real good."

Trying to find a firmer foothold in the recording business, Wally then signed on with Columbia as a singer. The contact was Chicago music store owner Alvin Sajewski, whose brother-in-law, Ed Terlikowski, had an orchestra with which Wally did four 78s for Columbia. But he was never happy with the results.

Many people who heard me asked, "Why didn't you record with your own band?" Terlikowski's people were good musicians, but they were choppy. You cut the notes real short, for Chrissakes, you ruin it. Terlikowski's band had a different beat. They were too fast for me. A little too much Eastern style. Chop, chop, chop, chop. That's why it didn't sell. In Chicago you couldn't sell that stuff. These people were very good in their respect, but they were not my style. The songs were fantastic. I sang the "Lucky Stop Polka," the "None Do I Care For Polka" . . . eight good songs. I could have sold them myself on a record by just singing and playing my concertina and drums.

Wally's reasons for insisting on his own band thereafter go, of course, to the heart of the matter. Chicago music had become a style, differentiated from the Eastern style. Wally ascribes a central place in the change to the tempo differences between the two:

You see, a polka was never supposed to be played fast. If you play it fast, you modernize it. I went to Europe, all different villages. I never heard a fast polka there. So why should I hear a fast polka here? My beat is more ethnic. People didn't used to understand that, but now they do. When I first began, DJs would send my records back and say there was something wrong. They were used to that other style, the Eastern style. They used to tell me this is too slow. I used to tell them it was ideal. Actually, it's not slow. It's a bouncy beat, but not fast. If you eat food, you chew it. What are you gonna get out of it if you just swallow it? You'll go to the wash room because it'll block you up. Same thing with this. Sure, certain people can dance it, but they have to be geniuses. They have to rehearse. Eastern style may be musicians' music, but I don't play for musicians—I play for the public. The public wants to hear melody, lyrics. They want to hear a song with a simple, real pretty story behind it that they can dance to. Real bouncy.

Listener participation is a major concern for Wally. He argues that because of the difficulty of actually dancing to it, the Eastern style separates an audience from the dance, makes people who would like to dance into passive observers of those few others who can "perform" the steps. In making this distinction, Wally once again reveals the degree to which his vision of polka music involves an event that is by definition an organic unity, that constitutes everyone as a participant and no one as an observer.

Now, don't get me wrong, don't misunderstand me. I don't say people who play Eastern style screw it up. They don't. They're good musicians. They play very well. I just don't . . . think they do justice to the polka. They may have dancers and teach them to dance real fast and then put them on television, but in the meantime a person who doesn't know nothing about polkas sees this, how they're moving their legs and hopping around like crazy and says, "I'm gonna dance this?! I'd die real fast! Impossible. Forget about it! Turn the channel!" Now, when you dance real nice, this they'll enjoy. Then you'll hit the other nationalities and all the other people.

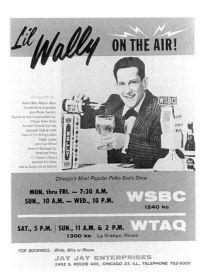

Li'l Wally flyer, 1962.

Ordinary people can't learn that fast stuff. They're not pros. They're hard workers. They work in steel mills, factories, they ain't going to be dancing like that. Saturday night is their time off. They dance to enjoy a dance. It's nice to watch someone else dance fast, but that is for a performance.

In 1952, Wally went back into the recording business. Separating himself from Columbia, he started a company of his own again, this time calling it Jay Jay, and opened a pressing plant as well. It was a way to work the market more effectively, to press and distribute his product according to demand, to achieve more control and flexibility in the process of musicmaking and distribution.

You see, the pressing companies . . . were too slow. I couldn't get my material fast enough or when I wanted it, so I gotta start off on my own. It's just like pancakes. . . . Especially when they're hot, you got to move them fast. Even if you come out with a hit real fast, it's impossible to cover all the states at one time. For a little organization, you'd need a million dollars just to have enough pressing to back you up to sell across the country at one time. So you cover some at a crack and just keep going on in a circle. By the time you

Li'l Wally and fans, Lackawanna, New York, 1972.

get to the last stop, you got another one cooking for the first stop. That's why I bought all the equipment and started off from scratch. Nobody taught me nothing. I looked for a bigger place, built recording studios, a pressing plant, and a shipping room. I had the whole works. It was a lot of work. I put in a lot of hours, but I enjoyed it.

By now, Wally had learned enough of the business to work its entire cycle. He could sell to the disc jockeys and he could place his records in the stores: both crucial links in the process. The DJ is, of course, central to any possible success, and Wally is acutely aware of how easily records can go astray.

Distribution depends a lot on the DJs—who plays a record, who doesn't. How many DJs got it, how many threw it in the garbage can, maybe gave it to the secretary and got an extra smooch. When it gets on the air, it starts moving. But still you've got to put in appearances. The record may be selling a little, but you're not there to help it. You're all occupied. Chicago, Wisconsin, Iowa. You got so many states to cover. How many places can you be in at the same time? It takes time to promote a record. It can bust open in one area—in Wisconsin, say—but that doesn't mean overnight it's gonna be a big thing in New York. There's a shift in merchandise by the time it's pressed. How do you know where it's gonna bust?

Over the next several years, Wally worked ceaselessly to expand and maintain his network. These were the years of his greatest success. In rapid succession, he wrote, performed, and marketed many of what have come to be seen as the classics of the Chicago style, songs such as "Puka Jasiu" and "Wish I Was Single Again."

That ceaseless effort took its toll. It had all the grind of a hard-driving small business as well as the literal hard driving a musician has to do. In the late 1950s the tours were booked as full as he could get them on a route through the Midwest and Northeast: "We'd hit Steven's Point on Tuesday, Minneapolis on Wednesday, Eau Claire on Thursday, Thorp on Friday, Wausau on Saturday, and Milwaukee on Sunday." In addition, the musicians, though many were very good indeed, didn't identify with the business the way Wally had to, and that meant he had to do even more work.

There were times I made myself sick, I worked so hard. I got my first ulcer in '52 when I was on tour. Touring is tough. You go out with some musicians and they don't want to share the work. When some of them go out on the road, they think they're on vacation. Driving, for example. Some musicians will help with driving, and some will fake it. "Oh, I'm so damn tired! I can't drive." There's nothing wrong with him. He just wants to sleep. He just wants somebody else to bust his ass. So many times I drove. Certain musicians drive much more than they are supposed to drive. And all because the other ones are con artists. They're waiting to get on the job all because they want to get on the job and smile and see some broads. They're stars! In the meantime, I got to carry all the shit, all the burden. "Hey, I come here to play. I don't carry no records."

The ulcer attacks increased, aggravated by the bitterness of the winters. "Don't forget, during the day it's forty and at night it's zero. . . . you're playing at night and you're soaking wet. When you get back in the car, you're dying. The next day, you've got a cold and your nose is running, you feel like hell, and you've got a job to play the following day. You know, you got to be built for this." And Wally was eventually forced to leave. At first he would retreat temporarily to Florida to recover, but a move to warmth and less pressure became essential to his survival. By 1965, Wally was living in Florida and trying to maintain his music business from there.

Down here in the winter, I do a lot of bar mitzvahs. I sing and I emcee. They have a three-piece or four-piece band. They get them from the union. The party directors at the hotels make all the arrangements. You can work a couple of hours here and a couple there, do two bar mitzvahs a day. You don't make much money, but you can get a lot of tips if you know what you're doing. It's nice, but it's not polkas. Once in a while you can sneak a polka in—like "Hava Nagilah" and all the other stuff. Much of the clientele is Jewish, and there are a lot of Polish Jews who like polka music, too.

I didn't leave Chicago forever. I still have my show there. I'm with Johnny Hyzny [on his radio show] now. I record the commercials from Miami Beach, but I always go back in the summertime. I show my face there. I go to the smallest places and to the biggest ones. I don't care where I go. I'm proud to see each and every one of them. Whether they're successful or not successful, healthy or sick. I like to see them because I've been with them, these people. We've been together. It's not only Chicago. It's all over the country. When I go to Cleveland, I want to see all my friends there. Steve at the Aragon

Walt Solek *(center)* and Jimmy Sturr *(right)*, Buffalo, 1976.

Lounge, Stas at the Polka Lounge. All of them. These are beautiful people. I love these people.

Even though Wally's career was cut short, he nonetheless remains a shaping force within the Chicago style. His legacy is clear, not only in his barely disguised imitators—such as Chicago's Li'l Richard the Polka General—but in the respect he commands from many musicians of the younger generation. Famous not only as a singer but also as a performer, Wally still brings an electricity to his work. When we first ran into him at Saint Michael's Church in Lackawanna, New York, on a bitterly cold winter night in 1974, he was leading hundreds of people through the hall in a huge dancing human chain and playing a concertina above his head. In the years since, he has continued to perform, using pickup bands hired for the particular occasion. He is still capable of dazzling us with his wit, ever able to give voice to our happiness and sorrows.

Eastern and Chicago Extensions

No major shift or upheaval has occurred in Polish-American polkas in the years since Li'l Wally took the sound of Chicago's Polish Broadway to points north and east. The changes of the past few decades are essentially modifications or variations of six well-established polka models: (1) the old big band Eastern style; (2) Li'l Wally's "honky" or early Chicago style; (3) the Connecticut Twins' use of improved sound-system technology to establish an influential small-group version of the big band Eastern style; (4) Marion Lush's innovative two-trumpet and accordion bellows-shake sound, which has become a hallmark of Chicago style; (5) Happy Louie's version of Li'l Wally's beat and energy, which could pass for a new "Bay State" style back East; (6) Eddie Blazonczyk's versatile Versa-tone sound that has made polkas seem current and modern year after year for over two decades.

Some polka fans might claim that Jimmy Sturr in New York and Dick Pillar in Connecticut have evolved something new from the Eastern tradition as they adapted to Chicago influences over the years, but their well-deserved reputations are due largely to strong summer festival promotional efforts that keep polkas visible and available, to be sure, but have not changed the music in any big way. Similarly, as Chicago style has been extended by driving bands like the Dyna-Tones, New Brass, and Chicago Push (Lenny Gomulka's spinoff from the Versatones), people talk about "push polkas" or "power polkas": more rock kicks and licks on drums, more chords and amplification on bass, and still more bellows shaking from concertina and accordion. But "push" and "power" describe energy levels; only time will tell whether they point to an evolving new style. A number of great and distinctive bands have developed in the various polka belts—for example, the Dynasticks in Detroit, the Tones in Chicago, the Canadian Fiddlestix in Toronto, Joe Oberaitis in Cleveland—but in making their

mark they have not opened up a whole new style of playing for other bands in other cities. Perhaps we are hearing a relocalization of polka styles and polka happiness.

The Connecticut Twins and Their Influence

As Connecticut Stas, leader and arranger for the Connecticut Twins (Stas and Jas Przasnyski), tells it, most people at a polka dance in the early 1950s didn't know what band was playing or how many musicians were performing.[7]

> On some of these records where there was a nine-piece orchestra playing, the accordionist would play his accordion solo, and the sax section would drop their instruments and the trumpets too. All you had was a four-piece band. So right then and there, it caught my attention: say, why do you have nine musicians? You don't need them. All you have to have is a trumpet lead, and harmony, and your rhythm, good rhythm, and that's it. Now, I did my own arranging and I picked out the best musicians, the most experienced musicians that I could find in the polka field. Then I went and invested in the best sound system to my knowledge that could take care of any hall and produce the sound. I think I was probably one of the first polka bands traveling around with fifteen-inch speakers back in 1953 or 1954.

With his big speakers and top-quality amplifier, Stas put one microphone on his accordion, one for the trumpet and clarinet, and one on the piano. (Already by 1952 the Ampeg electric bass was giving relief to the calloused fingers of the bass player so the balance was perfect and could fill any hall. Stas says the Ampeg bass was invented by Bernie Witkowski's bass player, Everett Hull, for polka purposes, but it went on to become the preferred bottom sound of Latin bands in New York City for three decades, whereas most polka bands soon switched to the guitar-style basses after they became available.) The Connecticut Twins' sound became a key model for Eastern-style polkas, not replacing the big bands so much as further marginalizing them. Ray Budzilek in Cleveland experimented for a

while with an enlarged big band that had two drummers, and a number of polka musicians who came
of age in the 1960s remember that band as a peak of
power and perfection, but it was a model no one could
afford to follow. By the late 1950s most of the new
bands with any Eastern roots at all were taking their
cue from the Twins.

When we began our research in Buffalo in 1969,
for example, two of the best bands around had been
inspired by the compact professionalism of the Connecticut Twins. The G-Notes and the Krew Brothers
were both excellent but had no place to go for broader
acceptance of their particular excellence. The Krew
Brothers—all six Krupskis—could have been a perfect complement to the lovely Lennon Sisters on the
Welk TV show if they had just been a little sweeter,
a bit cuter, and more commercial. Their musicianship was certainly of the same high standard as the
best national rock, pop, and country groups—as they
proved by playing in those idioms with great poise. But
they wanted to play polkas for people close to home
as well. Tony Krupski—a better singer and musician
than Bobby Vinton, better looking too—wanted to
lead a quality polka band and probably never thought
seriously of crooning to teens for a living. Similarly,
had the Karas brothers kept the tenor and accordion as
hobbies and put all their energies into another musical idiom, or another profession for that matter, they
might have garnered a lot more money and fame than
they got from fine-tuning polkas as the G-Notes. In
1975 as now, there was no "market," no national arena
or medium for bands, no larger public space or consciousness within which to compare, say, a Bobby
Vinton with a Tony Krupski. Musicianship that could
command the respect of anyone anywhere—all class,
ethnic, and neighborhood loyalties aside—was the
goal of Eastern style. The Twins, G-Notes, and Krew
Brothers achieved that goal and deserved recognition
outside Polonia, but in the 1960s and 1970s they could
not command the respect that a national audience had
accorded Frankie Yankovic in the late 1940s.

Think of this "Eastern combo" sound as the musical
equivalent of the New Ethnicity movement in the early
1970s, a conscious effort to be completely bicultural

and therefore acceptable to all. The Krew Brothers and
the G-Notes took great pride in their "English books,"
combing the charts for good songs in all styles, keeping
their 1950s rock medleys at a high energy level, aiming
to have at the ready anything a suburban working-
class listener or dancer might enjoy. "Suburban" may
be the key adjective for this style. It was during the
same period when the Dyna-Tones were beginning to
abandon their "English book" altogether and make the
Broadway Grill in the heart of the old Buffalo Polish
neighborhood their Sunday base of operations that the
Krew Brothers were giving peak performances at the
Jolly Roger out in the Cheektowaga suburbs.

More than a competition between two bands and
their fans, there was a competition between New
Ethnicity and Old Ethnicity, a struggle for the soul
and sound of Polonia. The Krew Brothers sought to
honor and reinterpret the whole range of American
working-class music: performing high trumpet dis-
plays in honor of Maynard Ferguson; covering the
Frank Sinatra and Tony Bennett classics sensitively;
learning the Latin percussion instruments well enough
to give a Motown medley the right touch. But seeking out a fiddler to get closer simultaneously to *gorale*
"soul" and country-and-western "soul" was definitely
a Dyna-Tones move, not something the Krews would
put high on their agenda. The Dyna-Tones wanted
to "get down" in a Polish-American way. The Krew
Brothers wanted to "get on up," "move a little higher,"
in a Polish-American way. African-American concepts apply in this instance, because neither band was
really understandable without reference points in the
soul and black pride movements of the late 1960s. The
Krew Brothers displayed in their "English book" a keen
awareness of rock, jazz, soul, and Latin techniques that
the Dyna-Tones never even attempted. The Dyna-
Tones tried to create a Polish-American equivalent
to the emotional core of blues and gospel, while the
Krew Brothers kept their Polish numbers very tidy and
quite traditional. Because the Dyna-Tones move was
down and inward, they were successful in their own
terms; because the Krew Brothers move was up and
outward, they missed, in their own terms, a similar
success.

Marion Lush and fan, Buffalo, c. 1973.

Marion Lush

Marion Lush's distinctive contribution to the evolution of Chicago style resists description because such a normal sound is at the center of the tradition. It *is* Chicago style, as distinguished from Li'l Wally's honky style and Eddie Blazonczyk's modern Chicago style, and it developed over a long time. Born August 10, 1931 (a year after Li'l Wally almost to the day), Lush too became involved in music as a child, joining a drum and bugle corps when he was eight. By the time he was ten or eleven he was playing for family and friends ("We had six families living in one house"), "switching off" on accordion and drums with a friend. At fourteen he

was playing the Lucky Stop, drumming with the Polka Stars. At fifteen, with some years of accordion study at Lee's Music School under his belt and lots of experience on drums, Lush taught himself the trumpet, taking his inspiration from Andy Day.

From around 1947 through the mid-1950s Lush played with the Polka Stars and then the Musical Stars. But not until the late 1950s, sideman Ed Benbenik remembers, did Marion's two-trumpet sound —Li'l Wally claims credit for the original innovation— emerge and Lush assume more leadership responsibility. In 1959 the Musical Stars included Stanley "Junior" Wozniak on trumpet, doubling on concertina, and that seems to have been the moment when

Marion Lush, Buffalo, c. 1973.

ances than the rest of the band members and took only the usual leader's fees on the road. "Back in the 50s we used to play for two dollars an hour per musician, seven hours on a Saturday night, fourteen dollars each, and we loved it," said Ed Benbenik. As touring became more and more important in the 1960s, however, the older partners in the band dropped out, and Lush became more fully the leader and star, eventually renaming his band the White Eagles in the 1970s. His is a very different history from the heavy-selling story of Li'l Wally in the 1950s or Eddie Blazonczyk's evolution as a polka organization man in the 1970s.

The early records were such big hits probably because the sound was matured and centered after a dozen years of evolution. In separate phone interviews, both Benbenik and Marion's drummer during the 1960s, Chester "Hoot" Filipiak, began with the same word to describe Marion's style, "dynamic," and shared a sense that the rhythm section was the basis of the band's success. As Ed put it, "Marion has always been hell on drummers; he knew what he wanted, the sound he wanted, and that's what he got. It was a relaxed, dynamic sound. Playing with other bands can be a lot of work, but with Marion it just flows along." Or, in Hoot's phrasing of the same phenomenon: "The most important thing in a good polka band is relaxation, to push it hard in a relaxed mood. If the trumpeters are playing tense, it can affect the whole band, and if anyone in the band is tense, the dancers can actually *feel* this on the floor. Lush's band was always relaxed."

Hoot brought his drumsticks to the phone to beat out a comparison between "Jeep" Machinya's snare drum rhythms and Li'l Wally's. As he talked about the beat of each drummer—the differences between Hoot's beat and Jeep's, and where Rudy Sienkowski's way with a snare drum might fit—it became clear that every polka drummer of reputation, every band with any local following, has a unique "beat." (Analysis of all these "beats" might produce a shelf of books on Chicago-style polka variations alone; indeed, there is an encyclopedia of information to be gathered on analogous music processes the world over.)[8] Talking about polka rhythm sections in general and Lush's "million dollar rhythm section" in particular (Gene

Marion's two-trumpet sound finally solidified. In the early 1960s when the band began recording, its members decided that having Marion's name as leader up front would help them get more work. Indeed, the records were very successful: Marion Lush was soon being called the "Golden Voice of Polkas," and his big sweet-boy image had a lot of charm. One of the "gold dust twins" at a polka fest some years ago was wearing numerous buttons, many Marion souvenirs among them, and she wasn't the first or last fan to have a crush on Lush.

Even as a leader with voice, charm, fame, and fans, Marion made no more money from Chicago appear-

Rydosz, piano; Stan Mikrut, bass; Mickey Lacny, accordion; Chester Filipiak, drums; and Wozniak when he doubled on concertina), Hoot pointed out that the articulation of the bass line has also been a crucial variable in defining "beat" and style and sense of tempo. The amplified bass from a concertina dictates a slower, looser pace and feeling than the bass from an accordion or the still "quicker" bass from a Chordovox. The old combination of string bass and piano working together creates still another "time feel."

It is easy to become lost in a discussion of Lush's highly danceable "relaxed dynamism" and lose focus on the man himself. His voice sounds better than everyone else's and is still like every man's. The two-trumpet sound and solid beat set the standard for the 1960s, and some very knowledgeable fans believe the classic Lush albums are still the best polkas on records, yet the band sounds like all the other polka bands of the 1970s and 1980s. It is Marion Lush's great achievement to make excellence seem completely normal.

Happy Louie

Just a few minutes into their performance at Idora Park near Youngstown, Ohio, in the mid-1970s, Happy Louie and Julcia justified its long-standing reputation as a great band. Louie is intense, all energy and smiles, as he sings from the heart one moment and pushes things along with his trumpet the next. With flashy costumes and strobe lights blinking, Louie Dusseault is there to make things happen. The band has to be into it. The people have to be fascinated. You feel a little foolish if you are not with the crowd in front of the bandstand or bouncing around the dance floor. With Louie's level of commitment so obvious, you had better be doing something to show you are alive.

After some wonderful moments when Louie and Julcia were joined on stage by Marion Lush, Louie talked between sets about the factors that shaped his style, highlighting the contributions of Walt Solek and Wally Jagiello.[9] He talked a lot about his French-Canadian father, who married Polish, spoke Polish, and took Louie as a child to dances and parish affairs

Happy Louie album, 1970. *Left to right: (front)* Happy Louie, Julcia, Louie Kaminski, Richie Woloss, Eddie Salomon; *(back)* Leo Olbrych, Walter Lech, Eddie Zieminski.

in Ware, Massachusetts, where the life was "very, very dominantly Polish." Louie could articulate his evolution so clearly because his commitment to Polish-American culture was a conscious choice and a celebration of participation in that particular community. His opening remarks—his response to the standard question, "When did you pick up an instrument?"—were equivalent to saying, "My instrument is the community, the history, the culture, the language."

Well, my parents being very active in the Polish community, both active in the church, St. Mary's, I went to Polish school there with Polish language and Polish grammar taught. . . .

We had nuns teaching in Polish. Not Felicians though. My wife was taught by Felicians in a neighboring town, that's Indian Orchard, Massachusetts, about eighteen miles from Ware, near Springfield. Yes, lots of old-timers there in Indian Orchard. Joe Lazarz, he's still going and he's been very influential in a lot of music that guys are playing nowadays. He

Happy Louie, Youngstown, Ohio, c. 1976.

wrote "The Fiddler's Polka." We recorded "Fiddler's Polka." I don't have my fiddler with me now, but it became very popular when we recorded it.

I play trumpet, saxophone, clarinet, flute, a little accordion. . . . the [Polish] school had a drum corps. I started on a bugle, a plastic bugle. I can picture the color of it, army brown. Well, I joined up, and we got instructions from a professional who led the drum corps. Week after week, rehearsal after rehearsal, you learned how to play the bugle. After about a year with the bugle I started playing trumpet. When I first started I couldn't read music; I did not know the keys or anything. All I knew were the fingerings, marked under the notes. I learned by ear basically. [Later] I went to music school. I'm a graduate of the Berklee School of Music . . . in Boston.

I went to St. Mary's parochial school for eight years. Then I went to the high school in Ware. Then I stayed around for about a year and a half, worked construction, tried to make a few dollars to go to school. I was playing in a polka band by then already. I played with a polka band since the age of thirteen. It was called the Golden Stars. They're all playing, every one of them. We started off with four, then jumped to eight men—a very big sound—with two trumpets, a whole reed section. Strictly Eastern style. . . . We were modeling ourselves after Ray Henry and Frank Wojnarowski, who were very popular. We had two leaders, myself and the accordion player. I did all the bookings, and he took care of all the music. At that time I did not know how to read music, and he'd taken lessons—Zigarowski was his name. He was two or three years older. Then he went into the service, and I was left behind with the band. So I took it over and renamed it after my name, my father's name—that's Dusseault, real French, from Canada. That was around '52 or '53. So I had my own band by the time I was sixteen, an eight-piece band: two trumpets, three reeds, a piano, drums, and an accordion player. No bass at that time—the piano gave us bass.

A band didn't just come up like that; you had to work for a long time together: I can't say the same now. It seems today a band gets organized and in four or five months is making records already. In those days it wasn't like that. You had to go through an apprenticeship. . . . You had to work to improve yourselves, go out and play and play. And you didn't get big money either. It was just a case that you were happy to play. And we *were* that way. Just happy to play. Eight men, and we were probably only getting sixty-five dollars for the band. It

was hard work. People would come up and say we had a great band and had all kinds of future and this and that, but it was always a hill that you had to climb. My first record wasn't made until I was about twenty-eight years old, and I was playing all those years. But with the big boys, Ray Henry and Gene Wisniewski, around my area, they wouldn't let you make a record till you proved yourself.

While in the army, stationed at Fort Dix, New Jersey, Louie played with Walt Solek on weekends.

When I was with Walt Solek he did not play; he fronted for the band. This is around '58, '59, and '60. We'd play places like Altoona, Pennsylvania, and Walt would come flying out of the side of the stage with a costume on while we were playing. And the people ate it up. And me too! I really would watch him. I found out that you can't just get on a stage and play music. You have to be an entertainer, you have to give your whole self. When you think there's no more left, you have to give more.

After I got out of his band, I reorganized my band. And my father-in-law, Julie's father (I met Julie when I was about nineteen, had known her about four years when I got married to her while I was in the service), her dad was very very much into polka music. He had a radio show of his own. And he did a lot of traveling. He was working with a company, heavy machinery, and he did a lot of work around Chicago and Buffalo. (During those years Buffalo was very strong on Polish music from Chicago. This was when Little Wally was so popular.) He would come home and say "Louie, you're missing the beat." I said, "Like what, Jack?" He says, "You gotta see this Little Wally." So I said, "I've heard his records." Now of course, we know that records are not the same as a performance.

So anyway, Little Wally came out to my area around '62. He played with Al Soyka; they played on a bandstand together. Al had ten men that day, Little Wally had five. And I saw a band of five men take an audience of five or six hundred people into his hand and do wonders with them. And that's where I really learned. After Walt Solek, that's where I realized I'd better change my whole format.

At the Berklee School I studied with a guy who was and still is the solo trumpetist with the Boston Symphony. And you know everything was exactness of tone, professionalism. It was perfect trumpet performance, but not for the

Happy Louie *(center)* in Poland, 1979; Big Al and Bette Mosztal waving at camera.

people. Basically I was doing that. I had a big band at that time in the early '60s, a stage band; the music was good, and people would come in and enjoy it, but there was no participation between the audience and the band. Which Wally had. He'd get out there and people weren't even listening to the music—they were watching this guy perform. It was the Polish singing, that whole thing. All of a sudden this guy is getting up there singing these old Polish songs, and the people really love him. . . .

Solek was entertaining. But he wasn't honky. The band was still very legitimate. He was honky but the band wasn't. Then Wally came around with a band that was honky. "Hey, gimme a glass of beer, we're gonna have some fun," and all that. And that's what was lacking before, that communication between the people and the band.

I remember Solek telling me when I asked what was the most important thing when getting a band started, he said, "Funny hats." He's a very good entertainer. Even to this day Walter is a good entertainer. He goes out on a date and he doesn't forget that. When I was playing with his band, if any guy got lax he would really get on him: "Hey, do your thing or get out." That's the way it should be. Everybody works. Unfortunately, a lot of bands coming up nowadays have gone over to the other extreme. They're going so much into entertainment, they're forgetting the music part of it. You can't forget about that. People can only be entertained for so long till they say, "Jeez, the music don't sound good." They notice. It has to be both things. Good music and good entertainment. It has to be clean fun . . . a family type of fun. My opinion is that polka music is family-type music. The mother, the father, and the

kids can come out and they don't have to worry about the kids being exposed to bad influence or bad talk or anything like that.

If the kids don't come out, maybe it's not the fault of the kids. Maybe it's the fault of the bands themselves. Maybe they gotta try and reach out to get the kids. It's a two-way street, not a one-way thing. You know one of the complaints is that "the people are dead." Well if the people are dead, it's up to the entertainer to liven them up, no matter how dead. . . . They're paying to see you entertain them and not vice versa. I never forget that. You get out there and you work. Sometimes you get in front of an audience and it's not easy. But just because it's hard doesn't mean you lay down and say the heck with it. That's how I do it.

That's how Louie did it that afternoon in Youngstown, and also during a tour of Poland with Julcia, the band, and a group of fans in 1979. Bussing around Poland, we were all American tourists together until those mysterious moments when the music started, the Am-Poles danced, and the Polish hosts and onlookers never knew quite what to do with us. When he sang "I Did It My Way" to a packed stadium in Poznan, Louie's way was certainly different from Elvis Presley's or Sinatra's, even though all these ways celebrate working-class identity and upward mobility at the same time.

Bill Mahoney, an Irish-American truck driver in Youngstown, echoed Happy Louie's story, giving a fan's version of the same themes.[10]

Well, the first ten years of marriage, polkas gave me a headache. I was out Friday night, Saturday night, and the wife would put them on Sunday morning. About eight years ago, all of a sudden, I don't know what happened, but now I am the one that puts polkas on and she is the one that complains. I'll tell you something, it's fantastic music. It's got a beat of its own and none of it is the same, if you really listen to it. . . .

I'm serious when I say this: you mature with age. You understand things a hell of a lot better, and nothing is going to be put on you, like it is now with the youth. The music that the kids have got to listen to is what is played on the stations. But once you get to your thirties . . . you start appreciating good things. You know, I've got a neighbor next door who is thirty-four years old. He loves it. He's a motorcycle rider and he loves it, loves polka music. He has a bunch of guys over, they play polkas and have a ball—where you'll go to somebody else's house, and they'll play hard rock and nobody does nothing. Just take your camera there and shoot the whole floor. When you see this many people on a dance floor, it's got to be fantastic, it's got to be something happening. You could go anywhere in the United States, a rock group—all you get is a bunch of people smoking up, or a bunch of people standing, listening. But when you've got a polka band, you've got a lot of people participating. And this is what it all comes down to. It is participating.

Eddie Blazonczyk

When it comes to helping people participate, no band has been more consistent the past twenty years than Eddie Blazonczyk and the versatile Versatones. Eddie and his boys are always the complete polka band—state-of-the-art, flawless, a summation of all that has gone before—and Eddie is the Renaissance or protean polkaman: simultaneously singer, musician, host, emcee, promoter, producer, record company executive, leader, disc jockey, composer, arranger, tour guide, studio engineer, and yet a good ol' boy and accessible friend who is humbly less than the sum of his many parts as he talks with people at dances and festivals. On stage, however, he projects the authority that comes from having mastered all aspects of polka production. Similarly, the legend of Eddie's mother, Antonina, as

A Versatones album cover.

the ultimate polka hostess and patron of young artists and the great story of her son "Eddie Bell," the rock-and-roller returning home to carry on the family and community traditions, are both part of an oral tradition that makes Eddie a man of the people and a star who is free of any tension or contradiction between these roles.

Even as a paragon of polka virtues, the current band is probably not as exciting as the one that had Lenny Gomulka's vocal blendings and clarinet solos adding lilt and sparkle. And the band before that, with Junior Wozniak's wailing violin and three trumpet climaxes, was still more exciting. Yet though the personnel may change, Eddie and his Versatones only have to be there to attract a crowd and electrify it. Never a wild and crazy guy like Solek or Li'l Wally or Happy Louie, Eddie very gradually lost his musical adventurousness in favor of matching evermore closely the fine recorded Versatone sound, and this tradeoff is acceptable to just about everyone. A few may resent the smoothness, but Blazonczyk is more in the tradition of a polka "king"

1988 (top) Eddie Blazonczyk (center) Jerry Tokarz, Al Piatkowski
(bottom) Ed Wolinski, Kevin Adams, Jerry Darlak

Eddie Blazonczyk's Versatones

OUR 25TH ANNIVERSARY

1963

In 1963 Eddie Blazonczyk's Versatones recorded their first album titled "Polka Parade" on the Bel-Aire label. Over the past twenty-five years they have recorded 41 albums and received over 100 miscellaneous awards from the International Polka Association, the United States Polka Association, United Polka Boosters, and the United Polka Association. Eddie Blazonczyk was elected into the I.P.A. Polka Music Hall of Fame in 1970.

The Versatones received a Grammy for their "Polka Celebration" album in 1986 and hold the distinction of being the only polka band nominated for a Grammy the past 3 years by the National Academy of Recording Arts and Sciences.

The band has toured all over the USA and Canada and has even performed in Poland, France, and Austria. Through the years Eddie Blazonczyk has lead his band in over 3,800 appearances.

1988

1963   **1988**

CHET KOWALKOWSKI & EDDIE BLAZONCZYK
singing together
"Good To Be Back Polka" & "I Want Some Lovin' Polka"

Versatones' twenty-fifth anniversary, 1988.

like Frankie Yankovic, upholding the highest standards of performance, than in the tradition of polka clowns.

The matter of upholding standards should not be underestimated as a force in the polka world across all its localities. Many of the musicians in the leading bands of Buffalo or Pittsburgh or the Connecticut Valley would say, in effect, "We want to do our music as well as Blazonczyk does his." Parents taking their musical children to hear him can say, in effect, "This is why you're taking lessons." The musical standard the Versatones set, their easy professionalism, their steady devotion to the music, and their commitment to serving the people are a challenge to polka musicians everywhere.

The Versatones *are* versatile. Their 1950s rock medleys have the ring of authenticity because Eddie was there and had hits in that style. You want to twist again like you did last summer—or decades ago? The Versatones have the groove. And for their "honky style" numbers Eddie B. gets behind the drums, and other musicians switch instruments to ensure a certain looseness and freshness of feeling. But it is the consummate skill with which Blazonczyk blends the polkas, waltzes, and obereks from the band's many albums that moves people the most: one recognizable song after another, short and sweet, each tune and lyric rich with specific associations for diverse members of the dancing crowd.

You will never confuse a Versatone waltz with a Versatone oberek, even though both dances are in 3/4 time: the waltzes are slow and sweeter than sweet in the vocal duets and trumpet harmonies; the oberek's two-against-three cross-rhythms have people stomping heavily if there is room enough on the dance floor. The polkas come with Polish and English lyrics, often switching back and forth in the same song. Songs about the functions of a polka band at a party are a Blazonczyk specialty. From "Opening Theme Polka":

> We'd like to play for you our opening number,
> We'd like for you to join and sing along.
> All the six of us are here to bring you happiness
>   and cheer;
> We'll try our very best to play your favorite songs.
> Forget your troubles with a smile and listen to us for
>   a while,
> We'll do our best to entertain you all night long.[11]

Polkas with country-and-western flavor are another trademark. All the bands have been doing country numbers as polkas for years, but Eddie's professionalism and the little bit of glitter that comes from his reputation as "the best" somehow make his borrowings from Nashville more convincing.

In fact, Eddie B. is the one polkaman who not only can dream about eventual popularity for polkas on the country-and-western charts but can actually set about trying to make it happen. Over the years the Versatones have been appearing at state fairs and looking for other places where country music lovers might be won over to the danceable polka beat beneath the familiar lyrics. Polka-country fusion songs have been common for twenty years now, and we may yet see a fusion of audiences; perhaps Tex-Mex and Am-Pol polka tributaries can help feed a country-and-western river threatened with being pumped dry by commercialization. Whatever openings there may be for a polka happiness closer to the center stage of American entertainment, Eddie B. and the Versatones are a good bet to find them.

polka
movement

Part II:

The International

Polka Association

IPA awards banquet, Rosemont, Illinois, 1983.

3. Organizing a Cultural Network

The International Polka Association (IPA) is synonymous with the good times of the polka fest the organization puts on every summer.[1] The majority of those hopping about and swirling across the vast dance floor at the festival are not involved in the organizational work of the IPA; that is carried on throughout the year by the few stalwart officers. When people say to one another that "the IPA is doing a great job!" they recognize the year-round effort that goes into creating a successful festival and that the festival itself is a lot more than three sleepless, polka-drenched, beer-and-cheer-filled days and nights in Milwaukee. The culmination of a year's activity, the festival is also the occasion for a membership convention, an annual business meeting with elections, and a banquet at which the annual polka music awards are presented and inductions to the Polka Music Hall of Fame are made. And for years it was the key money-raising event on behalf of the Polka Music Hall of Fame and Museum, established in Chicago in 1968 and continuing to fulfill their mission into the 1990s.[2]

Clubs, associations, and organizations of all kinds are a standard feature of Polonia, U.S.A. A stroll on the East Side of Buffalo, for example, will convince anyone that organizational life has been an abiding interest of the Polish peasants and workers who migrated to the New World. The residential neighborhoods are studded with "public" buildings, testimony to the intense organizational activity of the community: churches, with their adjoining social halls, parochial schools, and convents for the hardworking, Polish-speaking Felician sisters; a profusion of Veterans' Posts; the "Polish Home" (*Dom Polski* or community center), complete with theater, library, and meeting rooms; Adam Misciewicz Hall with bar, library, and theater; the Polish Union of America. Even the ubiquitous corner gin mills host a variety of social and athletic clubs. Indeed, organizations flourish so profusely in Polonia that sociologists who study such matters are hard put to explain why there are so many of them.[3] The IPA may proclaim itself international, but it remains very much a Polonian organization in membership, leadership, and inspiration; as such, it

Polka Music Hall of Fame

Year	Inductees	Year	Inductees
1969	FRANK YANKOVIC / LI'L WALLY JAGIELLO	1983	WALTER OSTANEK / JOHNNY HYZNY / LAWRENCE DUCHOW (Deceased) / EDDIE OSKIERKO (Pioneer)
1970	FRANK WOJNAROWSKI / EDDIE BLAZONCZYK		
1971	WALTER DANA / BERNIE WYTE WITKOWSKI	1984	BERNIE GOYDISH / JIMMY STURR / FEZZ FRITSCHE (Deceased) / CHARLIE HICKS (Pioneer)
1972	MARION LUSH / RAY HENRY / EDDIE ZIMA (Deceased)		
1973	GENE WISNIEWSKI / RAY BUDZILEK / MATTIE MADURA (Deceased)	1985	JOE WOJKIEWICZ / LARRY CHESKY / COUSIN FUZZY (Deceased) / STAN JASINSKI (Pioneer)
1974	WALT SOLEK / DICK PILLAR / MARISHA DATA (Deceased)	1986	WALT GROLLER / BRUNO MIKOS / PAT WATTERS (Deceased) / BRUNO "JR." ZIELINSKI (Pioneer)
1975	HAROLD LOEFFELMACHER / STEVE ADAMCZYK / JOHNNY PECON (Deceased)		
1976	DICK RODGERS / CHET SCHAFER / "WHOOPEE JOHN" WILFAHRT (Deceased)	1987	EMILY PINTER / JOHNNY VADNAL / JOHNNY MENKO (Pioneer) / ANTONINA BLAZONCZYK (Deceased) / MATT HOYER (Deceased) / JOLLY JACK ROBEL (Deceased)
1977	LEON KOZICKI / JOE LAZARZ / BRUNON KRYGER (Deceased)		
1978	ALVIN SAJEWSKI / "JOE PAT" PATEREK / IGNACY PODGORSKI (Deceased)	1988	LENNY GOMULKA / JOHNNY HASS / AL GREBNICK (Pioneer) / JOE STRUZIK (Deceased)
1979	MARV HERZOG / AL SOYKA / ROMY GOSZ (Deceased)	1989	LUCIAN KRYGER / VERNE MEISNER / JOE CZERNIAK (Pioneer) / KENNY BASS (Deceased)
1980	JOHNNIE BOMBA / STAN E. SALESKI / TED MAKSYMOWICZ (Deceased)	1990	MYRON FLOREN / JOLLY JOE TIMMER / NORMAN MARGGRAFF / BRUNON (BRUCE) KRYGER
1981	CASEY SIEWIERSKI / RAY STOLZENBERG / LOU PROHUT (Deceased)	1991	JOE MARCISSUK / CHET KOWALKOWSKI / JOHN CHECK (Pioneer) / HENRY JASIEWICZ (Deceased)
1982	HAPPY LOUIE DUSSEAULT / JOHNNY LIBERA / JOE FIEDOR (Deceased)	1992	BILL CZERNIAK / FREDDY BULINSKI / JAN ROBAK (Deceased) / ERNIE KUCERA (Pioneer)

From International Polka Association souvenir program, 1992.

73

Pulaski Day at the Rivoli, Buffalo, 1973.

draws upon a long tradition of Polonian organizational activity.[4]

The early 1960s were a watershed for the development of the polka scene within Polonia, U.S.A., as the powerful new style that had crystallized in Chicago in the 1950s swept fans and bands across the land. In ethnic and ideological terms this meant that the more raw, painful, powerful—and therefore "embarrassing," "shameful," and "stereotyped"—aspects of being a *"Polak"* or a *"Polka"* in America were being expressed in a style that had strong connections to the homeland yet was obviously born in the bars of "Polish Broadway": Division Street, Chicago.[5] Almost simul-

taneously with the reaffirmation of Polish-American identity, however, Polish-Americans were leaving their deteriorated city neighborhoods for the suburbs, and entertainment was being dominated to an unprecedented degree by electronic mass media that tended to ignore and exclude ethnic working-class cultures. The economic and social relationships that supported polka performance were eroding.

In Buffalo, the Eastern-style polka orchestras were replaced by five-piece neighborhood bands improvising polkas in the "Li'l Wally," "Chicago," or "honky" style.[6] The bands in the city were faced with declining neighborhoods, boarded-up bars, and a population

Street in Hamtramck, Michigan, 1986.

were growing at the expense of the Polish Catholic parishes. The characteristically American rotation of ethnics in the working-class neighborhoods took its toll as racism, fraudulent real estate practices, federal highway subsidies, bank "red-lining," and dreams of a better life turned the old neighborhoods into hostile territories where groups of various nationalities contested one another. Mexican-Americans were the strongest contenders for the places left by the Poles. The demise of Chicago's Polonia meant the end of the big ballrooms and the closing of the ethnic community bars that had housed polka bands. The Caldwell Woods picnics slipped from dependably regular Sunday social events, sponsored by Polish organizations, to occasional affairs sponsored by promoters. Word-of-mouth communication, a natural form of cultural bonding within an ethnic neighborhood, suffered as a result of these changes.

Polish-American recreation was also hit hard by transformations in mainstream society: postwar prosperity shifted the emphasis from labor and production jobs within an ethnic community to the American dream of suburban consumer heaven. Television took up leisure hours and shaped the tastes of viewers in non-ethnic directions. The consolidation of the 1950s rock revolution and the rise of country-and-western to the status of a national style, plus the general softening of ethnic identity after four and five generations of assimilation pressures, eclipsed a great deal of Polish music as well as the social activities where the music was performed. Polka enthusiasts faced a generation of young ethnics who were not so much rejecting polka music and polka dancing as taking the easier path into music produced and marketed by big companies. British working-class youth helped make rock-and-roll the music of working-class youth everywhere but did so at the expense of specific ethnic traditions.

Responses to the rock-and-roll deluge were similar across the large cities of the Midwest with similarly affected Polonias. As the polka scene began to shrink on the neighborhood level, fans and professionals responded by searching for new forms of organization and by pooling resources through wider geographic areas and social networks. In almost all cases the new

made up largely of scared older people who could not afford or bear to move to the suburbs, away from their once thriving parishes. The slicker, bigger bars, usually on the large thoroughfares crisscrossing the Polish-American suburbs, were responding to a wider clientele as well as to what an Am-Pol student once called the desire for "cultural mobility" in the young: the desire to embrace and be identified with mainstream culture. Some establishments featured a polka night once in a while, but they were not polka bars.

Chicago's experience was similar. The suburbs

75   Organizing a Cultural Network

East Side store, Buffalo, c. 1973.

Hamtramck, Michigan, 1986.

organizational forms were polka fan clubs. In the East and in Chicago, polka associations appeared. Designed to ensure the existence of polka music, they were also a tacit recognition of polka shrinkage under free market conditions. What we call "the polka movement" testifies to the need for "consumer" co-ops (the fan clubs) and "producer" co-ops (the associations). The realization that the well-being of the polka could be guaranteed neither as a byproduct of ceremonial associational life in the ethnic community nor by touring professional bands fueled the growth of booster activity. The continued survival of the polka required a concerted effort on the part of those who cared about it to replace the old waning resources with ones adapted to the new social conditions of the evolving ethnic community. Like Polish-American identity, consequently, the polka survived the territorial demise of Polonia.

With the growth of television as the main medium of marketing and official ideology on the national scene, it was possible for the polkas to become a distinct genre on local radio and TV programs that were looking for business. Radio kept the polka's connections with the broad ethnic community alive; at the same time, polka musicians and entrepreneurs began to reshape a public for records, bands, events, and dances that did not depend on a specific neighborhood's activity. This "new" audience was a public that could integrate polka listening, record buying and an occasional picnic into suburban life away from the day-to-day cycle of most Polonian institutions. The polka radio shows were also cultivating a somewhat broader audience, an audience not entirely Polish, perhaps, but "polka prone": German, Czech, Bohemian, and so on. The resulting eclecticism in musical borrowing fertilized the growth of the genre and in turn increased its potential appeal to a larger audience. The radio shows provided a steady outlet and incentive for polka record producers.

South Side bakery, Chicago, 1988.

The developments that culminated in the establishment of the International Polka Association are located in this dialectical relationship between the weakening ethnic neighborhood and the simultaneous development of the polka mini-media: local radio shows and special trade publications to reach a dispersed audience. Before the territorial diffusion of Polonia, polka musicians could play every weekend night—for weddings, retirement parties, anniversaries; in corner bars; at fraternal or church socials—and no one was particularly concerned that the polka did not exist for the primary mass media: TV, major AM radio stations, and national circulation magazines. Once the ethnic neighborhoods broke up, however, and there were no more central locations where an ad on the wall would reach 90 percent of the polka audience, the polka media emerged as the primary means for reaching the polka public out there.

The Radio-TV Polka Club of America, established in 1958, was one of the first organizations that attempted to confirm the concept of the polka professional. Most of its members were polka musicians, band leaders, radio disc jockeys, bar owners or combining three or four of these roles. The *Polka Guide* was first published in Chicago in 1958 by Leon Kozicki (editor) and Johnny Hyzny as "an authorized publication of the Radio-TV Polka Club of America."[7] It was an efficient means of bringing together polka professionals and their public. Early issues of the *Polka Guide* look like prototypes of the IPA souvenir programs and the *IPA News*.[8] They feature information about polka radio shows and bands, boosting interest by keeping the names of bands, radio shows, record companies, performers, polka personalities, the newest records, dances, and festivals in focus. The fact that so many of the key protagonists and activities of the polka world today were already part of it at the beginning reflects the economic and professional success of these early polka enterprises.[9]

An emphasis on the Chicago Polonian polka scene dominates the *Polka Guide*, despite a disciplined attempt to include Eastern-style polka.[10] In one issue from the mid-1960s there is a page of Chicago polka radio shows and a two-page directory of Chicago and vicinity polka bands.[11] Almost all the nightclubs and ballrooms listed under "Polka Nite Life" were in Chicago: Baby Doll Polka Club, Joe & Jean's Lounge, Club 505, Lucy's Wisconsin Rendezvous, Zima's Squeeze Box, Brothers Two Lounge, Manor Ballroom, Pulaski Ballroom, Polonia Grove and Ballroom. The Polonia Grove under Ed Zimmerly gives the impression of being the most dependable polka establishment in the area; it advertises a variety of bands and dances every Friday, Saturday, and Sunday, featuring top Chicago bands and the dances of such organizations as the Young Democrats, St. Peter and Paul Church, and Club Osolwoni. "Polka Time USA," however, heads two pages of about thirty radio programs in twenty-three states in which the polka belts of Connecticut and Massachusetts, upstate New York, Ohio and Pennsylvania, Delaware and New Jersey are well represented. This listing is an impressive beginning of a network of disc jockeys providing exposure to bands, records, and information for an emerging polka world.

To quote one of its contributors, John Lewandowski, the *Polka Guide* "enriched the music field, it enlivened the dances. Increased the dance attendance. Brought about closer ties in the polka personnel and increased the hours of clean wholesome fun for today's public."[12] The *Polka Guide* is presented as an ideological instrument in one of those origin myths that abound in the polka world. In reminding polka fans to spread polka values, Lewandowski tells the story of four friends who wanted to do something about "today's changes of values": "One nice evening . . . they met in a Chicago pub," and "noted that morality and common decency [have] been over-ridden by today's sex outlook." Fashions in movies, clothes, "dance steps," and "new societies and clubs" were promoting the glorification of sex, they concluded. They included abstract painting and contemporary music, propelled by the marketing of fame and hits, in the list of value-eroding developments. Significantly, they called these threatening values "off-beat," thus associating them with rock-and-roll and other African-American-based music. They saw mainstream cultural institutions and the market as alienating not only art but also self-expression and recreation.

The activist spirit is unmistakable: "And what do

Buffalo, c. 1973.

Polonia, South Side Chicago, 1988.

we choose to do about all this?" The friends decided that "there was a common ground on which to build true values. Their common ground was the happy polka and all those happy polka people behind it." The choice is pure New Ethnicity. They did not try to revive Old Polonia. Rather, focusing on the dynamism of the cultural complex of the polka, the members of this legendary foursome committed themselves to the support of the old values. "The rest is history," and it happens to be the prehistory of the IPA.[13]

Polka fans in and around Chicago say that the *Polka Guide* was a reminder that no matter where they might live, there was a polka land in Chicago and elsewhere open to those who sought it out. The *Polka Guide* influenced the fans to turn off the TV, get in the car, collect family and friends, and travel ten, twenty, or two hundred miles for a memorable polka night. Stories of miles and miles of travel to get to a polka bash attest to a far-flung polka audience dependent on the promotional media of radio and trade publications as well as the motional media of cars and vans. Passion for the polka, rather than identification with an ethnic community organization that used the polka as a drawing card, became the basis for promotion.

According to Chet Schafer, Ed Zimmerly contributed to the development of the "family spirit"

Polonia, North Side Chicago, 1988.

among the polka professionals who were midwifing this transition from Polonia to the polka world in the early 1960s.

Zimmerly owned Polonia Grove in Chicago. He was originally from Erie, Pennsylvania. He was a sponsor on my program. He always talked to me about bringing out some of the Eastern artists to Chicago. Because we had so many artists of our own, we never thought of bringing any out-of-town artists. Wojnarowski once came to Chicago. George Istvan promoted him, and they bombed. On the South Side at the Pulaski Ballroom, which Mrs. Blazonczyk owned (it burned out later, and it is no more), they had a good crowd, but really it was not enough to profit the event. The North Side booking was at the Lyons Ballroom, and that was very poorly attended. This was back in 1951. The first out-of-town band that came to Chicago, it bombed.

Then Ed Zimmerly attempted to bring in some out-of-town bands. He started correspondence with Gene Wisniewski. And Gene, on his own, made a trip here. Zimmerly decided to run a party for Gene . . . at the Tangiers Motel. It had just opened over there at Archer Avenue, close to Polonia Grove. And he invited musicians, myself, Chet Gulinski who is a DJ, some band leaders, and Joe Salomon from Joe & Jean's Lounge that featured polka bands. And we had this little reception welcoming Gene Wisniewski.

There is a photo taken at this party. It shows us all around an organ singing Polish songs: *Zosia*, *Wesoly Stas*, *Eddie Penway* with his accordion; Joe Pat was playing the organ. Some of these musicians are dead today. . . . That was the beginning of this polka family, the IPA.

It is not clear exactly why Ed Zimmerly wanted to bring Eastern bands to Chicago. Perhaps it was out of nostalgia for what he had known back in Pennsylvania, or perhaps he thought that out-of-town attractions could boost his gate. As Dolores Schafer put it: "Records were available and Ed Zimmerly could hear what was going on elsewhere and it was just simply out of curiosity maybe. He probably said, 'I wonder what would happen if Gene came here. He had big crowds in other cities.'" Chet attributed Ed's enthusiasm to the fact that he was a "real promoter": "He paid $100 out of his own pocket for that cocktail party for Gene. He was willing to gamble. Sure, he wanted to make a living out of it, but I don't think it was the almighty dollar he was after."

A real promoter, while managing to stay in business, takes risks for the sake of innovation. He seeks to develop a bigger, better, and more exciting polka business. Fans and musicians complain about specific promoters who will sponsor excellent events with good bands but will not take risks with less well-known bands whose drawing power is not established. Such business practices are considered an unscrupulous milking of the polka scene and a self-seeking refusal to share the cost of its upkeep and growth. In the polka world, not shouldering the cost of the future is considered cheating: "How are these bands going to start if the big promoters do not give them a chance?" Everyone who enjoys the polka, but especially anyone who profits from it, has the responsibility to contribute to its maintenance and survival.

Ed Zimmerly focused his promotional talent on transforming Polonia Grove, with its open space and outside dancing floor, into a polka club with the aura of the declining Caldwell Woods. Polonia Grove thus became the center of new efforts to attract a far wider audience of polka enthusiasts. Schafer cites Ed Zimmerly's promotion of the Connecticut Twins as a good example of his taste for innovation:

Zimmerly brought in the Connecticut Twins to Chicago for one of his picnics at the Polonia Grove. We had a good crowd because Ed called it a "Polka World's Fair" and featured good bands. Marion Lush was playing and whoever was popular. Blazonczyk was not around yet. I was on the radio with a remote broadcast from Polonia Grove at the time the Twins arrived. Zimmerly asked the [local] band to leave the stage and come to the gate. "Let's welcome them," he said. As soon as the Twins came in, [the band] started playing. Were they surprised! After they performed, Zimmerly had a dinner for all of them. It was all on him.

The Twins were real hot then. Actually, to this day, the theme song of my afternoon show is "Holiday in Poland" by the Twins, their biggest hit. When it first came out, I started playing it right away. They were hot, those Twins. That's why Zimmerly selected them.

Whether or not it was Ed Zimmerly who coined the term "polka world," by the early 1960s it was an idea whose time had come. The notion of a "Polka World's Fair" must have dazzled the fans with its ring of inclusive wholeness and its echoes of dominant institutions like the legendary World's Fair. But a basic set of concepts remained to be worked out before the IPA could be launched.

In 1960 Leon Kozicki and Johnny Hyzny organized the first annual moonlight dance, sponsored by the Radio-TV Polka Club, as a way to bail out the deficit-plagued Polka Guide. Though the fact it went unnoticed then, this was the first time that a professional cultural organization dedicated to the polka had sponsored a dance for its own benefit. The Chicago bands who played this and subsequent moonlight dances proved very popular with "the thousands of polka lovers from all sections of the U.S. and Canada."[14] The model of a polka organization sponsoring regional dances proved workable. The entire Midwest and Northeast, if not the nation, could be drawn into a polka world with Chicago as its musical and organizational center.

Zimmerly's summer picnics and the moonlight dances at Polonia Grove attracted, among others, Johnny Libera, a polka DJ from Southbridge, Massachusetts, who had older ties to the Chicago Polonia. During the war he had been stationed at Navy Pier and later, through friendship and common interest, had become part of the Chicago "polka family". It was Libera who, on one of his trips to a Polonia Grove summer picnic, conceived of a modern, all-American idea: an expense-paid professional trip to the dances.

Chet Schafer recounted:

He told me, "You know, we should have an organization. I would like to come to Chicago every year. . . . But it's expensive. If you have . . . a nonprofit association for the promotion of polka music, I can get my station owner to finance the trip." So I wrote an editorial arguing that we should have an organization and a polka convention, and it was published in the next edition of the Polka Guide.

Leon Kozicki liked the idea and we called a meeting. Jeanie Salomon . . . called the meeting at her place, Joe and Jean's, and we got together and started talking about these things. Emily Pinter attended. We had some more meetings. Something was getting going. Johnny Hyzny and Leon called their affair "The International Polka Convention," and that's what we had. We got started on our organization.

These developments were followed with interest by the polka public. In the beginning the change in the name of the event was just a change of words, but in time the concepts behind the words took hold. The notions of a big polka party, professional networking, and an international cultural organization coalesced: a major step was taken toward the establishment of the IPA. The 1964 schedule of the "International Polka Convention, presented by *Polka Guide* and the Radio-TV Polka Club, representing the Polka Music Industry," is the prototype of IPA convention souvenir programs.[15] Chicago and its polka family, as the polka professionals are affectionately (or derisively) called, were hosting the polka world of North America.

Except for its size and cultural richness, Chicago was not unique; across all the polka belts, people were casting about for a strategy to bolster the music's position in their localities. The notion of a polka convention, with its cheeky and at the same time tongue-in-cheek solemnity, was accepted enthusiastically. The times were calling out for encouragement and new ideas. The International Polka Convention emboldened fans across the country and resulted in widespread local polka revivals.

The International Polka Convention was held in Chicago for a few years before it was decided to try other localities. The desire for a national polka event that would invigorate local activity was so strong and the Chicago leadership so welcome that the 1965 convention was held in Cheektowaga, a suburb of Buffalo, New York. The 1966 convention was held in Detroit's Cobbo Hall and the 1967 convention in Depew, another Buffalo suburb. Taking the convention to different cities was intended to invigorate polka activity in the polka belts; to solidify cooperation of polka professionals from Chicago with their local equivalents; to allay grumbles about "Chicago taking over" by courting the Midwest and Northeast; to introduce the hot Chicago sound and bands to the country; to knit a national network out of the many disparate local polka scenes—in short, to demonstrate the possibilities for recreation and adventure inherent in the polka-party format by inviting polka lovers to participate in the biggest polka party ever.

The fans responded with enthusiasm to Chicago-style polkas, and Chicago's notions of voluntary organization and networking were taken to heart and put into action. In the wake of the 1967 convention, Buffalo fan clubs mushroomed. Local promotions grew into regional festivals: polka musicians formed their own union; polka dance lessons were organized by Polonian organizations; booster clubs planned annual affairs. The annual International Polka Convention began to be written into every fan's and each polka club's calendar.

The organizational and economic motivation fueled stylistic and musical creativity. Young polka musicians from different localities had a chance to stand at the feet of legendary Chicago greats, learning in person from their musicianship and showmanship. The convention became a clearinghouse for polka music, and a spirit of empowering competition developed. Bands everywhere aspired to play for the next convention; musicians began to listen to each other's records with an ear to learning, surpassing, creating a stir at the next convention. The Annual Polka Awards were still to come.

It was not all smooth sailing: though the meeting in Detroit was a "conversion experience" for many a fan and musician, the 1965 convention in Buffalo (Cheektowaga) was an organizational disaster. Yet it was precisely this flop that brought the inherent contradictions forward. Speaking with hindsight years later, IPA stalwarts pointed out the lack of well-articulated accountability in those early days. Informal camaraderie and old-fashioned individual or partnership enterpreneurial activity were intertwined in all the early functions, but by 1966 the polka movement had whipped up enough sales and enthusiasm to make its potential obvious and the stakes high. Organizational clarity was on the agenda because the polka world would continue to be of necessity both an "industry" and a movement. It has remained so ever since.

In the intricate jumble of private entrepreneurship, volunteerism, club membership, friendly activities, and shared profit incentives that constitute a polka promotion, contradictions can explode in fights or smolder as recurrent difficulties. Conflicts of interest, bitterly analyzed, can split people and groups apart. Most of the time such conflicts are kept glossed over, and collective interdependence is projected as the good of the community. Competition between "not for profit" organizations and private promoters sometimes breaks out, but on the whole, cooperation is safeguarded by avoiding date conflicts in a given area. This informal means of "sharing the turf" is taken for granted, but when (rarely) it is ignored, mediocre attendance results in hard feelings that have the quality of irreparable rifts.

In the case of the IPA, private entrepreneurship and public service had to be disentangled from the very beginning. It took a bit of doing, but the convention finally passed under the control of the new organization. The International Polka Association was incorporated in August 1968. This may seem like a small issue. But to those who, time after time, have seen polka clubs and larger organizations unable to overcome their dependence on single entrepreneurs or unable to solve conflicts of interest to their advantage, it is no mean trick. A very appropriate comparison can be made here with the United States Polka Association, whose days of greatness corresponded to its identification with Dick Pillar's "Polkabration" in New London, Connecticut. By Christmas 1968, when the USPA was incorporated with Pillar as its founder and first president, the Polkabration itself was a well-established concern under Pillar's personal control, and it simply hosted the USPA convention for the first few years. When the two separated, the USPA suffered appreciable loss of morale, and it never consolidated a localized base of strength or the complex of festival plus convention plus year-round polka advocacy that would have made it a major factor in the polka life of the Northeast.

But that is another story. It is enough here to under line that in Chicago the "polka family" stood fast. How were they able to succeed where others failed? One could study with great profit the role of John Hyzny as an entrepreneur and Leon Kozicki as an organization builder, since both figures recur as types in Polonia as elsewhere. According to Chet Schafer:

Johnny was taking care of the financial end of it, and Leon could not get a financial report from Johnny. Why? Because they were just the two of them. They got people to help collect tickets and what not, but Johnny took care of the money,

and Leon never knew how they were doing financially. They ran another convention in Buffalo, and Hyzny was still in charge of everything. It was a disaster; they never got a permit! It was after the Buffalo disaster that Joe and Jean decided to run a testimonial for Marion Lush and invited some out-of-towners who knew Lush very well—people like DJ Johnny Simms of the Pittsburgh area, DJ Joe Marcissuk, and the composer from Detroit, Zoltan Music Company's Wally Weber. We had this dinner and testimonial. Father Wally Szczypula was there, said grace and gave a little talk: he encouraged us. Another time we called a special meeting at Joe and Jean's with Dick Pillar when he visited Chicago. There was no IPA yet, but by getting together these people from out-of-town, we got them all to like each other. We got especially close with the people from Detroit.

Schafer emphasized the slow process of association that concluded with the agreement to establish the IPA; Leon Kozicki gave his own crisp version:

The IPA organized by a steering committee consisting of Leon Kozicki, John Hyzny, Ed Blazonczyk, Jean and Joe Salomon, and Don Jodlowcki. After some resistance from John Hyzny, who wanted to reactivate and resume publishing *Polka Guide*, the group decided to sponsor the International Polka Convention when it was returned to Chicago (after a three-year absence) in 1968. This group (except Hyzny) advanced personal money to be available as "seed money." After some discussion the group agreed upon the formation of a not-for-profit polka organization dedicated to the establishment of a Polka Music Hall of Fame and was committed to the advancement of polka music.

The question persists: Why put money and energy into a nonprofit organization rather than into one's own projects? The answer from the participants is unambiguous: "The feeling that the promotion and preservation of polka music is important."

Ethnicity was an essential element that made pulling together the obvious choice. The people who have been talking here, the Schafers and those who initially banded together to promote the polka, had known Chicago Polonia in its prime, both the bitterness and the sweetness of life there. Some of them tried to be traditionalists by holding out in the old neighborhoods. Others, most of them, embraced the new trends and tried to make the best of it in white-collar jobs, with more education, in newer homes with larger yards out in the suburbs. But both groups had a passion for the polka and wanted to hold on to that. It could not be done individually. There were ample signs that a fresh approach had to be found. Take the case of the missing young people as an example. Those actively involved in keeping the polka alive are always measuring their success not only by how many people come out to a dance but also by whether the youth participate. The falling off of polka interest among the young is always pointed out as a sign that the polka is in trouble. "We noticed that the youngsters did not go for polka music," said Schafer. "Rock-and-roll was their thing. When we were young, polka dancing was the big thing. We just had a ball going to the dances and picnics. There was nothing better. So, we've got to do something; we've got to get these kids interested."

It was a matter of realism. The IPA would promote the polka in a constantly developing ethnic situation. Using a form that exists throughout Polonia, the ever present not-for-profit organization and club, the founders of the IPA moved to institutionalize fan and industry cooperation because the polka and what kept it alive had begun to decline, and individual promoters could not turn this situation around.

The seriousness and intensity with which the IPA pushed both the convention and the polka business over the next decade are reflected in the dense 84-page 1976 *Souvenir Program of the IPA Convention and Festival*. Roughly the first third of the booklet is devoted to the program of the festival, the schedule of events, biographies and pictures of Hall of Fame and annual Polka Music Award winners, and pictures of bands appearing in the festival, followed by lists of their sponsors, both commercial and fraternal. The rest comprises advertisements from businesses that support the polka and in turn are supported by the fans. The souvenir program is obviously another fund raiser. It advertises polka bands, the famous ballrooms of the northern Midwest, the equally legendary bars of the industrial heartland, the record companies unknown to anyone but polka lovers, and a list of 247 contributing "Well Wishers." But it also boosts commitment to the polka field as a whole. An introduction to this field for budding enthusiasts, it exudes solidarity and is full of information about the small-scale economics (promotions, advertising, sponsorship), status competition, and polka commitments on which the entire polka world depends. It is a *Who's Who* of the polka world, referred to by fans throughout the year.

The program is especially informative in presenting the organization. All the officers and directors of the IPA are represented by individual photographs and their places of residence given. Brief histories of the IPA and of the Polka Music Hall of Fame are presented by Leon Kozicki, first president of the IPA, acting chairman of the board of trustees of the Hall of Fame, and generally acknowledged leading light of the IPA from its very beginning. Listed also are all inductees since the Hall of Fame's inception in 1968, and deceased members of the association (under the title "Lest We Forget"). This concern to explain to the public what the IPA is and how it came about, and to celebrate its own members and the work they do, suggests a self-reflective and highly motivated organization. It is the first Polonian volunteer organization focusing on the polka to make a serious bid for a central place in the life of the ethnic community.

Here is a summary of purposes as it appears in the language of the charter and is reproduced in the souvenir program: The IPA is "an educational and social organization for the preservation, promulgation, and advancement of polka music"; its goals are "to promote, maintain, and advance public interest in polka entertainment; to advance the mutual interests and encourage greater cooperation among its members who are engaged in polka entertainment; and to encourage and pursue the study of polka music, dancing and traditional folklore." Through popular vote of its delegates, the IPA also accepted "the challenge of responsibility" to establish a professional academy and selection procedure and to raise funds for the Polka Music Hall of Fame in order "to bestow proper honor and recognition to performers, DJs, and others who have rendered years of faithful service to the polka entertainment industry."[16]

Without quite saying it, the program defines the IPA as a professional association, a badge of pride and legitimacy. The role of the polka musician in the Polish-American community is governed largely by community rather than by professional standards, and this relationship of tension and balance between the specialized network of musicians, promoters, disc jockeys, bar owners, and the ethnic community is reflected in the variety of terms used to describe the polka complex: polka industry, polka field, polka world, polka lover, polka people, polka entertainment, polka power. Each term emphasizes a different aspect of the complex, and each one remains unsatisfactory if taken alone. Some terms echo populism; others point to professionalism and specialization—it is the mix that is essential to the IPA. The fans are included right next to the musicians: "engaged in polka entertainment" is an identification broad enough to include the entire polka-loving community and reflects the balance between "professionalism" and "community" that keeps the polka alive.

Although musicians may be called "artists" from time to time and composers of popular new polkas are recognized as such, the IPA does not generally glorify polka music as "art" and polka musicians as "artists" or "composers." There is no fetishizing of "music" and "art," only a pragmatic concern for the health of polka music. The recognition that the polka needs serious study, however, responds to the realities of the situation and is a message of self-affirmation to bruised polka identities. The IPA seems to be saying, "Chopin is fine, but our polkas are worthy of serious study and honored preservation too." This affirmation is aimed not only at the non-polka, non-ethnic community but also at that image-conscious and "gatekeeping" section of the Polish-American community which, until quite recently, has not wanted to acknowledge the polka people's existence at all.

The Polka Music Hall of Fame is part of the IPA's struggle against the belittlement of polka music from

Emily Pinter and Chet Schafer presenting Lawrence Welk *(center)* an IPA Special Recognition Award, Chicago, 1982.

both outside and inside the ethnic community. The Hall of Fame is an appropriate mark of seriousness and success, not only to those who make unconscious or conscious comparisons with the acceptance, popularity, and unassailability of baseball and country music but also to the vast majority of Polonians who tend to recognize virtue in an organization only when they see it materialize in a building, a landmark of substance. In this desire to put the polka on the map, the two themes of ethnic pride and class pride are interwoven.

A long-standing member of the IPA emphasizes this point:

The IPA is for the Polish-American people and the young people. They [the IPA] want them to still have that feeling of Polish music.

Q.: So you say the IPA is a cultural organization, not a promoters' organization?

A.: Oh, yes. A culture. I donate my time. . . . I pay my dues, and I still put in thirty hours in three days for them. I want to see Polish-American music, our culture, I want to see it always there. When I'm older, when I'm maybe sixty-five or seventy, I want people like these dancing. Do you understand? I believe in our Polish culture. They can tell all the Polish jokes they want. It goes in one ear, out the other. I laugh just like anyone else. I'm not like some people who want to kill somebody. To me, Polish jokes, Italian jokes, it's all the same. One of the things that the IPA is doing: they are taking a lot of Polish shows off the air, and the IPA is trying to keep them on. They [IPA members] are writing their congressman, their senator to get the shows back.

Q.: How can the IPA keep the culture alive?

A.: Look at Eddie Blazonczyk now, what he is trying to do. He plays Polish music, right? He plays it in the Polish-American style. He sings a little English for the young people and then he does it in Polish. Eddie tries to play for all three classes, you understand? The old, the middle class, and the young people. When he goes on the air he tries to sing half in English, half in Polish. The USPA [United States Polka Association] is trying to do the same thing. Help everybody. They were disorganized before. Maybe now they are a little better organized. [But] there is so much jealousy in this thing. There's always one man wants the big power. Then if you have one leader other people do not have the power.

You see how much friction there is in the polka field! You travel over all the country, people are jealous of this, of that. You are trying to bring them all together. They are squabbling about money. I don't believe in politics. I know a man who has been in politics for fifty years. He's got kids and they are all crooks. They pocket money on the side and everything.

This way we have it in the IPA, you change every few years. You put new people there. They have new ideas. If you are going to get along you've got to listen to them, to new ideas. You got to listen all around. There's jealousy. . . . they say you've got $100,000! Wow! Now it's nothing. You've got to have $500,000, $600,000 to get something decent. But they are jealous when they hear about money. Eddie and Johnny Hyzny, they put $1,000 to start it. They never took the money out of it.[17] It benefits Eddie but it benefits these people here,

IPA Festival, Milwaukee, 1976.

too. They come from all over. You see no bare hall here. You see people. They benefit.

I like music. What is good I like it. Not only polka. TV is a disease. You understand? TV is a disease? Violence, that's all there is. Nothing beneficial. What's in a polka? Happiness. When you go out of here, you say: Oh boy, did I have a ball! Did I enjoy myself! When you watch TV you say, what a miserable show I watched!

The Polka Hall of Fame is a monument to ethnic pride—not just for the Polish, but for the Bohemians and Slovenians and others as well. They see a Country-and-Western Hall of

IPA Hall of Fame induction ceremony, Rosemont, Illinois, 1983.
Leon Kozicki introducing Eddie Oskierko (right); Steve Adamczyk looking on.

Fame, Baseball, TV stars, movie stars in a Hall of Fame. Why can't the little people have that? Why should it always be the big people with millions of dollars that have that? Why not the little people too? That's all. Eddie B. is not a millionaire, Marion Lush is not, Wojnarowski is not. They are like us.

Not only is Eddie B. a hard worker, but he works for the public. The polka DJs are putting on a dance. Six, seven bands that will be paid. Music and hall are free to the public. They are to pay only their drinks and eats. Blazonczyk is on the committee to hire the bands. He works for the public. . . .

There are never any polka millionaires. There never will be. The only way to make millions is to cheat. That's why. So Eddie is building it for his sons. You know, he is not going to be thirty-four anymore. Thirty-four years from now, he is going to sixty-eight. He's going to be an old man after all the hard work he is doing now. Not that he anticipates making any big money out of it. They do it anyway.

Museums and halls of fame, like other visible institutions, are respected in Polonia, U.S.A. But respect never comes unadulterated. By the time an organization is doing something clearly enough to command

IPA awards ceremony, Rosemont, Illinois, 1983. *Left to right:* Eddie Blazonczyk (Versatones),
Scrubby Seweryniak (Dyna-Tones), Jimmy Weber (Sounds).

respect, it has also crystallized an opposition that is
eloquent on the subject of its demerits. The Polish-
American's deep sense that nothing gets done without
many people pulling together, without organization,
cooperation, communal work, and appropriate institutions, is threatened by enduring rifts in the community. On the one hand Am-Poles claim to love freedom
and democracy so much that they cannot compromise
on such important issues; on the other, they say they
"cannot agree on anything." What Helena Znaniecki
Lopata calls "status competition" is taken for granted.[18]
"Jealousy" is the word for it, and it is the most preva-
lent explanation for unresolved disputes between
people who are not divided by substantial conflicts of
interest. "Jealousy," assumed to motivate any criticism,
is deprecated when it seems to be the main motivating force in a person's behavior. In fact, however, in
a community where status competition and having a
pleasant time in a companionable group are such preva-
lent motivations for social activity, both jealousy and
good common sense unite behind the following crucial questions: What's the leadership in it for? What's
happening to the money? Is this a democratic, open
(noncliquish) organization with legitimate procedures?
Are the leaders active? Are they doing something for
the community?[19]

These are perennial questions through which every
old and new organization is scrutinized in Polonia.
The standards of selflessness, scrupulous handling

of money, and legitimate procedures are extremely
high. While leniency in these matters may be possible
toward an individual member, strict skepticism fuels
the examination of anyone who presumes to act in an
official capacity.

Since polka activity is expected to pay for itself,
those who assume organizational positions are usually
adept at handling the economy that sustains the polka.
Such talented individuals are admired yet scrutinized.
The fans are practical and accept as a matter of course
that in helping the music survive, polka professionals
are also working for their own futures; they point to
this interdependence as an intelligent compromise between private and public welfare.[20] Greed, however, is
an ever present threat. Concern for monetary profit
only is completely out of place within a polka ideal that
demands cheerful service to the public. Sharp gossip is
constantly used to limit excessive profit seeking.

While the IPA cannot avoid the skepticism that
readily accompanies financial success, it has managed to put its best foot forward. Most of its functions
are benefits for the Polka Music Hall of Fame and
Museum. The IPA makes contributions to charitable
organizations such as the March of Dimes. Through
a calendar of such affairs the IPA ensures adequately
paid work and good publicity for the polka businesses
of its members (bands, halls, bars, caterers, and so on).
Such moderate compensation, however, falls within
the limits of what the practical polka public consider

IPA dance at Glendora House, Chicago Ridge, Illinois, 1988.

reasonable. And there is nothing like donating money to the community to allay suspicions of personal gain. Furthermore, the IPA is run completely by volunteer labor, and the *IPA Bulletin* maintains a high standard of open information about finances and meetings. Nonetheless, there are jokes. Elections are greeted by a jovial response: "Fixed—do it again!" Most of the time, these jokes are good-humored—people poking fun at themselves and exorcizing the ever present suspicion and danger of crookedness—but may include a pointed challenge to the legitimacy, the fairness of selection: "How come your cousin won, Stan?" This is why the broad membership in the academy of electors for the

Annual Polka Music Awards and the professionalism of the consulting firm that tabulates the votes represent a solid base from which the legitimacy of the IPA decisions can be defended.

Although the association's purpose and activities are remarkably coherent, there is one gnawing inconsistency in its stated goal. The IPA proclaims itself international, yet in many important ways it has always been a Polish-American organization. Some fans see this contradiction as an indication of bad faith in the very nature of the organization, but most ignore it or interpret it as a pious wish that for practical reasons has not yet been fulfilled. The feeling in polkaland is

IPA dance at Glendora House, Chicago Ridge, Illinois, 1988.

always "the more, the merrier," and everyone within the polka world is aware that the polka is a true international phenomenon.

Like other active members of the IPA, Chet Schafer accepts this dual nature of the association as a pragmatic reality, the way things have actually worked out. The IPA came to life out of the experience of the polka people in Chicago's Polonia; hence, it is not only a Polish organization in its membership, its leadership, and the cultural ideals it embodies but, more specifically, a Chicago Polonian organization. Nevertheless, as Schafer puts it, irrespective of the original and present membership, "the idea is to unite all the ethnic groups interested in preserving the polka." The consciousness of the international nature of polka itself is very strong in Chicago. In Buffalo and the Eastern states the polka essentially means Polish music, since there are no other substantial styles and constituencies to be accounted for. But Chicago is home to great numbers of Bohemians, Germans, and Mexican-Americans who have their own styles of polka. It is neighbor to Cleveland and Milwaukee, where the Slovenian style is very popular (in fact, Wisconsin is a checkerboard of different polka styles). And it is almost within hearing distance of New Ulm, Minnesota, which is a center of the German "oompah" style.

Still, all the IPA activists are well aware of the ways in which their organization is more international in theory than in practice.[21] Leon Kozicki, speaking of the conditions that made the IPA necessary, defended the polka itself from what seem to be a set of basic if unverbalized criticisms. His comments had a definite "civil rights" drift that is almost completely absent from the polka party. Polka is usually kept separate from the kind of thinking that asserts "our rights," analyzes the way they are eroded, and plots strategy to get them back. The tough aspects of life are never mentioned at the party, never appear at the motivating center of the polka happiness ritual.

Leon began by establishing that the rhythm of the polka appeals to many different people, not only the Slavs but some of their neighbors—Germans, Finns, Greeks—for whose parties he had played. The 2/4 polka beat is the major rhythm in some countries, and in the music of many others there are some 2/4 rhythms that are very much like the polka. This rhythmic similarity is the basis for the often touted "natural" appeal of the polka and its historically documented ability to cross cultures and spread happiness around the globe.

As to the financial question, although he acknowledged the fact that just about all polka musicians support themselves by working at other jobs, Kozicki resisted definition of the polka musician as an amateur.

I am a musician. I do not make my living as a musician. I've been on radio for twelve years. I have my own radio programs, also on television, promoted various events, but that would be only one little segment of my livelihood. Yet I am a musician. I am not just an amateur.

My indoctrination to music was through my father, who had one old-type accordion, the old type that had button keys. He knew something of music and perhaps that was the motivating force that inspired me back in grammar school, in third and fourth grade. . . . I came home with the cornet, but my parents did not approve. Instead I learned to play the clarinet and later studied the saxophone and trumpet. So, I play clarinet, saxophone, and the trumpet . . . I play almost all the standard dance music and popular music.

Some polka musicians do make their living from music, he added. For Kozicki, Eddie Blazonczyk's bar business, record studio, distribution company, and dance promotions made him no different from "the classical musicians who make money teaching, composing, and arranging." In the polka world there is no concept of the struggling artist who lowers his or her standard of living in order to become a full-time "great." Polka musicians are well-integrated members of society, and they put together a life that includes laboring for a decent standard of living. Playing polka music is a congenial way to raise that standard a bit— and quite different from the financially motivated rock concert created by big-time promoters.

We still emphasize dancing. We have not got much in the way of concerts. Occasionally someone will produce a show, but essentially we are talking about dancing. Contact. Not the kind of dancing where you are in one part of the room and your partner is in the other part of the room.

I must also emphasize that there are a lot of people who just listen. I myself am a musician, and I don't dance. Most musicians don't. There is also a large segment that comes to listen, just to listen. They come to the ballroom, hall, or lounge and they want to be entertained merely by listening. They want to hear songs, melodies and tempos.

Those who are involved in polka, they enjoy it, they find happiness, which is part of what life is. Some people enjoy car racing, some horse racing, others football, sports, art, and so on, and I say those who get involved with polka music find happiness, jubilation, time for camaraderie, time for joy and for friendship. They say, let's get together and forget our worries, our problems of the day. Let's get together and enjoy ourselves.

Particularly with the young people, there is a form of propaganda that goes on. They get indoctrinated. The major radio stations, television channels, and record companies are part of a combine that . . . gives them only part of the picture. As I understand it, they do this for commercial reasons. Apparently they feel that there is more money to be realized from such promotions than from polka events. If we could have the media do for us as much as they do for country-and-western, I think that we would be equivalent to them.

Emily Richards, Jeannie Johnson, and small fan listening to Gennie "O" Okrzesik, Cicero
American Legion Post, Chicago, 1988.

But for some reason, when we pursue this matter, their explanation is, "Yeah, that's ethnic, and nobody is interested in anything being ethnic. It's not cosmopolitan!" Of course, the polka all over the world is the rebuttal. They use the argument that a lot of our songs are foreign vocals. Then we say, "Why, *you* play such and such that is Spanish, Italian, or what have you." And we document it; we give them the exact artist and the album and title and language. We have done that repeatedly. Actually, as the national laws have changed these last years, we are very close to invoking legal action, because we think that many of the radio stations and others—agents, artists, promoters—are really discriminating. We have brought cases before the FCC against local stations when they wanted to replace polka programs or not have polka programs because they said it was not profitable, because there was no market. We were not initiating legal complaints but providing information and documentation. And we proved to them that there is a market.

You see, this is what we say: within the format of twenty-four-hour broadcasting, we hear—you name it, everything. We ask, give us our fair share. Put a polka or waltz in there. What are they afraid of? Money. Their own personal ignorance, they don't recognize fairness.

I also have to include the educators. They have told those students, or implied, that it is not fashionable to be ethnic, that European heritage, and so on, is bad. You are an American. Speak up and be a cosmopolitan. You know, it's not too cool to have a foreign name. We should all be Smiths and Jones and Jacksons. I have to blame some of this on the educators. They are not really teaching what the world is about.

In fact, many times we come up to the point where many people, particularly in the business world, frown upon ethnicity. They seem to put it down, downgrade it. They fail to realize their own background, that we are all ethnics. We all come from some place, some derivation.

Kozicki's framework places the problems plaguing polka music not in Polonia but in the larger society, and more specifically in the economic establishment. Within the market there is no place for "musical values" or "community" or "seeking happiness, jubilation, joy" if these are not accompanied by maximum profits. Furthermore, in a slow and unconscious way

the mass media shape a view of the world that takes its clues about what *is*, what is real, from what is on the tube. The major broadcast media shape tastes not only by what *is* on the tube and the air waves but also by what is *not*. What is not reflected in the major media is effectively defined as *not there*.

Kozicki describes eloquently the IPA's attempt to lobby, to reason with, and even to cajole the media, as well as the IPA's plan to use, if necessary, existing legislation and regulation through court action. Both these civil rights routes have been followed again and again by victims of discrimination in American history, and both have proved to be very long routes indeed. Kozicki believes that the IPA's greatest resource lies in the polka people themselves: "For one thing, they know who they are, and they do not pretend they are someone else. There is strength in acceptance of oneself and one's past."

Groups that fend off the pressures of homogenization and discrimination fight on two fronts at the same time. First, they must fight the effects of mass culture on the outside; second, they need to keep intact their own special culture and coherence. Amid general agreement on the IPA's success, there is also a consensus that much remains to be done. No working committee has yet been established to introduce young people to polka music, even though the desire, the ideas, even models and pilot programs exist. Mrs. Chet Schafer muses, "They know that's what they should be doing, but they haven't gotten to tackle *that* problem yet." It is a problem partly rooted in the more general one of not having enough members who can take on demanding jobs. The day of the festival there are great numbers of volunteers working in different capacities, so it is easy to forget that the bulk of the planning and day-to-day programming is done by a handful of people who are already overworked.

A plan has been worked out, however, according to Chet Schafer. A committee will contact the big "ethnic" Catholic high schools—Weber High School, Madonna, Mother Garan, Notre Dame—and talk to each principal about having a polka night at the school. The IPA will furnish the band and buy Cokes and some potato chips, all just to introduce the kids to polka

IPA dance at Glendora House, Chicago Ridge, Illinois, 1988.

IPA dance at Glendora House, Chicago Ridge, Illinois, 1988.

music. This is a simple enough idea, but no principal has yet been persuaded to accept a potentially controversial program of polka parties. Once a breakthrough is made, however, the IPA is confident that American youth will accept—or at least will not reject—what it has to offer. The brassy Chicago bands could catch the attention and imagination of young people accustomed to rock music. There is nothing "old country" about these bands, nothing backward or "old time." Their polka music rings modern and echoes contemporary contributions from other American styles even as it springs out of the ethnic experience. The polka's ability to recruit dedicated young musicians who continually make the crossover from rock-and-roll is an indication of the inherent power of this music to attract and inspire modern Polish-American youth—though the crossover has yet to attract youthful fans and dancers in large numbers.

Polka people can remember well the not so distant past of their own adolescence when they "had a ball at polka dances . . . nothing could be better!" And those among the youth who *are* fans express their love of the music very directly: "My folks, we all go polka dancing, so I love it." The parents, not to overstate the case, see their mission as providing an opening to the *possi-*

bility of polka music and keeping the connection alive. Chet Schafer expresses this limited yet desirable result: "Like, my kids know how to dance. Maybe they don't love it like we used to, maybe they'd rather listen to rock-and-roll, but then they go someplace where there is polka music, and they enjoy themselves."

The IPA can draw some hope from the fact that there still are areas of the country which have seen no break between the generations when it comes to dancing polkas. In Wisconsin, for example, young people have never stopped dancing the polka, even though they may also be rock-and-roll fans. Actually, it is the unusually high attendance by the young that made the IPA convention at the Red Carpet Inn in Milwaukee look like such a youthful event. The same convention in Chicago, and certainly in Buffalo, would draw a much older crowd.

As she considered the ebb and flow of polka enthusiasm over the different generations, Dolores Schafer observed: "Johnny Libera said it's like a completion of a cycle. It dies out in one area; it picks up in another area. Now figure-dancing is big where he is in Massachusetts, and in Chicago it is out with the youngsters." The IPA wants to make sure that it does enough to keep interest alive so that the cycle can repeat itself.

IPA dance at Glendora House, Chicago Ridge, Illinois, 1988.

They see this cycle not only as a function of what goes on outside the polka community but also as a function of how available and attractive the polka events are.

The cycle operates not only among teenagers but over the entire developmental range. Dolores Schafer continued:

> Because the polka died down so completely, let's say in the East—and it really went down—people in the third and fourth generation are seeking it now: what are my roots? And they are picking it up again. People in their late twenties, early thirties, who married, have a couple of kids, got out of the city, are now at loose ends. They who were so anxious to reject their parents' way of life, now they are looking for some place to have dance lessons, a thing to do, a club to join, something like a community. . . . In the last IPA meeting there was a young couple, they were the youngest there. They came into the IPA meeting and said: "We've been living out in Schaumburg [a Chicago suburb] not too long now. It's a relatively new community. And we've discovered that there are a lot of people of Polish heritage, and we would like to start some Polish dance classes, if we can, and get some Polish club organized!" The IPA is there to help people like this. They do not have to start from scratch.

Chet Schafer spoke again out of his own experience:

> One of my daughters, Tessie, is a freshy at Good Counsel High School. They had a Valentine's father-daughter affair . . . and we heard this concert. They sang songs from musicals and what not; they did a very good job. And the school band played. After the program, the band teacher announced that the band will continue to play and asked the fathers to dance with their daughters. The first tune they played was a polka— the teacher happened to be Polish. They played a polka, and that floor filled up real fast because the biggest percentage of parents were Polish. Then she played "Blue Skirt Waltz." When I passed her by I said, "Mrs. Marcin, can you play an oberek?" And she says, "Oh, we have not gotten that far yet, but we are working on it." Now what I think is, next year I can work in a polka band for that night. They can have their concert and then have a regular polka band play, a good one. Then they will really be exposed to it.

His story suggests the support the IPA can give the polka-loving professionals in educational institutions, but the ethnic community is not unambiguously behind them. They need the moral and logistical help of a strong network to keep on pushing.

The exciting young bands, good up-and-coming bands, booked by the IPA for its festival are another tool for attracting the youth. At the 1976 festival the Polka Towners from Muskegan, Michigan, were decided favorites. Their supportive and enthusiastic fan club, all of them teenagers, presented an attractive example of how much fun teenagers can have in the polka world. They enjoy traveling to conventions, being a part of the big show, meeting people, dancing and partying all night long within a healthy "family" atmosphere. They are accorded respect, basking in the reflection of the shining band to whose success they have contributed. Being a teen polka fan is much more actively involving than being a rock-and-roll fan; polka fans are truly essential and they know it.

Most organizations in and outside Polonia seem to be running on the enthusiasm and disciplined work of a few members, and the IPA is no exception. The amount of hard, efficient, and consistent work that the central core of officers accomplish is exceptional. They meet almost every week—their "quorum time." The need for so much collective effort, identified from the very beginning, was one of the reasons the IPA's by-laws specified that half the officers and directors are to be from Chicago, Illinois, the state of incorporation. They were determined to learn from the experience of organizations that collapsed because their officers were scattered all over the country, making frequent meetings nearly impossible. The IPA's founders were willing to brave the likely chorus of accusation that they were cliquish, keeping everything under their own control in Chicago. They took the practical view that it is much better to have a workable organization that can be maligned than to fail altogether. Their position is that whoever cares enough to take a close look cannot fail to be impressed by the seriousness and honesty of the officers.

Moreover, board members who point with pride to their history of effort and accomplishment also note that some non-Chicagoans have developed into enthusiastic, committed, and hard-working supporters. They hope that this can be a model for IPA expansion in places other than its traditional strongholds in Chicago, Milwaukee, and Detroit. "Essentially," Chet Schafer pointed out, "the contributors in other states are convinced that we are honest in Chicago and committed to the cause. That's why they trust us and why they contribute. We are very close with John Libera in Con-

necticut and Joe Marcissuk in Michigan. . . . There are disagreements also, but they are wise enough to realize that you just disagree; you don't give it up. And the show goes on."

Jerry and Bonnie Brevig from St. Paul, Minnesota, are an example of active non-Chicagoans. The Brevigs joined the IPA not only because they enjoy the exciting innovations of the Chicago-style polka and the energetic, happy people who follow it but also because they were convinced that the IPA is effective in supporting polka entertainment nationally. Here is an organization that is "giving something to others and not looking for a profit. In Minnesota, our home state, you can belong to the Polka Lovers of America Klub and you get a reduction of admission to a dance—there are certain benefits you get—while the IPA is always asking: what can you do for the organization?" This concern for the community, this enjoyment of working and accomplishing a common good, is reported to be a major motivating force for those who give their time.

The following poem reprinted in the *IPA News* reflects the ideal of high commitment cultivated by the organization.

WHICH ARE YOU?
by Larry Sladek from "The Columbian"

Some members keep their organization strong,
While others join just to belong.
Some dig right in, some serve with pride.
Some go along just for the ride.
Some volunteer to do their share,
While others lie back and just don't care.
On meeting nights some always show,
While there are others who never go.
Some do their best . . . some build, some make.
Some lag behind, some let things go.
Some never help their organization grow.
Some drag . . . some pull . . . some don't . . . some do.
Consider, which of these are you? [22]

The IPA has a pragmatic approach to marshaling polka energies. Its officers plan an annual calendar of events, community service, and affordable recreation, and they promote ethnic (at least pan-European) cul-

The Brevigs and friend, IPA Festival, Milwaukee, 1976.

tural unity. That the promise of being "international" has not been fully realized is common knowledge. But perhaps in the future the barriers between Slavic-American and Hispanic-American polka worlds will come down.

Jerry and Bonnie Brevig are also attracted to the IPA by their love for "the festival" and for "people." The IPA gives them the framework they need to act on their generous inclinations and their well-developed capacity for service. They have, for example, made a tradition of appearing in matching original costumes that they design afresh every year especially for the IPA festival. Their love and talent for that extra bit of glitter and for the fun that can make an occasion memorable was honored when the organization named them Chairpersons for Special Projects. It is especially interesting that the Brevigs do not make any portion of their living from the polka. They are not even Polish. As they proudly put it, they are "enthusiasts."

As such, the Brevigs are excellent ambassadors for the IPA in the Twin Cities. In April 1976 they sponsored two benefit dances for the Polka Music Hall of Fame building fund, involving two local ballrooms (the Majestic and the Medina), three local bands (Bill Czerniak and Polka Soul, the New Whoopee John Wilfahrt Band, and the Macko Orchestra), and the Polka Lovers

of America Klub in an all-out effort that allowed them to present a check to the IPA for $1,337. The money is welcome, of course, but equally important is the achievement of cooperation and identification between the Minnesota ethnic recreation scene and the IPA. The Brevigs also organized a busload of friends to attend the 1976 IPA festival along with their hometown band, Bill Czerniak and Polka Soul, which was featured at the festival. This is the kind of expansion that the IPA will have to depend on if it is to realize the promise of its title. In this sort of cooperation all interests dovetail. Those two dances meant jobs and exposure for the bands, two successful and relatively inexpensive affairs for the Polka Lovers of America Klub, and business for the ballrooms, as well as money for the Polka Music Hall of Fame. And the public could feel virtuous about participating in a community effort and a culture-building project while having a ball.

It is precisely such piecing together and balancing of financial interests and cultural values that keeps the polka going. The balance is fragile and can very easily be upset by any one of the participants if greed enters the picture. In a profit-oriented economy it is a constant temptation to go for the most you can get. The polka scene falls apart with dismaying speed when people succumb to such pressure. "Who Stole the Kiszka?" is only the comic version of potentially bitter distrusts and divisions. By upholding a cooperative mode and by pricing polka events to be widely affordable, the polka association performs an essential service. In its promotions it attempts to demonstrate that the forfeiture of immediate large profits will be rewarded by continued and dependable business.

In balancing economic and cultural concerns, the IPA activists are only doing what people used to do in their neighborhoods and parishes: deliver polka happiness with maximum cost-benefit efficiency. But every living tradition is the result of constant invention in the face of changing conditions, and the IPA has had to cope with the difficult conditions of community dispersal through upward social mobility, outward geographic mobility to the suburbs, and "cultural mobility" into "the popular." In the era of TV, malls, theme parks, and the consumption of mass-produced leisure products and experiences, the IPA and similar organizations have ever harder and more consciously strategic decisions to make.

Red Carpet Inn Convention Hall, Milwaukee, 1976.

4. An Annual Ritual

The annual festival of the International Polka Association is the quintessential polka party, bringing together polka enthusiasts from widely dispersed locales.[1] For the uninitiated and the devotee, this chapter offers a sense of polka as both a lay ritual and a cultural movement, two aspects of this recreational activity that are usually camouflaged by the mundane particularities of Polish-America's urban and suburban surroundings.

Contemporary discussions of recreation and music, even "classical" or "art" music, tend to center on a view of recreation as profane and "art" as solely inhabiting the realm of aesthetics. "Ecstasy" has become a label that elicits derision; "enthusiasm," mere good-humored tolerance. We forget that "ecstasy" originally meant "outside of this world or this body" and that "enthusiasm" stands for "in God" or "God within." The contemporary use of science to legitimize some concepts while invalidating others has robbed public discourse of the concepts of "spirit," "the sacred," "ritual," and "ecstasy," which are centers of meaning for some of the best recreation around the world. We tend to lump together under "recreation" both the market-imperialized leisure time spent in or around expensive gadgets and the kind of life-restoring sociability laced by poetry, myth, dance, music, and culinary alchemy that occurs in what we call "polka happiness."

Furthermore, most of us have been negatively sensitized to ideas of "spirit" and "enthusiasm," as they have been diminished through their association with fraudulent cults. Even the Polish-American reader who is likely to be less resistant to discussions of ritual is nevertheless conditioned by a parochial schooling that has insisted for generations on the distinction or division of the world into sacred and profane realms. The church and Poland are sacred; everyday life and worldly pursuits—especially socializing with food, booze, music, jokes, and dancing—are profane. So the Polish-American reader is likely to be most shocked by our discussion of the polka as a ritual. Those who perceive the polka as a quaint but suspect or even unfortunate ethnic preoccupation might accuse us of reading too much into a simple or, to their ears, "simplistic" musical form.

We invite the reader to step beyond contemporary prejudices polarizing the sacred and the profane into the transformative mysteries of community recreation that turn polka music, dance, and sociability into polka happiness. The special signs of this transformation are all around: myth and lore making; ritual space and ritual time defined as distinct from utilitarian or quotidian space and time; ritual garb and gestures and motions; ritual friendliness and avoidance of strife; the subjugation of profit to the community-building functions of the occasion.

Prologue to a Legendary Polka Party

Polka people love to reminisce about good times. Every great polka party is enjoyed not only as an experience but also as a story to be related again and again. People check the stories, laugh at the jokes, and prod for juicy details, expanding the power of the polka event through space and time. There are many legends in every local polka scene. In fact, almost as soon as a polka function is announced, the criticism, the discussion, the gossip about its progress and likelihood of success begin to weave future polka lore. Whether the story will become a classic depends on the intensity, the absorbing brilliance, of the event itself.

By all accounts, the 1975 convention in Milwaukee had become a polka legend within the following year. The Buffalo fan clubs had been represented in large numbers, and spirits were high. Buffalo was on the map, conspicuous, united, full of energy, strong; some of the best music was played by Buffalo's own bands. Funny jokes were constantly elaborated into larger ones, ensnaring more friends in the general mirth. The after-hours parties in the hotel rooms lasted all night, spilling into the corridors, out on the lawns, and into the pool.

And so, on Friday, August 6, 1976, as we arrive for the opening day of the International Polka Association's annual festival at the Red Carpet Inn near Mitchell Field in Milwaukee, Wisconsin, the stories of 1975 are vivid in our memories, and our anticipation rises. Three kinds of activities are planned for the three days ahead: the Polka Fest in the afternoons and evenings, the Polka Music Hall of Fame and Annual Awards ceremonies for every polka lover with a ticket for the banquet, and the annual business meeting for the membership of the IPA. Word is out that Eddie Blazonczyk and his Versatones have captured four out of five awards: best polka album, best single recording, best male vocalist, and best instrumental group. Only the award for best female vocalist or vocal group is going to someone else—to the Langner Sisters.

The announcements of the annual awards are a high point of the polka year. Everyone wants to know who is voted best, and the choices are criticized or approved in lively discussion. But once the results are known, attention turns to the festival. Barring a scandal, a shakeup, or something out of the ordinary to change the normal state of affairs, the existence of the annual organizational meeting is hardly noticed by the majority of revelers. What the fans look forward to is three days filled with the music of good bands from all across the polka belts and the prospect of continuous dancing. The IPA meeting is a specialized business for the polka "elite": band leaders, disc jockeys, promoters, fan club presidents, and the like.

In the polka world it's hard to meet someone who does not have some direct connection to the music. The driver of the courtesy airport limousine is soon explaining his own relationship to the polka. Sure, he's Polish, and he has played in a band himself. But more important, his father, now seventy-four, had a band touring Central Wisconsin in the 1930s. His dad, whose contemporaries were such musicians of fame as Romy Gosz, Lawrence Duchow, and Frank Dukla, had made a name for himself; even now, retired from his job as "a foreman in a plant," he does some arranging for a publisher in Chicago. The driver's two sons, both teenagers, play a variety of musical instruments that he has taught them himself.

This chance conversation confirms the family as the central institution perpetuating the music; through the influence of parents and siblings the passion for the polka and the craft of musicmaking are nourished. What does it mean that the masters for an entire group, an entire generation—like those masters of the Wis-

consin polka scene that this driver takes so much for granted—are not even known to the general public? What does it mean that the wealth of the different polka traditions reaches the general public only via the homogenized show of a Lawrence Welk?

The Red Carpet Inn is obviously designed with an eye to convention business. The bedrooms are hidden behind ample common rooms: lounges, banquet halls, bars, bowling alleys. Across the huge parking lot stands the sprawling Expo Hall: the hangarlike building of cinderblock architecture that will house the Polka Fest. The space between is ideal for the cars, buses, trailers, and campers that will bring the bands, families, groups of friends, and fans clubs to the scene from the far reaches of Middle America. The lot, far from full as we pull in, is reverberating to Eddie Blazonczyk's current hit, "My Mary Lou Polka," on the tape system of some impatient early arrivals. These tape systems, the object of so much discussion and pride, transform the long highway travel into a warmup for the polka weekend.

The main entrance of the motel is framed by two large signs: WELCOME POLKA BOOSTERS and WELCOME TO THE IPA CONVENTION. A swimsuit-clad man is playing the concertina for a bunch of young people who sing along: friends singing to each other. Aquatic roughhousing is sending water and peals of laughter through the air: the fans have taken possession of the pool in the name of polka fun and games! In an indoor kidney-shaped pool, several children are swimming sedately. The contrast is characteristic: it is precisely the rigors of adult life that require the healing magic of polka playtime. The children at polka functions are usually involved in the serious business of learning how to dance or showing off their already expert steps. Absorbed by the challenge of mastering another intricate community affair, they dance, they listen, they help with this or that; but except for toddlers and infants, the children are not "childish." At polka functions, if the children are not dancing, they are decorously poised in that comfortable manner characteristic of those who have grown up participating in social activities with all the generations.

In a visible corner of the lobby, a long table covered by a Bicentennial tablecloth (it's 1976, remember), red

The Buffalo crowd, IPA Festival, Milwaukee, 1976. *Left to right:* Joanne Nowakowski, Jim Rykowski, Donna Nowak, Dan Buciur.

with white stars evenly splashed all over it, welcomes the delegates. ENJOY, ENJOY, ENJOY is emblazoned on the cloth. On the table are dolls dressed in a variety of national costumes. Well-ordered piles of IPA convention and festival souvenir programs are being amiably but insistently peddled by a man and a woman, also in Bicentennial colors; they both welcome us and sell us a program. Everyone seems to know them. Some new arrivals stop for short, vigorous greetings filled with references to past meetings and dances. Their name tags proclaim them to be Bonnie and Jerry Brevig from Minneapolis, Minnesota.

The conventioneers pouring into the hall are dressed in the casual assortment of shorts, halters, and bermudas that one might find at the shopping plaza on Saturday or around the house and lawn on a summer Sunday afternoon. In contrast to the Buffalo fan clubs, whose members tend to be mainly in the grandparent generation with a sprinkling of younger couples and a few youth clusters, here the dominant age group seems to be a decade or two younger: men and women between thirty and fifty. There are also fans in their twenties and teens, as well as children.

The noise level in the lobby is comfortable, despite the incoming commotion. Constant greetings and sudden bursts of recognition give it the sound of reunion.

IPA Festival, Milwaukee, 1976. *Left to right:* Mike Nowakowski, Joanne Nowakowski, Donna Nowak, Dan Buciur.

Small clusters of people enter, greet and mingle with those already present—people they have met at past conventions or other dances, or friends from back home who have traveled separately to the convention. Some backslap, embrace, kiss, talk, joke, reminisce, plan for a while, and then go their separate ways. Others move together toward the rooms, the dining area, or the pool.

Now and then a group with outstanding convention spirit and polka enthusiasm enters the scene. Here comes a rowdy bunch who seem to be in their twenties and thirties, mostly men, all hell-bent on a loud good time. Most are wearing Bicentennial convention

hats that read "Ray Kaminski and His Merry Makers"; one sports a huge yellow Mexican sombrero that is also dedicated to Kaminski. They are concentrating in discordant and contrapuntal unison on a mischievous rendition of EEEYI, EEEYI, EEEYI, OOOOO. The first impression they give is of drunkenness: the out-of-tune harmonics, the hilarity bubbling through improvisations on the lyrics. The statement of life-bolstering narcissism comes through loud and clear.

We remember that today, August 6, is Hiroshima Day. Against the backdrop of our murderous century, we experience this ritual of "drunken narcissism" as a flash of socially responsible sanity. The song seems to say: "It is us, world, universe. Hey you over there, take notice, it is us." No matter what the lyrics, this is the message of the group. They cannot be drunk. They are preparing themselves—and inviting everyone present—to enter the ritual space of polka happiness. The "wet-tuned" harmony (to borrow an expression used for accordions and concertinas) suggests drunkenness to the uninitiated by implying a lack of the control required for well-tempered (or "dry-tuned") harmony. But this bunch is working hard to achieve the eerie chords that pierce the complacency of the mundane with intimations of the vibrations of the spheres. "Wet-tuned" harmonics have sent vibrations heavenward from humans of all continents and all cultures. It has been one dependable way of "talking with the gods"—though polka devotees tend to be good Catholics and speak in terms of "fun," "good times," "happiness," and "entertainment," words that obscure the perception of the ecstatic element in "polka happiness."

In the lobby, Kaminski's Merry Makers manage to create a stir without really disrupting the scene— an excellent example of polka spirit mingling with polka politeness. Farther down the lobby, past a sign announcing the IPA reception and banquet, a small cluster of men and women congregate at a bar. Cocktail waitresses in red miniskirts move around, leisurely, smiling. In the restaurant we find no rush of people; most of the crowd will eat later and more cheaply at the concessions in the Expo Hall as they take breaks from polkaing and waltzing. Two couples in their fifties come in speaking Polish. One of the women, lean and very upright, is wearing a cotton dress and a handkerchief on her head. The style is incongruous, reminiscent of village life in another era, another world. The Polish conversation asserts itself without apology over the hushed atmosphere of the restaurant. An old, frail-looking couple are enjoying a whitefish meal, commenting on how large the portion is. In the corner, four robust women in their forties are talking, every so often dissolving in laughter. One makes repeated honking sounds, and they burst into uncontrolled giggles: "Oh, Alice!" "It's my hiccups." When the food comes, they fuss over their large portions. Diet considerations. "Enjoy it—you're on vacation,"

somebody says. A large family group comes in with three children of grade-school age. They dine with soft but animated conversation. The kids are well behaved.

Five young men and two women from the Merry Makers enter with a flourish of talk and laughter. They extend their loud but inoffensive sociability to the entire room; everyone there is a potential friend. Their gestures and comments draw the attention of people from neighboring tables. They order food and drink amid a great deal of banter. Out of someone's pocket come narrow, sausagelike balloons, which they blow into colorful phallic shapes with glee. The guy under the sombrero attempts to stand up with a bunch of balloons in his hands; an older woman with a rakishly poised Kaminski hat on her red hair pulls him down with a lot of joking and laughter. After serious discussion, two of the men get up and start offering the balloons—now innocently twisted into a variety of animal shapes, giraffes and puppy dogs—to the pretty waitresses and the even prettier cashier. The women accept them coyly, with giggles and thanks.

It is the ever present public sexual joke! After a riotous mock wedding at a Buffalo polka fan club, similar balloons were whipped out of pockets and filled the atmosphere with colorful flying penises. Men chased women with them; women slapped them away with laughter, took them to their bosoms with mock caresses, undulated exotically in front of them. Nudging and poking and laughter, laughter, laughter. Among friends at the Buffalo fan club, the balloons were part of a direct, explicit, carnival-like, sexual pantomime. Here, the same sexual joke is tamed by the public nature of the restaurant, but the need for decency in this "foreign" domain is only a disguise. As the men offer their balloon "dogs" to the waitresses, we can almost hear Eddie Blazonczyk's warm high tenor:

> I'll take you walking in the park,
> I'll buy you puppy dogs that bark.
> Why? Because I love you.
> I'll take you swimming in the sea,
> Oh how happy we will be.
> Why? Because I love you.
> I'll write love songs all about you

Cause I just can't live without you.
Why? Because I love you.
I will climb the highest hill,
I'll be Jack and you'll be Jill.
Why? Because I love you.[2]

These innocent, childlike love lyrics and the joking with balloons proclaim in public that sexual energies can be fun for the whole family, safe, a fuel for love and joy, part of polka happiness. What a contrast to the way sexual energies are man-handled at rock concerts.

The Brevigs—an excellent choice as official hosts for the weekend—have agreed to an interview with the same good grace that makes their selling of the souvenir programs an act of welcome. After leaving the restaurant, we talk informally at the welcoming table as they tend to their duties.

These Minnesotans are not Polish but Norwegian, two of many "cultural converts" at the IPA. They were not born into a polka culture but have adopted the polka scene by choice. Precisely because they do not take it for granted, they are able to be articulate and analytical, whereas born-to-the-polka fans may be puzzled by questions about their enjoyment of polka.

Jerry works at Honeywell and Bonnie with an insurance company. They met at a dance years ago and became involved with the IPA through their love of dancing. Theirs was an "enthusiasm beyond what was the German, Bohemian in our neighborhood. In the state of Minnesota we have many lovely ballrooms, but the music is repetitious. The same thing, the same thing." Their search for novelty in music and dance, as well as a live scene where innovation is both a matter of course and an ideal, led them to the Chicago Polonia and the IPA. They see the Polonian polka integrating and assimilating diverse elements, and they appreciate this concern with innovation:

Eddie Blazonczyk, now, when he takes a country-and-western song, he arranges it, but it is put across beautifully. The tempo . . . everything. Some of the country-and-western stars and some of the polka fans are against the mixtures. We are not, because the polka will still have its place. You have the greatest talent in country-and-western; therefore, you will

have to adapt some of their songs to polka and waltz. And it works. Eddie does it good. There are others too, in all parts of the country. Like Marv Herzog in our area—he came with four men, and you should hear the music those four made.

To emphasize the vitality of the polka, Jerry begins to discuss the polka Mass.[3] Not only can country-and-western music be digested and transformed, but the polka can become sacred by fusing with the Catholic Mass itself. "I have goose bumps and I am not a Catholic. They do not dance, but it is the same music and religious words. It is sacred—it's beautiful."

A newcomer rushes over and kisses Bonnie on both cheeks—"the custom everywhere"—and the Brevigs focus on the polka people. They "love people" as well as dancing. To love polka music means to support the functions that keep it going and to appreciate polka happiness.

We have been going to Chicago dances since 1960. We traveled around with Polish bands, and the IPA convention was in Chicago at that time. We became interested and started supporting the IPA because we were so enthusiastic about this music and the kind of people you meet—wonderful, happy people. When we were in Chicago, a group of people following Marv Herzog from Michigan were so taken by this music that they told us of a festival, and we went. And you know that when people come back, they must have had a very good time. . . . Frankenmuth, Michigan, is a town of 2,000 people, and they have more than 80,000 people for their festival. Omaha, Nebraska, has Omaha Days in September. Last year we were at Hartford, Connecticut; Dick Pillar was there. We go all over. We are old-time dance enthusiasts. If we can't drive, we fly; if it got bad, we'd hitchhike.

Neither TV nor movies will do for the Brevigs' entertainment. They find their greatest joy in doing things with people. Their other hobby is also people-oriented: "We are both professional clowns. We belong to the Clowns of America, out of Baltimore, Maryland. We play for the underprivileged, a hospital,—give us a call and we are there. We are independent, but we can call others in. All you have to do is give the word."

Father Wally Szczypula celebrating a Polka Mass, IPA Festival, Rosemont, Illinois, 1983.

IPA Festival, Milwaukee, 1976.

Let the Dance Begin

The Expo Hall entrance is mobbed. Most people have their tickets already (part of the package deal that includes fare to and from Milwaukee), and they are standing in line to get in. Others approach a ticket booth, efficiently staffed by IPA members, which has the quality of a Mom-and-Pop store. In 1976 the three-day tickets cost $10, and one-day tickets go for $3.50. The price is very good for what you get: on the average, eleven or twelve bands play, and the Expo Hall is scheduled for eight or nine hours of continuous music every day.

A bottleneck forms at the door, which is lined on both sides by about half a dozen men, women, and girls in "Eddie Blazonczyk and His Versatones Fan Club" vests. The women wear the ever present simplified generic form of a peasant Polish costume: white blouse with tight red bodice and full red skirt, sometimes referred to as a "club dress." Older volunteers, age and labor embossed on gnarled hands, collect the tickets. Their manner is careful, insistent. They double-check everything and hand you from one to the other in a complicated ritual, putting a string bracelet around your wrist and then a clip that identifies you as somebody who has handed in a ticket. The process is slow,

intimate, deliberate—all these busy hands gently but firmly making sure that you have paid your money and that you've got what's rightfully coming to you. It's like being reborn with all kinds of solicitous care as you pass through this narrow, well-tended corridor of welcoming, slightly anxious hands and faces. The intensity of the entrance seems out of proportion to the situation; it has the intimacy of a group of aunts and cousins checking you out as you emerge all dressed up for your confirmation. The exit, next to the entrance, is guarded by a lone member of the fan club. There's no action there. No one is leaving.

The same concern for not letting any freeloaders in and not cheating any honest people out of their due operates at the Buffalo polka clubs, where matter-of-fact matrons check tickets with the strictness of custom officials at a sensitive border. Yet ticket and money collection at polka affairs almost never has a mercenary air; rather, it always feels like a ritual of welcome into the polka world, the special brotherhood and sisterhood concerned with the transformation of food, beer, polka music, and dance into polka happiness. In the effort to support the polka, money is transformed into the sustenance of the community. This is so different from some upper-class charity affairs where money stands out, distinct from and incidental to the content

Eddie Barczak *(left)* and Irene Paterek *(center)* selling souvenirs, IPA Festival, Rosemont, Illinois, 1983.

of the affair. In this working people's ritual there is so much volunteer labor and widespread concern for the survival of the polka that the money transaction, reduced to a very reasonable price, feels thoroughly appropriate.

The Expo Hall is capable of accommodating about three thousand people. Portions of it are brilliantly lit, others lost in semidarkness. People are everywhere. Against the left wall, men and women are tending the polka souvenir booths as they would at a parish bazaar or at their favorite charity carnival. Buttons, most of them three inches in diameter, proclaim KISS ME—

I'M POLISH, POLKA POWER, or I'M A POLKAHOLIC—IN CASE OF EMERGENCY PLAY ME A POLKA. Some simply carry the picture of Eddie Blazonczyk. One features a photo of Eddie B. as a wistful ten-year old. Mixed with the polka buttons are stickers in red and white, the Polish colors, and other insignia of ethnic pride. These trinkets promote visibility and solidarity, and bring in cash; they are the same whether you go to a lawn fete in Buffalo or a national convention.[4] The mass-produced items are marketed along the national networks which—with the help of promoters, fan club officers, disc jockeys, and other institutions of the

Tom Mrozinski *(left)* and Mitch Biskup, IPA Festival, Milwaukee, 1976.

ethnic community—gather polka people together. But how is uniformity achieved in the handmade crafts sold by the women fans? Here at the IPA Convention 1976, hats made of panels of straightened-out beer cans crocheted together with bicentennial colors are particularly popular.

Another booth sells tickets good for purchasing food and booze. The association is obviously controlling the liquor sales, and the greatest crowds are directly in front of the tables set up as bars, where well-groomed young men are pouring drinks and taking in concession tickets. It's 50¢ for a glass of beer, $3.50 for a pitcher (obviously the better buy), $1.00 for a mixed drink, and $1.50 for your choice of liquor brands. Good prices—even in 1976. Behind the liquor stand is another room with the food concession. It is run by a group of women—young and old, mothers and daughters or members of a family—very much again like the lawn fete. But this is a food concession operated by the Red Carpet Expo Center. Hot dogs, Polish sausages, cole slaw, German and French potato salad, ham sandwiches, coffee, and chocolate cake with white icing are all sold at low prices. Business is brisk and the service efficient and fast. It is obvious that the low-cost food is subsidized by inexpensive women's labor. Young and old women going to and fro between the kitchen and the counter look like cousins and aunts, friends and neighbors helping out with the food at a family celebration.

The polka economic strategy, which is also a community-building ideal, is very much in evidence here: cheap prices, made possible by lots of volunteer labor, attract big volume and generate enough profit to keep the effort worthwhile. No one ever makes a killing; labor and profit are always precariously balanced to keep the polka going. This ideal is also a pragmatic necessity because of the constant pressure of the mainstream economy not only on polka music but also on polka people.

At the other end of the hall is the bandstand, big enough to accomodate two bands at a time. It is bounded by two huge black speakers and heavy with the electrical equipment and instruments of two bands, one playing, the other getting ready. The promise of continuous music is given and taken seriously. The stand is festooned by very legible business addresses of the bands and their sponsors: polka lounges, sausage and beverage manufacturers, fan clubs, fraternal associations, disc jockeys, and printing firms. Just about every firm is a small one known only in its hometown; together they constitute a representative sample of the business underpinnings of the polka. Whether or not this advertising is effective for sales, it is important to hometown pride. These signs are another reminder that a polka performance depends on the solidarity of the community. Sponsor, band, and fans are all asserting their particular localities' significance in the national scene.

The hall is divided into three approximately equal sections. Long lines of tables, each seating ten to four-

IPA Festival, Milwaukee, 1976.

teen people, fill the two sides. In the middle, facing the bandstand, there is a spacious dance floor. The ceiling is decorated with rows of brilliant balloons. Banners announce the fifty states, with a riot of red, white, and blue streamers filling any gaps. It looks like a political convention on TV. Most of the states are not represented by fans in this hall, yet nationwide scope is symbolized: polka happiness engulfs the entire United States! Under this canopy of bicentennial color, patriotic hoopla, and polka "nationalism," the dance floor is dense with couples whirling in a variety of styles, shuffles, and hops—a kaleidoscope of motions, ages, and smiling faces.

The Ray Kaminski crowd surges onto the dance floor with characteristic fanfare. This is no "audience," just coming to listen and dance a bit. The Merry Makers on the floor are as much a part of the proceedings as Ray Kaminski and the Merry Makers on the bandstand. Most of them wear some token of belonging to an organized fan club: a red vest with their favorite's name stitched in white on the back, a painter's hat. Arm muscles bulging, bellies thrust slightly out, big hairy hands and arms, bare chests with medallions of the Polish eagle all proclaim almost aggressively the stereotype of a hardhat out to have a good time. The

Merry Makers are the biggest and most energetic fan club in the hall. Kaminski seems a perfect choice for the early hours of the festival. His fans don't need to warm up. They are very visible: a large mass on the dance floor, and a groundswell by the bandstand. Two men with a huge paper banner have stationed themselves in front of the band. Other fans rhythmically raise large red, white, and blue paper pompoms. The atmosphere is electric.

The Merry Makers expertly dramatize a simple affirmation of existence, the bedrock of all well-being. Clowning, prancing, posturing, yelping, they seem to proclaim: Here we are! Again and always. Us, Us, Us. Pride in existence is the first casualty of social evil. Pride in existence is also very difficult to affirm in a meritocratic society deeply divided by class and caste divisions. So the Merry Makers are at the center of healing performance, the symbolic healing of basic pride. The crowd is engulfed in laughter and body-warming enjoyment, feeling good and talking about it as "foolery," "fun," "craziness," "a good time."

The Merry Makers are also celebrating their existence as a fan club and a band—an achievement not lost on this gathering. These people know how difficult it is to keep a band together and the momentum rising.

IPA Festival, Milwaukee, 1976.

They know how special it is to spark the fans' imaginations and to maintain enthusiasm and solidarity. "Ray Kaminski and His Merry Makers from Grand Rapids, Michigan!" the announcer shouts above the storm of local pride.

Great musicians
Wonderful people
We love them
As much as you do.

The riotous demonstration that follows is punctuated by shouted ya-hoos, jumping, the shaking of hats and pompoms in jagged patterns. Resplendent in white slacks, red shirts, and baby blue vests, the men on the stage stand pleased and flattered, facing their loving fans. And the fans, represented by their heroes on the platform, are validated as well. The entire polka scene of Grand Rapids, Michigan is being cheered.

This almost Slovenian band (with a banjo) from Grand Rapids has a raw honky sound echoing Polish Chicago! The first number sounds like an outlandish imitation of the Versatones—elements of harmony searching for each other and finally plopping next to each other, almost tempered chords but not quite. It takes a lot to be that close to temperedness and not give in. You can see why their fans love the Kaminski band: that out-of-tune wail echoes not only the Polish mountains but the peaks up and down the unruly Balkans as well. The sound is raunchy, evocative, unsettling, discordant. Whatever these fans are excited about, there is no question that everyone in the hall is dazzled by the spell of fan enthusiasm.

Devotees of brilliant, arrived bands like Buffalo's Dyna-tones count on dependably excellent performances and consistently good times. But the most determined and energetic fan clubs seem to surround bands that are still developing. It's as if the fans perceive the energy, the determination, the "something special" of the up-and-coming band and give their utmost in devotion, enthusiasm, and support to push the musicians over to greatness. Bands in a determined-if-ragged climb to the top capture the imagination of fans, who respond to this demonstrable

need and the implicit promise that goes with it: "You root for us and we'll make it. We will *all* make it." Maybe this is true of Ray Kaminski too. Perhaps the Polish-from-Michigan quality of the two-style mixture is exactly what grips the fans. And they, knowing Ray and His Merry Makers, are able to sense that the band will achieve the synthesis they crave.

Eddie B., his great proportions elegantly suited in white slacks and baby blue jacket, starts moving equipment on the stage, slowly, methodically, noiselessly. His sidemen, equally plush in matching red, white, and blue, begin to set up. They work discreetly. They've done this a thousand times before; they could move with their eyes closed and still not bump into anything. They do not detract attention from Kaminski, still performing on the other half of the stage. Every so often Kaminski shouts out "POLKA" like a battle cry and gets a big rise out of the audience. The band is wound up with excitement. Its obereks are a little too fast; there's no time to dance, so people simply whirl.

The Merry Makers next number is "Because Your Blue Eyes Blink Polka." Another Blazonczyk number, it is dedicated to "all the people from Michigan." The response from the crowd is so huge, you might think everyone in this hall is from Michigan. Eddie and his sidemen have finished arranging their equipment, and he has retreated to the bar nearby, which is comparatively calm now; most people are intent on the dance or riveted on the drama of fan devotion near the stage. Eddie B. approaches the impeccable young bartender, gets his drink, and leans on the bar in his last few moments of repose before stepping on stage. He appears to savor the quiet.

Eddie Blazonczyk comes close to being the central figure of this festival. He is the top polka singer and composer-arranger, the leader of the top band, an innovator and perfectionist whose new compositions are awaited with the expectation that they will top his previous landmark best sellers. He is also one of the top entrepreneurs in this field: manager of his own band, producer of records that are widely distributed throughout the polka belts, owner of Club Antoinette and the catering business that serves the fraternal and familial ceremonies of Chicago Polonians. Further-

The Versatones setting up, Niagara Falls, c. 1973. *Left to right:* Junior Wozniak, Jerry Tokarz, Jerry Darlak, Eddie Blazonczyk, Lenny Gomulka.

more, he and a few others are at the core of the polka lovers and professionals who have been pushing the IPA and its Polka Hall of Fame and Museum as a means of promoting the polka not only in Illinois, Michigan, and Wisconsin but nationally.

Even given the immense amount of organizational work that these three days represent, it is easy to imagine that Blazonczyk as an active IPA member had something to do with every level of detail from general policy to decoration: the concessions, the selection of bands—everything. Yet that's somehow as it should be. Everyone here would take it for granted that

Eddie B., star of the show, "Number One Polka Man of the Nation," would be doing all this work to promote his field and remain number one. The "art" of singing that wistful Polish tenor and producing his exquisite polkas, waltzes, and obereks is inseparably intertwined with the endless detail of administrative work, business details, and attention to public relations. This is assumed to such an extent that almost no one except an outsider trying to plumb the mysteries of the polka scene thinks of it as extraordinary. Just about everyone would concede (either enthusiastically or grudgingly) that Blazonczyk does all this very well, and no one

Jam session with Eddie Blazonczyk (accordion), IPA Festival, Milwaukee, 1976.

doubts that he should be attempting it in the first place. Making so much hard work look easy is his special gift. Eddie B. is a model of grace under pressure.

Rock stars, by contrast, are supposed to shine as blinding images of sex, energy, and fame. Mick Jagger's magic would be destroyed if, when we looked at him, we thought of all the hard work involved in putting him on stage and getting an audience there to watch him. All *that* is left to an invisible army of managers and usually presided over by some kind of promotional whiz kid or businessman intent on the bottom line. The infrastructure of performance is kept

separate from the "star" and his art. Who is Mick Jagger's mother? What does his father do for a living? The questions themselves—so basic, so central—seem unreal. Rock stars, disembodied symbols of human energy, are defined in their very nature as "other," as outside the everyday details and drudgeries of life and community.

But Eddie Blazonczyk is expected to shine from among his comrade-sidemen and fans, to radiate his profoundly social being into the daily and ceremonial life of Polonia. His brightness is sweet and potent precisely because he is at the center of all that daily work, the everyday struggle to make a living and to steal time for play in a community vibrant with hard work, discipline, rivalries, fidelity, heartbreak, and humor.

In the hall, Ray Kaminski and his Merry Makers are approaching the end of their performance, wringing every bit of partisan feeling and "drinking day" rowdiness out of the crowd by playing "Everybody Do the Ladida." It's a coarse little song, almost a jingle, that has little meaning unless you are in the center of a group of drinking buddies and announce to the world that you are set to make merry in any way imaginable. Then everybody "does the Ladida" and the devil take the hindmost. An amazing amount of noise from people stirring, talking, coming and going to concession stands, bar, hotel rooms, and poolside fills the hall, but somehow the sound of the amplified band turns it into background "white" noise. The crowd's roar asserts itself whenever the music breaks. Of the two or three thousand people here, only about five hundred appear to be under the spell of the stage, the dance, the music; the rest stand or sit around socializing, eating, buying. There is a slow and constant shift of people from the tables by the far-off shadowy walls of the immense hall to the brightly lit dance center, and then back again to the perimeters. The circular movement is reminiscent of something biological.

Eddie B. is still alone, drinking slowly at his quiet spot by the bar; a six- or seven-year-old girl in neat slacks and shirt and shiny patent leather shoes is confidently leading her mother by the hand toward him. The mother, in her late twenties and quite pregnant, wears a cheerful cotton maternity dress. The pair seem to be emissaries from a world of rowhouses, neat lawns, modest homes in the new working-class suburbs or perhaps from the old working-class neighborhoods—a world ringed by grimy train yards but one in which great care has been taken to keep life neat, clean, and livable under the noxious shadow of the industrial plants. The girl, not a coy bone in her body, approaches Eddie B. and offers her hand. She introduces her mother and then proceeds to give Eddie her program to autograph. The poise of the six-year-old, the big man bending to greet his diminutive fan—it's nothing extraordinary in the polka world; the polka man is friendly, sociable, and polite to everyone, just as he's supposed to be.

As the last noisy demonstration for Ray Kaminski is taking place, two elderly women—gray-haired and bespectacled—step up on the stage, holding between them a banner reading "Nation's Number 1, Eddie Blazonczyk." Their blazers proclaim them members of the Eddie Blazonczyk Fan Club, Chicago, Illinois. These fans neither need nor wish to make a lot of noise. They just want to say they are there. That's enough when you are backing Big Eddie B. and the Versatones.

The Versatones are already playing their "Opening Theme Polka." A quick burst of drumming, a few measures of smoothly blended brass, the concertina, the steady drums, and then Eddie B.'s sweet, strong, high tenor rises slightly above the balanced texture of the band.

> Forget your troubles with a smile
> And listen to us for a while.
> We'll do our best to entertain you all night long.[5]

Eddie is smoothly polishing every single word within the snappy yet flowing rhythm. Lenny Gomulka's matching tenor seconds Eddie's and goes even higher on key words: "for you," "to join," and "favorite song." The high-pitched sound is powerful and lighthearted at the same time as the song simply and directly states the polka ideal. The trumpets repeat the melody, and then Lenny and Eddie repeat their promise:

> All the six of us are here
> To bring you happiness and cheer.
> We'll try our very best to play your favorite song.

The crowd standing in front of the band starts to grow. It's a compliment when polka lovers quit dancing in order to concentrate on the music.

Eddie B. now turns to his important job as emcee. The master of ceremonies in polka events builds solidarity with the fans, entertains them with jokes, reflects the communal bonds that bind individuals and groups, affirms the life crises or landmarks of individuals within the group, and, finally, advertises and sells the constant stream of dance festivals that make up the polka scene. He works with a number of stock phrases and expressions but must also improvise to suit the exigencies of each dance and the special demands of each audience. There is rhythm, meter, and sometimes even as much rhyming as in some polkas. The band leader is usually the emcee, and every band leader is known as much for his emcee style as for his musical accomplishments. The special character of each band is reflected in that style as well as in its music.

Chet Lasik, who is scheduled to appear at this convention, and Walt Solek, who is not, are examples of polka musicians who have developed the job of emcee to a special art. In front of the irrepressible 47th Street Concertina Club, Chet keeps up an incredibly funny commentary in both English and Polish and advertises his sponsors by tossing kielbasa to the fans. Walt Solek's performances develop into separate comedy routines, complete with special props and costumes. His style has its roots in peasant fair performances and in American vaudeville.

Eddie B.'s approach is very much in tune with his band's style. In a clear, well-articulated tenor, he moves rapidly through dedications and requests, acknowledging names and places and (for the polka trade people) mentioning bands and radio shows. In so doing, Eddie charts a network of friends, fans, and professionals with whom his audience can identify, each name adding its specific image to a shared picture of the polka world. Eddie's style, punctuated by crisp breaks and stresses on key words, has a peculiar rhythm that permits him to move quickly through the dedication and yet leaves the audience with an impression of a casual, unhurried presentation.

> OK, ladies and gentlemen
> We thank you very much
> We'd like to welcome you
> To the 1976 IPA convention and festival.

Enthusiastic whistles and yells from the audience.

> It's really great to see a lot of our friends
> And all your faces from around the country here
> At the convention
> Saint Paul, Minnesota

> Up in Green Bay, Wisconsin, and
> Grand Rapids, Michigan.

Yells follow each place name as if a roll were being called.

> And we'd like to introduce to all of you
> Our new album
> *Polka Spotlight*
> And we'll play one titled
> "Sweet Bippy Polka."

The band breaks out again in brilliant, brassy sounds. This time Lenny Gomulka is singing lead, with Blazonczyk accompanying him. The effect is of two buddies talking about their girlfriends. Lenny looks sweet, serious, and intent as he sings to the microphone. The singing and the instruments are precise, while the lyric is innocently raunchy. The combination is dynamite. The special deadpan double-entendre turns this childish ditty into a song of affectionate sexual teasing.

> I got a girl named Skippy
> With freckles on her bippy.
> The men all stare, the women giggle
> When they see that bippy wiggle,
> Three cheers for Skippy's bippy.
> The men all stare, the women giggle
> When they see that bippy wiggle,
> Three cheers for Skippy's bippy.
> When Skippy goes out walking,
> Everyone's looking, talking.
> Look her over, oh by golly,
> She's got dimples on her jolly,
> But you should see her bippy.
> Look her over, oh by golly,
> She's got dimples on her jolly
> But you should see her bippy.[6]

The song is over, but the crowd is still roaring. Blazonczyk reads from a piece of paper a request for Tony Krupski's "Judy Polka." The acclamation from the floor is deafening.

> We dedicate this to all of you from the State of
> Michigan.

The acclamation continues.

> This is especially for Don and Dennis
> Also, I would like to dedicate this for Phil and Josie
> All the folks here from the State of Michigan.

The crowd quiets as the song begins.

> I first saw you at a dance,
> And you were talking with your girlfriend.
> Staring at you you gave a glance;
> Your warm smile made me break my trance.
>
> (*Chorus*):
> Judy, you are a beauty,
> I love you truly, with all my heart.
> Judy, you're such a cutie,
> I'll love you always, we'll never part.
>
> I walked over, said hello,
> Although I'm as bashful as can be.
> We got acquainted and we danced;
> I knew then you were the girl for me.
>
> (*Chorus*)
>
> After two years of happy dating,
> We both decided that it's time.
> Let's make arrangements to get married;
> Give me your love, I'll give you mine.
>
> (*Chorus*)[7]

The crowd's enthusiasm is running high. About one-third of the dance floor is packed with fans standing in front of the band and taking in every phrase. As you stand there, the feeling is that there cannot be a better song than this last one. Experience will surprise again and again, but for the moment the judgment is absolute.

Eddie moves on; he gives the delirious fans no time between songs but drives the crowd's feeling still higher by launching right into his intro for the next number.

> This one is for all the folks here
> From the states of Ohio and Pennsylvania
> Also from Buffalo, New York
> For the Versatones Fan Club from Buffalo, New York

> Also the Versatones Fan Club of Milwaukee and
> Also the Versatones Fan Club of Chicago
> So here we go now
> One titled
> "I Love Everybody."

The waltz rhythm slows things down a bit, and the standing crowd starts to sway back and forth with the music.

> I travel around the country.
> There's many sad folks that I meet.
> They ask me how I keep so cheerful.
> My method I think can't be beat.
>
> (*Chorus*):
> Oh, oh I love everybody,
> And everybody loves me.
> If you love everybody,
> You'll see how happy you'll be.
>
> My folks started to get worried,
> So Pa had a little talk with me.
> He said I had too many girlfriends.
> I said, "Pa, there's a reason you see."
>
> (*Chorus*)
>
> I never had too much money,
> Still I always have a good time.
> My friends still gather around me
> When they know that I haven't a dime.
>
> (*Chorus*)[8]

Now there is a dedication to the United States Polka Association. Given the friendly rivalry between the two associations, Eddie's dedication stands out as a gesture of solidarity and statesmanship in the polka world. Indeed, it foreshadows the grace with which the USPA's beautiful and talented president, K. J. Robak, will preside over the ceremonies of the formal IPA banquet later in the weekend. Her very presence there says: "No matter how competitive we may feel, no matter how many clashes, ultimately, we want solidarity in the polka field." The song is "My Mary Lou Polka," voted the best polka single of 1975.

Eddie Blazonczyk *(left)* and Junior Wozniak, IPA Festival, Milwaukee, 1976.

Why did you go away and leave me, my Mary Lou?
You ran away and left me alone and so blue.
Please come on back,
Oh baby come on back,
Come on back and live with me,
My Mary Lou.[9]

"Why'd you go away and leave me?" Eddie bursts out with both anguish and anger, permitting us a glimpse of the power and passion that usually lie decorously hidden behind his smooth control. The effect is exquisite excitement. "You ran away and left me alone and so blue." The word "blue" stands out to rhyme with Mary Lou, the special emphasis wresting the word from its usual connotation and making it a part of well-articulated and crisply enunciated polka English. A studied care for correct pronunciation is as much a sign of the cultural distance of Polish-American from mainstream American culture as the muddy, slurred, hard-to-understand English of the old-timers. Of course, it was Lawrence Welk who wedded the two and offered them to the television audience in an unparalleled synthetic version that echoes reality without being a part of it.

The second verse of "My Mary Lou Polka" is sung in Polish, and hearing Eddie's attack—his voice hurtling out of a tight throat, sweet no more but urgent and anguished—brings to mind the passion that marked the rise of the great Chicago polkas. It pulses through Jerry Darlak's concertina. The hurt of the voice and the intricate density of the band together provide the basic contradictions between bursting emotion and masterful form. Gomulka's clarinet rises above the concertina and is weaving sweetly around the Polish verse. Tension builds between the voice and the horn. It feels like someone crying in anger and pain on a sunny spring morning. Concertina, clarinet, and violins finally overwhelm the song in a sustained hop or polka-twist that manages to echo both the Tatra Mountains of the old country and the hills celebrated in country-and-western, U.S.A. The convergence of disparate elements that history has brought into the lives of Polish Americans underlies the power of these deceptively simple songs.

As if "My Mary Lou Polka" were not enough to complete the emotional outburst, the band launches without announcement into the Polish song "Oj Danna." After that, Eddie breaks in to dedicate an instrumental from his new album, "The Potatochips Polka," to "Johnny Libera and his wife, Stasia. He is here with his son, Jack. . . . Johnny is polka disc jockey at radio station WESO in Southbridge, Massachusetts. Also Ed Menardi, here with us. Also, Dick Mitchell and his family are here with us. Here we go."

Thereafter, polkas and waltzes alternate with dedications to polka DJs and fellow orchestras (every time a state is mentioned, there is a rise from somewhere on the floor) and with announcements of coming events.

I'd like to remind you
of the famous polka weekend which is going to
        take place
at *the* Playboy Club, Lake Geneva, Wisconsin
Three big days, Friday, Saturday, and Sunday,
        March 26, 27, and 28
Featuring the
Jimmy Sturr Orchestra from Florida, New York
Frankie Yankovic and his orchestra
Dick Rodgers and his polka band, also
yours truly and the Versatones
If you want more information for this polka weekend,
        stop at the record stand.

It's hard to imagine the local polka of family picnics, lawn fetes, and fan clubs in the context of the Playboy Club; it's probably Blazonczyk's brainchild, the product of his constant push for an expanding market and for respectability in terms of conventionally defined success. Losing no chance to advertise, he keeps on plugging.

We also
Would like to have you with us
For a week in Florida
October 4 to October 10
Starting out at Orlando, St. Petersburg, and ending
At Miami and Hollywood
If you want to join us in this tour
You can find more information at the record
        concession.

Finally, the Versatones bring their session to a close with the unsurpassable "Clarinet Polka." A roar of satisfaction rises from the crowd. Then Bill Savatski, leader of the next band, is introduced by "Fritz the Plumber," Milwaukee's most famous old-time polka DJ. Polka bands will succeed each other every forty minutes till 2:00 A.M.

Standing on the sidelines of the hall is Concertina Patti. She looks thirtyish, her smiling face framed by an efficient short permanent. Her red "club" vest is plastered with polka-boosting buttons, especially the favorite "I'm a polkaholic—in case of emergency play me a polka!" An ardent fan, she is also one of those rare creatures, a woman polka performer.[10] The polka world is dominated almost exclusively by men. The few shining exceptions include the excellent and irrepressible mother-and-daughter team, Buffalo's own Wanda and Stephanie Pietrzak, "America's Polka Sweethearts." They are individual performers of force and demonstrated musicianship—one DJ called them "the ultimate honky act"—and their "presence" as mother and daughter have made them stars. Yet this very fact has also turned them into a specialty show rather than a popular polka band—precisely because by definition a polka band is a male scene.

Few women are members of polka bands, and they generally portray feminine familial roles on stage: wife, sister, daughter. The Langner Sisters are a good example: prim and proper little-sister types, their singing is defined by smoothness at the expense of expressive force. They are decorative, there to draw the residual interest of the audience. As "the girls next door," they cater to the appetite for female image, an appetite whetted by the mass media, without breaking the polka prohibition against sex symbols on stage. The Langner Sisters, despite their talents, have nowhere to go. Similarly, Julcia's role in the Happy Louie and Julcia band is to sing and glow in Polish peasant costume. Although a participating wife and mother and a great symbol of family solidarity, she is not an equal musical partner, and fans often note this.

The two bellringers in Buffalo's Happy Richie (Bojczuk) and the Royalaires reveal another version of women's auxiliary role: polka cheerleading, in which "polka dolls" in thigh-high gored skirts, tight bodices, and knee-high white boots act out the enthusiasm of aroused fans. Theirs is an image that fuses fan club costume with school cheering, national folk finery with dance-school competition. The symbolism is complex, especially when one considers the unrelenting beat of their sleigh bells, which seems to echo from a mountain road or the fairgrounds of old world villages. However, when all is said and done, they are

The 47th Street Concertina Club, IPA Festival, Milwaukee, 1976. *Left to right:* George Stevens, Eddie Slats, Chet Lasik (throwing salami), Lillian Kovac, Casey Puzio.

only a "touch" and nothing more. Some categorize them as an undignified gimmick, "those go-go girls up front!"

The 47th Street Concertina Band from Chicago has an older woman who also rings the bells and exhorts the musicians and dancers by shouting "Hopa Hopa Hopa" with enormous energy and authority. Probably the wife of one of the performers, she represents all those wives who manage the logistics of getting their husbands and their instruments and their equipment to the stage on time, who form the core of the fans, who sell their share of tickets and buy their share of raffles. She's earned her place through her work, and her auxiliary bellringing gains authority not only as a representation of all that necessary labor behind the scenes but also as a reflection of the figure of the old woman clown or soothsayer who officiates at the carnival. She's bawdy and awesome at the same time. She embodies the power of the postmenstrual older female at the peak of her social power and independence.

Concertina Patti, however, is a different kind of woman polka performer: she is the leader of a regular four-piece band that goes by the same name and is beginning to gain steady jobs and a growing reputation around the southside of Milwaukee. Like most other polka band leaders, she holds a day job—Patti is a housewife and mother to five kids, six to sixteen years—but her evenings and weekends, her "second shift," are devoted to the polka.

I play the concertina. I've got a drummer, bass guitar, and a fellow who plays lead guitar and trombone. We play in Milwaukee and the suburbs so far. We play bars, anniversaries, weddings, everything. This is our third year in the bars. I've been playing since 1970, a total of six years. . . . I started giving one of my kids lessons. I sent him to a teacher and everything he came home with, I learned and he didn't. So we switched. He quit and I took lessons. I like every kind of music, but polkas are something special.

Before I started to play I went polka dancing. All these years I had it in my mind. I never could take lessons when I was a kid. We came from a big family, and we couldn't afford it. . . . So I really wanted to teach my kid, send him to a teacher to teach him how to play. He never learned anything,

but I sure did. I love it. I love polkas. I play every weekend. If I'm not playing, I'm out dancing just like tonight. Always did love polka music.

The Milwaukee area has Frankie Yankovic here all the time. They're brought up with Slovenian style. Now I come from up Stevens Point. That's my hometown. I lived there seventeen years, then I graduated and came to Milwaukee. And all you hear up there is Polish music. So then I came to Milwaukee and I've been here seventeen years, and I learned Slovenian from hearing it all the time. I got both in my blood now from living in both places. When I first came here I could not get used to Slovenian because all we had up there was Polish. I can sing in Polish. I do not understand the language but I can sing. My dad taught me the words because he understands. So he'll sing and we'll pick it up from him. . . .

A lot of these fellows here are in our club: Bill Savatski and Joe Marsolek. Mostly everybody in our club plays Slovenian. Some Polish but mostly Slovenian. I like both styles. I love Eddie Blazonczyk's style and Savatski's.

The polka is more popular now, really, than when I was growing up. Two weeks ago on a Wednesday night we did a benefit dance for the drum and bugle corps at Bay View. The place was jammed with kids, all high school kids from freshmen to seniors. And I went there thinking we better know some rock. This is all kids and they'll be bored stiff. You know that we did less rock than we do for weddings? They wanted polkas all night. So you just know they love it. Even at the bars nowadays, kids have to be eighteen to come in, they dance the polkas all night. Even here there're quite a few young ones. And they do the polka real fantastic.

The polka spots here are real busy. Veteran's Park, Kossins, and the Blue Canary are the top spots here in Milwaukee. Veteran's Park, it's just unbelievable the crowd he draws. The road is parked down there for half a mile. And the Blue Canary is the same way. He had two bands on a Saturday night. We played and this fellow here, Savatski, played right after us. At nine o'clock you could not find parking. He's got a great big parking lot, and they were parked on the road. People told me on Monday, "We'd come and see you but there was no parking." Every bar that I play is free admission. They never have a ticket—no cover charge.

Initially, fans didn't accept Patti as a performer, but she and another female concertina player, Millie

IPA Festival, Milwaukee, 1976.

Kaminski, have gained a strong following. However, it's hard to mesh the work of a professional polka musician with family responsibilities.

> My husband does not like me being gone all the time, but he also loves the polkas and he likes the money I make. . . . We play every weekend and we make sixty dollars a night each. That's good. It certainly beats an ordinary part-time job, and I love it.

Concertina Patti moves on, greeting friends and fans as she ambles closer to the action on the bandstand and the dance floor. She looks just like another mom, a polka fan. She appears completely impervious to how unusual she is. Her fans don't seem to notice either; they accept her, and they delight in her.

At the tables, where the dancers come to catch their breath, the loud music impedes conversation, and even those not dancing are rapt in the sound and the rhythm of the dance. Friends are drying the sweat from one another's backs and foreheads. Partners lean against each other, beatific smiles on their drenched faces. A bunch of seated older people, bending over their thighs, play spoons to the rhythms of the band. Whole parties are leaving, some swaying, others limping and carrying their shoes in their hands. There is no question that polka happiness has touched these people and has transformed them from an audience into celebrants. This experience of euphoria as part of listening, dancing, and even just watching a polka is the essential mark of a polka event.

This huge bash, the IPA Polka Fest, is both more and less than the best moments in each local polka scene, when the local band is cooking away and their fans transform the music into dance and joy. Polka happiness can be achieved in both the familiar intimacy of the back room of the neighborhood gin mill and in this relatively cosmopolitan mammoth hall where most people do not really know one another. As long as good polka music is played and the event is defined as a polka dance, as long as it is not marred by dissension or disappointed expectations or fights, the conditions for the ritual creation of polka happiness are present. The local and national polka scenes, though they create different social and emotional contexts, are complementary. Both allow people to become completely absorbed in the moment while immersing themselves in all the festivals of their people that have been celebrated in the past and anticipating the celebrations to come. This paradoxical quality of a thing done, redone, and predone simultaneously is one of the sources of all ritual power.[11] Every annual IPA festival enhances that power.

polka

p l a c e

Part III:

The Polka Scene in

Two Cities

Record display at Milwaukee Polish Fest, 1990.

5. Milwaukee

When Dick Blau left Buffalo in 1975 and relocated to Milwaukee, we all looked forward to expanding our polka horizons.[1] A conference on ethnic studies soon brought the Keils to Wisconsin and gave us a few days to investigate some very disturbing reports of missing persons and mistaken identities. According to Dick and the people who were giving him his ethnic orientation to Milwaukee, Polish-American polka bands were conspicuous by their absence, and a considerable number of musicians with Polish last names were found playing in the bands and musical organizations of other ethnic groups. All this would have seemed less mysterious had the Poles been just one small minority group among many trying to find their way in "a German town," but in fact, the Poles were easily the largest ethnic group in a city whose population approached half a million. A large Polish population in the city, its surrounding suburbs, and the farm country to the west and north was surely one of the reasons why the International Polka Association had chosen to hold its convention and festival in Milwaukee for many years in a row. So how could Milwaukee be a polka center with plenty of polka bands, host to the big event of the year, and not have any Polish bands of its own? Why were all the Milwaukee polka bands Slovenian?

The conference participants from Milwaukee told us that Poles were quite solid in their South Side parishes, well represented politically, doing all right economically—just not so visible culturally or musically. Nor were the Germans any more visible, having had their high morale of the nineteenth century lowered severely by World War I and eliminated by World War II. The Slovenes, never a large population, were split by factions of some kind and had lost their old neighborhood to Mexicans and Puerto Ricans twenty years before. Yet their style was the people's music of Milwaukee. Why?

The day after the conference we wandered down Lincoln Avenue, in the heart of Polish neighborhoods. As always, the churches were impressive, the basilica a fit place for even the Pope to hang his hat if he should come to Milwaukee. And every corner had its tavern.

Polonia. In a big music store that must have seen better days, the record racks had old albums we'd never run across before: *Gene Wisniewski Presents Walt Jaworski and Eddie Olinski*, from an era when a Connecticut band leader's introduction could help two Buffalo bands find work out of town; an old Solek album with terrific pictures of Walt in twenty different costumes on the cover; records by other Buffalo bands—Big Steve, the New Yorkers playing rhinelanders—on Li'l Wally's Jay Jay label. There were many rows of 45s as well, with titles and leaders' names neatly tabbed. We looked for 78s, but that big inventory had been divided between a collector and the junkman a few years earlier. An old employee who had played many years with Max and the Merrymakers and might have been able to answer questions about the Polish bands had passed on the year before. Many hundreds of Polonia's young musicians had taken lessons at that store, but it was too late to get much information there.

On down Lincoln Avenue there were more bars, some advertising rock bands, others country-and-western; the office of Representative Clement J. Zablocki; over a tavern, the headquarters of the Polish Roman Catholic Union of America; a funeral home; Roman's Jewelers. Jimmy Maupin's tavern, the one with pictures of people playing accordions in the window, was deserted—no regulars, apparently the kind of place that exists mostly for weekends and evenings, but it wasn't quitting time yet. Jimmy introduced himself with a brandy and presented his credentials as Frankie Yankovic's second accordion player for many years and leader of his own Slovenian-style band.

CK: Why so many Slovenian bands in Milwaukee?

JM: Honestly, it was all Frankie. He hit big with "Blue Skirt Waltz" and "Just Because" back in '47 or '48 and it's been that way ever since. Before Frankie, say fifty years ago, the north side of Milwaukee was all accordion music, buttonboxes, German music, and south of the viaduct it was Polish concertinas. There wasn't any big Slovenian community in Milwaukee. I'll be honest with you—I lived in Milwaukee all my life and I didn't know what a Slovenian was. To me that was probably Czechoslovakia; I never heard of Yugoslavia. But Frankie changed all that.

Left to right: Jimmy Maupin, Denny Boneck, Bobby Chick, Joe White, and Frank Yankovic in Canada, 1977.

CK: You discovered there were Slovenians in Milwaukee?

JM: Yeah, they brought him in. There was a tight-knit old community, say from 1st to 16th Streets and from Pierce Street to roughly Greenfield, where it's all Spanish now. They held all their doings out at Arcadian Park or a place called Turner Hall. Frankie packed 'em in. And not all Slovenians. Of course, they hosted him. He was like their hero, and everybody else came around.

CK: But what was there before Frankie in '47? Just concertinas and accordions, no bands?

JM: That was about it. . . . I think the Poles just had their concertinas, with maybe sax and drums—no big bands, just Milwaukee-style Polish music. I remember Max and the Merrymakers because they were on every Tuesday night from the Wisconsin Roof Ballroom for years and years, about thirty years, ten or eleven pieces, more of a dance band that played a lot of everything. And Irv Mattey had a well-known band, I think it was maybe two concertinas, a horn and drums. A couple of other bands. Hey, you should get a hold of Fritz the Plumber for examples. All the early bands, he has 'em: Norman Marggraff at WYLO. He could sort things out for you.

At this point, an old-timer came in with an old accordion, and overhearing our conversation, he stated flatly and swiftly:

I was the first commercial polka band leader in this area! There was polkas for a coupla thousand years, but that was only weddings and parties. I organized it. I had Maupin here playing for me in '48 and '49, didn't I, Jimmy? [Maupin nods, but his smile says it's not quite like he's telling it.] And George Baltz on accordion, a German, but he played by ear, everything. We had bass fiddle, drums, banjo, but there wasn't a well-known Polish polka band in Milwaukee. There was the Jolly Polecats, you'd have to say they were number one for a while. But they played Slovenian music, and they were Italian! All five Italians, all five of 'em, every damn one of 'em.

Jimmy started to tell me about Chet Ubick and the Ubick Brothers, a strictly Polish band that was popular after the war, but the old-timer would have none of it.

Frankie hit it with "Blue Skirt," and them Italians smelled a buck. If you want straight Polish, you gotta got to Pulaski, Wisconsin. They play it all day long in the taverns, all night too—like they do rock down here. Polkas, polkas, polkas. One hundred fifty miles from here, 154 miles to be exact, Green Bay to Route 32. Band leaders run the place. Dick Rodgers owns half the town—he's a *Polak,* don't let the "Rodgers" fool ya—and Alvin Styczynski owns half the farms. Put them two together in a knot. Nothing like that here in Milwaukee. It's all Slovenian here. The originals before Yankovic even were Slovenians. I'd say Frankie Bevsek was on top for a while, and Rudy Pugel, and Louie Bashell, he's on top now. Pugel's dead, and Bevsek is retired.

CK: Those are all Slovenian names? What about Maupin? What's your background?

JM: Well, basically, Irish and German and some Indian. It's

Jeff Winard with photo of Frank Yankovic, Jolly's Inn, Milwaukee, 1990.

good to have that Indian, you know, they can't deport you. My father was Kelly, a railroad man, and my mother was from West Bend, but I was adopted.

The old-timer jumped in again:

You know, he's more adopted by the Slovenians than anybody else; because they actually think he is a Slovenian. You know that yourself, Jimmy.

Sensing, perhaps, that the old-timer was running away with the interview again, Maupin asked him about the accordion case he was carrying. Indeed, that was the basic purpose of his afternoon visit, to get the

recently repaired accordion checked out by Jimmy before turning it over to his son. This led to a technical discussion of accordions. In the case was an original "musette" accordion built by the father of George Karpek, who had just repaired it. (It was also George who built the special "no-bass" accordion for Lawrence Welk.) The owner of this antique explained that all real polka accordions are "musette" or "wet-tuned," because "it gives more polka bounce to the music. See, originally they had buttons." Jimmy played a few bright polka choruses and explained:

See, it sounds louder up to twenty-five feet away, because it's really slightly out of tune, it's shrill, the waves go out like

Yankovic fans at Jolly's Inn, Milwaukee, 1990.

this [gestures of overlapping waves]. But after twenty-five feet, it defeats itself because you're not playing a true tone. The wet-tuned sounds sharp to the ear. I like a dry-tuning because I have an amplifier, perfect pitch at 76 degrees in 80 percent humidity. I always like that sound, and it was Frank's sound. He was amplified from 1952 or so, and before that it was stand mikes, so you could say he was amplified from the start.

As the old-timer packed up the accordion and headed for the door, he said, "Tell him about the first time you ran your hand down the accordion and Frankie said, 'Don't you ever do that again.'"

JM: It's true, you know. One of the first times I played with Frank in 1958, I got excited and did a run, a gliss really, down the keyboard, and Frank turned around and said that, and meant it. He wanted to hear every note in every run.

CK: You were playing a lot of runs with Frankie? Tell me about his style. How would you describe it?

JM: Sure. Single-note runs are the only thing that works. We tried doing little things with harmonies, but it doesn't sound right. So the second accordion plays the fills; he plays twice as many notes each night as the lead. Lead sticks to the melody, with some harmony maybe, and the second can play harmony, or harmony over the melody, or maybe a counter-

melody, and all those single-note runs that fill up the spaces. I ride off of what Frank is doing.

CK: Mainly those runs. What do you do with your left hand?

JM: Not much really. It's basically just the two right hands, two balanced accordions. Real simple. Really, I like all kinds of music, but Slovenian comes easiest. Basic peasant simplicity is best. But clean. Clean and sharp. You want to hear every note.

CK: So with Frank you had two accordions plus bass and banjo?

JM: Right. Simplicity. You can listen to the melody. It's easy to dance to. You know, with the banjo in 4 [four strums to the 4/4 bar], Slovenian music seems to flow—Frankie's style, Cleveland style, whatever you want to call it—it flows.

CK: What about drums? Don't you have to have drums?

JM: I have drums in my group now and no banjo, but almost all the Slovenian bands have banjo, usually he doubles guitar for other stuff, like country songs. But Frank didn't take drums on the road, took up too much room in the car and took too long to set up once you got there. You have to understand, all Frank's work was touring, one month, five months, two months. I hit all forty-nine states with Frankie over a ten-year period, and the four of us with instruments, suitcases, amps, could just fit in the station wagon. Always on the road. If Frank plays in Cleveland, forget it. Slovenians are

Frank Yankovic, Jolly's Inn, Milwaukee, 1990.

Dancers at Jolly's Inn, Milwaukee, 1990.

Eddie Blazonczyk *(left)* and Frank Yankovic, Milwaukee Polish Fest, 1990.

Yankovic and fans, Milwaukee Polish Fest, 1990.

funny people, awful jealous of each other. I'll tell you that 90 percent of the people Frank plays to are Polish, just like most of the people who come in here are Polish.

CK: Who else comes in?

JM: Some German, some Slovenian, about 75 percent Polish. It's a Polish neighborhood, a few Croatians, a few Mexicans.

CK: Mexicans?

JM: We got some Mexicans down here, too; they filled in where the Slovenians were, and the Slovenes went out to West Allis, West Milwaukee. Now there's a guy—Doc Perko's place is on the border between the two. He grew up on National Avenue and knows the '30s and '40s. He can talk for hours about the music then.

CK: I'll try to look him up. Is there much friction between all the different groups?

JM: Yes. Between the Mexicans and Puerto Ricans. They look down on each other.

CK: I was thinking more of the people who come in here.

JM: Not really. Everybody gets along, has a good time. It's just that you'll never change a Polish mind. They won't cross the line. Most Polish equate a Mexican with a knife and a mustache. The Polish can't understand how the Mexican is more fatalistic, blows all his money on a Saturday night because maybe he won't be here on Monday. Whereas the Polish work

hard to get where they are; he takes care of his lawn, he's clean, keeps to himself. It's their own Mexicans exploit the Mexicans most, believe me. A lot of wetbacks taking jobs from the Polish people doesn't help relations any. And then they don't pay taxes either, that really hurts. The Polish are very conscious of the taxes. Welfare checks are killing them.

CK: So any frictions between the Slavic and Spanish communities are sort of built-in, coming from the economic side?

JM: Yeah, I don't have any trouble in here. You know who could tell you a lot about Slovenes and Mexicans is Tony Beyer. Beyer isn't Polish, but he came out through Poland, I think, after the war, and had the National Ballroom at 6th and National when the neighborhood was still Slovenian but changing over. He's been sick a lot lately, but his wife Zena would know. They booked strictly Mexican for a while, Latin, Mexican polka bands right where the Slovenian polka bands were. Ask the Beyers, ask for them out at the Blue Canary by the airport. They'll know.

CK: I've never heard Mexican polka. What's it like?

JM: Beto Salinas is the best known around here; it's button accordion, wet-tuned, real staccato, like "Peanut Polka"—do you know that tune?

CK: No, maybe I've heard it and didn't know it. So nobody from this community goes to Mexican polka dances or likes that style much?

Badger Button Box Club, Jolly's Inn, Milwaukee, 1990. *Counterclockwise from left:* Hank Magayne, Hank Junemann, Rudy Kotras, Frank Murn, Jim Galbraith. Not pictured: Ed Gallun, Joe Krevs, Rudy Maierle, Ed Sterbenz, Stan Stevens.

JM: I don't think so. Some old people are still living in the old neighborhood, but they wouldn't be going to dances much.

CK: With every community so attached to its own music, how was Frankie Yankovic able to take over Milwaukee?

JM: "Blue Skirt Waltz" was a big hit, something over two million copies over the years, I'll bet. You know, somebody else in Cleveland recorded it before Frankie, but he had the promotion, I guess. And "Just Because" was a million seller. That's big time—not just another polka band.

CK: But what did he push aside, so to speak? What were the established styles here?

JM: I guess Lawrence Duchow was the biggest draw in the area before Frank, sort of sweet German-Bohemian style.

CK: I heard a 78 of his that sounded like Guy Lombardo.

JM: Right. And Romy Gosz was big in the whole area, another Bohemian.

CK: Li'l Wally was telling me that his trumpet could make you cry.

JM: Cousin Fuzzy was coming up in the '40s—also German style.

CK: Well, why didn't the Polish South Side generate a lot of bands? I still can't figure it out.

JM: I'll tell you what it is on the South Side. It's probably their independent nature. Instead of five or six ten-piece bands, you might have two hundred three-piece bands. They were playing all the time, weddings and that, that was the big thing. So nobody really got organized outside of Max.

CK: And after 1947–48, if you do get organized it will be in the Slovenian style?

JM: Sure. You had to. That was the thing that was going.

We spent more time looking over Jimmy's albums of photographs and clippings, most of them documenting his work with Yankovic over the years. We discussed the finer points of Slovenian style as it evolved in Cleveland and Milwaukee: Frankie Yankovic's range of keys and "patented endings" of an extra bar or two; the high standard set by Joe Trolli's early arrangements for Frankie; the intense competition between excellent bands in Cleveland—Johnny Pecon's pride, the Vadnals' perfectionism, Timko's push to the top of the Cleveland pile. It seemed that everything important in Slovenian-style polkas happened in Cleveland first. The pace, the actual tempo was faster; Cleveland banjos were swinging in four while Milwaukee's still clumped along on the off beats. Perhaps the key factor in Yankovic's success in Milwaukee was the solidity of his Cleveland foundations: he took off because he had a better launching pad. The blend of competition and cooperation that it takes to make any music, any style, any culture cohere and then grow was somehow better managed in Cleveland.

Leaving Maupin's, our heads were full of Slovenian style as a set of interesting "problems in ethnomusicology." We couldn't, and still can't, hear it as the flowing, clean, glowing thing that Maupin described; what was "flowing" and "clean" to him sounded stiff and a little sterile to us. But this was probably because we had not yet listened long enough to get inside the music, and of course, our acquired bias for Am-Pol polkas was getting in the way. Yankovic's "Blue Skirt Waltz" swept Milwaukee in 1947; interest in the why and how of that kept us from hearing what Jimmy was saying about the "independent nature" of the South Side Polish and their "two hundred three-piece bands." Those two little phrases eliminate a lot of unnecessary mystery. Polish traditions were probably strong for a long time inside the community but weak outside it: strong because the old-country village traditions of small "pickup groups" for weddings and parties were maintained in the parishes, weak in that there was no demand (indeed, probably considerable scorn) for such music outside Polonia in the German and Slovenian neighborhoods. Polish-American polkas were probably alive and well in Milwaukee through the 1940s and 1950s but just not very audible or visible to the rest of the city.

Back at the Blau house we met David Paul Winkler, known to his friends as "D.P." America's ethnic cities should be full of Winklers: "cosmopolitan workers," "organic intellectuals"—how should we identify those people who get high on the histories, languages, and world views of their fellow citizens? As a philosophy major and bartender, D.P. likes to know about those forces and events in Austro-Hungarian history that might account for some of the emotions bottled up inside his older patrons. As a lover of fine wines and music, he has to find out where Milwaukee's "best vintages" and "village bands" are located. Why? Maybe

because his people were from contested Poznan. Maybe because his grandfather insisted that English be spoken in the home but kept a large picture of the Kaiser over the piano throughout World War II. Such threads of explanation would fit with D.P.'s own predilection for getting to the nineteenth-century root of things. But why do so few want to remember and so many want to forget? It's a hard question for New Ethnicity and Old Ethnicity theorists alike, and one that D.P. couldn't answer except to say that "America was made up of shit from the start; all the respectable people stayed in Europe. The German '48ers who started this city were decent, but everybody else was running, poor, desperate. So why look back?"

CK: Why do you look back?

DP: I can't get enough of the "old style," old village styles like *gorale* fiddling, the minor keys, something barbaric about it. That's why I go for Chicago-style polkas; they still have some of that mountain music sound. John Zurawski's band of old-timers in Chicago had some of that Eastern European sound. All the Chicago bands, the AmPol Aires, even modern Eddie B. has some of it.

But what's interesting to me is how people talk about jazz, how a theme is picked up and how they keep going and working at it, but, hell, these clowns in the villages were doing that for a hundred years already. They start some little weirdo line, somebody stands up and chants out one verse or just one line, and then they grab that and just grind on it till they exhaust the possibilities. A wild thing. Develop it, work it up into this great big bang!

CK: So why doesn't this sound survive at all in Milwaukee? How did Frankie Yankovic sweep the field and establish himself so easily?

DP: I think Yankovic created the first new sound—a silly thing to say, but in a sense he did. It was a complete mixture, taking all the old styles and just making this thing. Because what Yankovic plays is definitely not of any one ethnic background. I've always kidded about it and called it pretzel-bending music because it was noncommittal. It wasn't the sound of a village in Upper Bavaria, or one in Slovenia, or a Bohemian village, or a Slovak village. It was one of the first things to come out of these old folk traditions; he sort of made it respectable. They didn't like when Uncle John would get half juiced up, grab his fiddle, and start sawing. . . . So Yankovic made it respectable—he irons it out, smooths it, not raw anymore—and other people picked it up. Now they don't make mistakes. Somebody doesn't kick over a drink or break a string; it's all the straight poop. I would never say I dislike Frankie Yankovic, but that music doesn't move my spirit at all. It seems too mechanical to me.

From "a wild thing" to respectable perfectionism, from grabbing and grinding up a "great big bang" to the smooth, mechanical "straight poop"—Yankovic would certainly not like this descriptive evaluation of his music, but he is proud of having cut the polka free of ethnicity: "You see," he has said, "I was trying to give the polka a certain beat where it wouldn't be tied to no ethnic group in particular. I never liked wind instruments. I found I had enough lead in the accordion."[2]

But it is those wind instruments that can keep the polka wild and Dionysian: a wailing clarinet or alto sax, the two trumpets of Chicago style. Though an accordion is technically a wind instrument, it is not blown; and though two accordions, like two of any instrument, produce a sum of overtones and harmonics greater than the parts played, the primary goal of Yankovic's music is clearly control: dry-tuned "perfect pitch at 76 degrees and 80 percent humidity," not too hot, not too wet and mushy, and none of those excited glissandos, Mr. Maupin, please.

Our own hot jazz biases and D.P. Winkler's similar feeling for the village sound could easily lead us astray here. Time to reassert a few basic points: Yankovic's music is (1) basically ethnic—that is, Slovenian—but also somewhat black; (2) working class, and (3) one of the most popular polka styles to have appeared in America. Taking these points in reverse order: the size of Frank's big hits in the 1940s and 1950s suggest a large audience "waiting" for that sound, second-generation people anxious to have their parents' old country passions Americanized: smoothed up, ironed out, machine-tooled—in a word, modernized. Uncle John became an embarrassment; his passion to get into the music and get everyone else into it with him produced a lot of false starts, broken strings, and spilled drinks—all aspects of involvement. The second generation doesn't want to fetch another drink, wait for a string to be replaced, or participate psychologically in a false start, even if that participation will be rewarded with a bigger bang at the end of the grind. Trying hard in public, what blacks used to call "soul," doesn't communicate to everyone any more. Passion makes for "mistakes"; perhaps passion itself is a mistake. Anyway, we want a finished product, say the children of the uprooted. And in the postwar boom, ethnic America could afford to pay for it, was happy to pay for it, happy to have jobs, happy the war was over, happy to dance the polka without having to worry about nurturing the music process.

Frankie Yankovic or, more accurately, Slovenian Cleveland was able to effect this transformation of collective practice into professional product, of first-generation ethnic working-class passions into second-generation ethnic working-class perfectionism. This "perfecting" process is paralleled by all the other strong proletarian styles of this century—African-American blues, Greek rebetika, Yoruba juju—and from studying these, one could predict the essential characteristics of the Slovenian-American process.[3] Describing this process for any of these styles with a set of ideal characteristics or material factors at work reduces the real complexity of what may have happened more or less simultaneously to a set of specifics that raise more or less valid sequential questions.[4] For example, from the set of four factors discussed below, can we determine which came first, "amplification" or "streamlining," "commodification" or "control"?

In any effort to define these features, a variety of answers emerges. The "amplification" factor makes a big difference in any style. Certainly it helps the Slovenian-Americans keep their bands small and mobile. It let Frankie Yankovic dispense with the blown and the beaten, those Dionysian wind instruments and drums. It allows the switch from shrill penetrating wet-tuned accordions to dry-tuned, perfect-pitch models. And improving sound systems in the 1930s and 1940s encouraged instrumentalists to become more vocal, vocalists to become more lyrical and conversational.

The "commodification" factor pivots on the change that occurs in the recording studio when a people's practice becomes a company's product. In some styles this exerts a strong "perfecting" pressure: for example, the three-minute time limit of the 78 RPM record cut a lot of conversation out of the blues, eliminated most of the taxemia (presentation of the modal "road" by the bouzouki player) from Greek rebetika, and did away with or compressed the gradual tempo shifts of Yoruba juju. But we suspect that perfectionism was an element of Slovenian style before the era of recordings, that beginning together and ending together very precisely, for example, was not a feature taught to Slovenian bands by recording session supervisors. Careful interviewing of the older Slovenian stylists might reveal some basic recording studio constraints on the style but, beyond the general pressure not to make mistakes, probably nothing specific. On the other side of the commodification equation, however, the power of promotion and distribution to increase consumption of the songs by an enlarged audience was certainly a force in keeping the lyrics prominent and in English, and probably a factor in keeping the band small so that Yankovic and others could tour easily to meet their new audiences.

Just as these first two factors, "amplification" and "commodification," can be boiled down to one complex efficient cause, electric technology's impact on a people's music, so the next two factors, "streamlining" and "control," could be reduced to a simple final cause or goal: happiness, feeling real and good, strong and in control of some new power. Song and dance can do that for people, temporarily; and it seems to be the case across cultures under capitalism that the further and faster people lost control of their daily lives and working conditions (moving from farm to factory, from craft work to assembly line), the more they wanted to hear and feel control in their music. Alienated from their bodies during the working week, they looked for reintegration, recreation, at the weekend polka dances. Their work/play dialectic shaped the style. The deep push for "control" in the music styles of the proletariat comes from the powerlessness of the working class, but the specific forms control will take have an ethnic di-

mension that might be called "streamlining." A class/ethnic dialectic shapes the style, too.

When B. B. King's and Bobby Bland's fans in the early 1960s (and in those days all their supporters were African-Americans) were asked what they liked in the music, the answer was always, "He's made it mellow," "It's smooth," or "They've streamlined the blues, made it modern." In other words, they kept the old music but distilled it, simplified it, controlled it, perfected it. Old wine in a new bottle, whether the distilleries are African-American and located in postwar Memphis and Los Angeles, or Slovenian and located in postwar Cleveland and Milwaukee.

The new Slovenian-American style, not really created by Yankovic but certainly polished, promoted, and disseminated by him (with some assistance from His Master's Voice), is controlled, clean, modern, streamlined in the extreme. Two dry-tuned and balanced accordions for melody and countermelody, lead and fills; no slurs or glissandos, every eighth-note run articulated; no mess in the superstructure. And the bottom? There is a difference in the beat because it's black—1920s black, but African-American for sure. Basically, a banjo downstroked in 4/4 time gives the music its drive. The bass moves inside this beat in 2, with occasional measures, pairs of measures, and whole choruses in 4/4. The bass notes are not German oompah, back and forth, root and fifth, but moving all over the chords and beyond in the 4/4 choruses, where the affinities with early Duke Ellington and Count Basie are most obvious. It is this combining of sounds—clear, clean accordions running and bounding along over the bass and banjo rhythm team (a white/black dialectic)—that constitutes "streamlining" and "control" in Yankovic's music. Finally, the vocals keep the perfected style accessible. Yankovic singing by himself sounds like you or me or anyone else, and much of the time he is joined by one or more other singers who create a participatory sing-along effect. It was this sound, a higher synthesis of three dialectical American dilemmas (work/play, class/ethnic, and black/white) that captured Milwaukee in the postwar period.

In dialectics, whether Marxist, Hegelian, or ancient Greek, a "higher synthesis" is never permanent, always

Louie Bashell with Loren Kohel (left), Milwaukee, 1990.

the history of Milwaukee's socialist city politics. Bits of information about the various ethnic communities in the city, portions of the conference proceedings, and general impressions of the city itself began to fit into place. Milwaukee was exceptionally clean and decent—wonderful parks, great library system, fine transportation—not at all like rowdy Chicago or depressed Buffalo. So it deserved a clean, decent, rational polka style, a compromise in taste and tempo between slow German and faster Polish. Within well-ordered Milwaukee the ethnic groups were perhaps more conservative than elsewhere, more clannish, more concerned with internal factions than with public relations. As ever, the Serbs and Croats were at one another's throats. The old Serbian community from Austro-Hungary and the new Serbian community from Yugoslavia each had its own orthodox church and politics. The early Poles from the northern fishing villages, the "Kashubs," once had their own village on Jones Island and didn't have much to say to the southern Poles who came later. So Frankie Yankovic didn't displace all these peoples and their music so much as define a public space for himself and the less traditionally minded.

On our last morning, D.P. drove us out to visit Louie Bashell, the "Silk Umbrella Man," generally acknowledged to be the top Slovenian-American stylist in Milwaukee. In our pleasant and efficient interview the basic outline of his life was quickly established. Louie was born on July 1, 1914, the day his father opened a tavern in a mostly German neighborhood. His father occasionally played the buttonbox, or semitone accordion, for back-of-the-bar entertainment and started his son playing at age seven. Louie switched to the chromatic accordion at age twelve, took lessons from Tony Martinsek, moved to the piano accordion at fifteen, and has been "playing out for public" ever since. He went to trade school in the early 1930s to be a plumber but couldn't find work when he graduated in the middle of the Depression, so he spent more time on music and worked when he could at the packinghouse. He married in 1940, did plumbing in the war factories, put his savings into properties; with the help of his first and only hit record, the "Silk Umbrella Polka" in 1946, he says, "I haven't worked in a shop since that year."

becomes a thesis that will be met by an antithesis. Now, polka lovers, if Yankovic's Cleveland Slovenian sound is the thesis of the 1945–50 period, what is the antithesis emerging 1950 to 1960? That's right: crazy Li'l Wally's honky style from Polish Chicago. And the higher synthesis emerging from *this* confrontation of polka kings? Right again: Marion Lush and Eddie Blazonczyk, the styles where Dionysian passion and Apollonian perfectionism meet.

As we talked with D. P. Winkler late into the night, we covered topics ranging from D.P.'s Big Church Theory (the more despised the people, the bigger the church,) through the problems of school integration to

CK: Was "Silk Umbrella Polka" a big hit in Cleveland?

LB: Well, only like a folksong. It had Slovenian melody and Slovenian words, so all the Cleveland bands recorded it at one time or another. But it wasn't like Frankie Yankovic's impact here at all. In fact, I've never played in Cleveland. And I have an uncle with a tavern there, who hires bands, too. No, you see Milwaukee's music is not like any other. It's slower. Cleveland is going twice as fast! Milwaukee is more relaxed. People set no pace, they just live it out and enjoy as much as they can that way. No rush to get nowhere.

CK: And your music fits that feeling?

LB: Yes, I think so. It's really a surprising thing about Milwaukee: the Slovenian population is rather small, but it's the most popular ethnic music in Milwaukee. The Germans or the Poles may start a band, but it will be 90 percent Slovenian music.

CK: That's the puzzle we've been working on. Why do you think that is?

LB: It's a very melodious music. Simple music and melodious; you don't have to be a genius to play it, you know, or have good technique, or anything like that. It's just a flowing music. Polish music has various frills and trills in it, a very distinct flavor, while Slovenian music is plain, simply notes that just move—nothing fancy. I've never come across a piece of Slovenian music that was difficult. The Slovenians are so easily pleased. They don't have to have nothing special. The way I see it, the Slovenians haven't got great composers or great writers—at least, I don't know about them, I don't think the world knows much about them, Slovenian opera singers or conductors.

CK: You should have heard this paper about all the Slovenian contributions this past weekend at the conference we came out here for—the first opera house in Cleveland was a Slovenian opera house—

LB: Yes. Yes, I'm sure—

CK: But Slovenians really excel in straightforward simple songs?

LB: That's right. That's my thought exactly.

CK: And so those songs dominate in Milwaukee. Aside from Veteran's Park, all I hear is Slovenian style, like Gentleman Jim at the Blue Canary—Slovenian and country, Slovenian and country. Is that fairly typical?

LB: Yes, I'd say so. Gentleman Jim, he's Polish by nationality, but he plays a lot of Slovenian music. It's a real odd

Bob Schamburg, Louie Bashell Orchestra, Milwaukee, 1990.

thing that Milwaukee with so much Polish ethnic stuff around here—they have Polish schools, great Polish churches, music stores, and everything—and I have yet to see or hear an organized Polish band play Polish-type music in Milwaukee like Eddie Blazonczyk in Chicago, or Walt Solek and Wojnarowski from Connecticut. But you can't get a group like that in Milwaukee to make music; they'll come right to the accordion and play Slovenian music.

CK: Why is that?

LB: I don't know, really. You think you'll find the answer, huh?

CK: It probably has to do with politics, the schools, a lot of German influence.

Bob Brusky, Louie Bashell Orchestra, Milwaukee, 1990.

A Louie Bashell album.

LB: I think it all exploded from Yankovic. When he came to town and his music became popular—"Just Because," "Blue Skirt Waltz"—then everything else fell in place for him, such as all the Slovenian songs he sang, Slovenian lyrics even on records. That was a very big impact.

CK: But Frankie didn't push the Polish style out of Cleveland; how did he do it in Milwaukee?

LB: He had a lot of Slovenian support here. He was not adopted by the Germans or anything like that. You see, they needed a hero back then, like Bobby Vinton is a hero to the Poles now, they were proud of him for representing them.

I remember in the late '40s there was a big promotion in the Milwaukee Auditorium, eight or ten bands, Lawrence Duchow, Six Fat Dutchmen, Sammy Madden, Yankovic, my band, and some others. Frankie was crowned polka king, and I was crowned number two. I was satisifed. And I've been holding my own here in Milwaukee; we're in the top position for fifteen or twenty years now.

The reason for my longevity is that we play all kinds of music. The banjo doubles guitar, and the bass doubles tuba. So I can take and play German music almost their style. And then I can play Polish music—I don't play fast enough to play Polish music like the real Polish people do, I play it actually in my own feelings. I was honored a few months ago when a lady from Europe thanked me for the finest tempo she had ever danced an oberek to. I just pick up the Polish songs by ear, kids have had them for lessons, Lush's "Hey Cavalier" I use. It all depends where I am playing. Some places no polkas at all; other places, like German parties or New Year's, we won't play much Polish.

CK: Aren't there German bands for the German parties?

LB: Oh, yeah, Johnny Hoffman, Johnny Walters, they have the German flavor, but it is still basically Slovenian music. The two accordions.

CK: Were there always two accordions?

LB: No, before the war it was usually a solo accordion, you know—Martinsek alone always had fifty to a hundred students—or just a trio of accordion, drums, sax. My very first records were like that; maybe my wife can find one.

CK: I hope so—we'd like to hear it. You made other records after those, right?

LB: Oh yes. One just before the strike and the ban on recording. RCA hired us, and later I did a few albums and 45s for them in the '50s, but RCA dropped us when rock came in, and then I was with Mercury a few years. The last record, about ten years ago, was with the King label in Cincinnati with all the other leaders, but the guy who hired us for that was fired soon after. It must have been a big flop.

CK: You don't go to a studio and make records of your own?

LB: No. There is no way to distribute them except off the bandstand. And I always say, I come to sell music, not records.

CK: And you don't need the records to keep the band busy?

LB: We work four nights every week, and I could have stopped years ago on the income from the properties. Wednesday we're at Music Land, Sunday at the Blue Canary, and Friday and Saturday are always booked ahead. My wife hasn't had me home on a Saturday in so many years we lost count.

CK: With so much work the personnel must stay the same.

LB: Some come and go and come back again. My fill accordion player left in '61 or '62 and then I took him back after ten years. The drummers come and go and I need substitutes; unless they do vocals they get bored, because I try to use the least amount of cymbals and half the banjo rhythm section, just the off beat. I insist upon that; that's the flavor I want, and that's the flavor that the people are buying for fifty years— two-beat, solid, no frills on the drums, nothin' fancy. Bass drum and sock cymbal, that's all a man has to do for me on that stage.

CK: Do you rehearse regularly to get the sound you want, break in substitutes?

LB: We've never had a rehearsal. Never. Except when we were doing records, of course. . . . If you are rehearsing a lot, you start playing for the musicians. I play what the people ask for, what they remember. I play for the people because they pay the freight. And there are bands that try to play just like I do, and bands with musicians who used to play with me. The country-and-western songs are standard, the old ones, not many modern ones, mostly Eddy Arnold, Gene Autry, "Cheatin' Heart," "Jealous Heart," "Never Ending Love." The men all have a lot of experience, so really there's no problem with a request. A guy asks for "Moonlight and Roses," we play it. I play "Sweethearts on Parade," they give me an ovation. They remember.

CK: Who are the musicians? I mean, are they all Slovenian and Polish? And what do they do aside from the band?

LB: I'm the only Slovene in the band. Let's see, Johnny Bello is Hungarian, and he's over at the County Hospital. Matuszak, the drummer, he's Polish, does some vocals; he's a food inspector, dairies, cheeses. Brusky, the bass, is Bohemian, and sometimes he can't play during the week because he's a vice-principal and has to be up for school. Robert Zir is German, and he's a foreman at a chemical leather company.

CK: So you all know each other's music in Milwaukee.

LB: Like I said, we keep it simple and solid. For the dancers. You need a good partner. My wife tells me when I play bad—if she has a hard time dancing, she'll tell me something is wrong.

Mrs. Bashell had brought a small pile of 78s from a hiding place—"Louie would just give them away if somebody asked, so I've kept them safe"—and we spent some time listening to records. Louie's first records, just the trio, were much wilder than expected: lilting alto sax and a very busy drummer kicking things along with breaks and fills that reminded me of Chicago Dixieland—the Austin High gang, Gene Krupa or George Wettling mixing it up on the tubs. A little later a 78 by the legendary Romy Gosz—buttery tone, vibrato, loose surging phrases—took us completely by surprise. If you played that next to a Bix Beiderbecke record, what conclusions could be drawn? Was that polka clarinetist related to jazz clarinetist Frank Teschmaker? Before we could begin to sort out the German contribution to jazz from the jazz contribution to polka, we were moving along to Louie's LPs of the 1950s, where the music seemed to get smoother and mellower with the years. They were still mostly two-beat, but the Yankovic influence was unmistakable, and the net effect was of ever increasing respectability.

Richard Yehl, Louie Bashell Orchestra, Milwaukee, 1990.

Within the Milwaukee Slovenian community there is some feeling that the Cleveland style became dominant just because the Slovenian community there was better off, better organized, coming from Steiermark (the supposedly better part of Slovenia), while in Milwaukee more people were from Kreinmark ("lower Slovenia") and struggling with factionalism.[5] According to this view, Cleveland has six or eight Slovenian Homes (community centers), while Milwaukee's community could barely organize one—and finally had to hire a Swede to manage it because the jealousies were so fierce. In the good old days there used to be regular two-by-four fights whenever a Krein walked

into a Steier tavern, but in recent decades the fisticuffs have simmered down to gossip, backbiting, and the hope that such old feuds are a stain on the Slovenian heritage that will one day fade away completely. This Steier versus Krein factionalism, however, seems to support the notion that the Slovenian style represents a compromise or mediation between Germans and Poles; the Steiers come from the area closer to Germany and Austria, and it is German values, German business sense, that they hold over the Kreins. Yet it is the Kreins who seem to make most of the music, probably (if other class/ethnic nexuses of musical creation are any guide) in an effort to transcend Steier standards and stereotypes.

Could it have been class antagonism within the small Slovenian community of Milwaukee (or a lack of it in Cleveland) that somehow contributed to the hegemony of Slovenian style? One notices, in just a few days of research, that class splits in the ethnic groups seem to go deeper in Milwaukee and are more easily acknowledged. Could this have anything to do with the long history of socialist city government as a context for ethnic identities? A lack of conventional ward politics and the usual ethnic alliances that mute class differences? A clearer ideological climate for identifying class interests and acting on them? Or is Milwaukee's mosaic better viewed as a series of historical accidents and particulars? The Poles called "Kashubs" happened to settle in one area; there happened to be enough Serbs immigrating at two different times to form two factions; for reasons best known to themselves, the Slovenes from Steiermark and the Slovenes from Kreinmark could never build a community center big enough for both.

Along these lines, one might retitle this essay "Milwaukee: The City Where Frankie Yankovic Happened to Be Most Successful," or "It's Krein Time Again: The Poles Learn Country and Slovenian." The very special particularities of style formation in Milwaukee need more research, but the few generalizations one can make from even so swift an overview are supportable by parallel data from other cities in the industrial heartland of America. To begin with, successful proletarian styles are often ethnic hybrids. Slovenian-

American polka style is an especially nice example because of its black foundation and white country adaptation, both factors personified in the banjo player who doubles on guitar.

Second, within working-class culture in any given locality, one ethnic group seems to prevail. A streamlined Slovenian-American style wins out in Milwaukee, but in Pittsburgh there are young bands (such as the Treltones) of Slovakian and German backgrounds who sing exclusively in Polish and play the Polish-American Chicago style made popular by Li'l Wally. In fact, the main polka clubs in Pittsburgh are only about 50 percent Polish, and there are a lot of Slovakian, Irish, and Italian members. New York City is the only place where the old-fashioned Eastern style of Polish-American polkas still holds sway, and its leading band is the pet project of an Irish-American banker, Jimmy Sturr. In Buffalo, polkas are maintained almost exclusively by a small core of fans within the Polish-American community. In industrial Massachusetts and the Connecticut Valley, Happy Louie Dusseault's distinct variation on "honky" style is the norm, and a number of other bands also have French-Canadian members who sing and play the Polish way. So each locality is different, but one ethnic style tends to dominate—most often a Polish one.

Third, perhaps a minor point, the leading stylists are often prophets without special honor in their own cities. Witness Yankovic, big in Milwaukee and taken for granted in Cleveland. The best Buffalo bands draw much bigger crowds and better money on the road than at home, and the big-name Chicago groups report the same pattern.

Fourth, a few of the older bands in each locality, feeling the pull of respectable culture, tend to become two-beat "society bands" or (the timeworn label in Buffalo) "radio-recording orchestras." The transition from "people's polka hop" to "businessman's bounce" is not difficult—a shift from one restricted code, in Basil Bernstein's sense of a kin- and community-based expression, to a still more restricted one perhaps.[6]

Finally, because the local style is ethnic and working class, it is also community-family centered and supported. This means that musicians and fans in one localized ethclass (say, Slovenes in Milwaukee) don't know or care what the musicians and fans in another localized ethclass (say the Poles in Chicago) are doing, and vice versa. There has been surprisingly little communication between the Slovenian, Polish, and Czech-Bohemian polka traditions over the past century or so of development in the New World, and almost no communication at all between these northeastern and midwestern Slavic styles and the flourishing polka traditions of the Mexican-American and Native American communities in the Southwest, which have also been evolving for more than a hundred years. That all these different segments of the working class have been dancing to the same beat for so long without being aware of one another is surely a fact worth thinking about.

Pages from a Polka Diary

The Julida Boys

BY DICK BLAU

The International Polka Association's great 1976 convention, at Milwaukee's Red Carpet Inn, was some affair.[7] Three days of dances and parties. Days that started at two in the afternoon and ended—if they did—at seven in the morning. Days that saw bands from as far away as Massachusetts and crowds of something like ten thousand. The movement was continual. After the formal doings were over, hundreds of people—young and old—would flow through the halls of the motel looking for *the* jam session of the evening. They weren't disappointed. The sound of those pickup bands was something else. The first thing you heard were the trumpets, bright and brassy, doing incredibly long and yet wonderfully quick runs up and down the scale. Then the electrified accordions and the concertinas filled the rooms with rich harmonic chords. This was a very special sound, a living presence punctuated only by bellows breaks that caught you down in the chest and seemed to replace your breath. The vocals

Members of the 47th Street Concertina Club, Veteran's Park, Milwaukee, 1986.

had that quality, too. They came out of the throat from the same place as the blues, and it was easy to see why "honky" and "dyno" are the Polish-American equivalents of African-American words like "soul." And finally, there were the drums. Intricate and powerful, the drums gave a drive to the tempo that couldn't help but set you dancing.

For three days people danced. It was hard to believe, but they did it.

> Whirling skirts, pretty girls, and smiling faces
> Is the happiness we have in Polkaland.
> Mom and Dad, Sister Sue, Cousin Bob and Mary Lou
> Dancing all night to the music of our band.
>
> So let the sunshine in, shake hands with your neighbor
> And happiness will never leave your heart!
>
> From Chicago to Milwaukee up to West Bend,
> People wishing all their friends hey, *Nazdrowie!*
> Happy feelings in the air, forget your troubles and
>   your cares.
> Join the ranks of people dancing everywhere.
>   [The Golden Brass, 1971][8]

The dance floor was almost always full, full of Moms and Pops and Sister Sues, Cousin Bobs and Mary Lous, all dancing with one another in every possible combination. *What* they were dancing is a little harder to describe. We are accustomed to thinking of the polka as an antiquated and somewhat bouncy one-two-three-hop—the South Side Gallop, one person called it. But

there is nothing old-fashioned about the dancing these days. Real polka dancing is an intense experience, marvelously quick and energetic, a moving communion between two people. When you dance it well, you feel it as a beautiful flow involving hands and feet and torso and head all at once. A good dance is a spontaneous performance. At its best it is like a high-wire act, with the dancers improvising to a music so fast that they seem within a fraction of a second of losing the beat and yet still manage to stay with the time.

"The feeling that comes from this kind of dancing is euphoric," one dancer told me. I think he hit it on the head. Euphoria, known long before the Greeks named it, is a feeling of great happiness and well-being. Another word for euphoria is bliss. It is one of the most prized of human experiences. What makes euphoria so special is that it is a feeling that can be shared. And nowhere is that sharing more evident than in the polka. Dancers coming off the floor at the IPA with their arms around each other's shoulders were laughing together, laughing as they panted to catch their breaths and got ready to dance again.

For those who tired, there was always some space in the crowd of five hundred or so standing next to the bandstand. At the very front of the crowd stood the fan clubs, outfitted in shiny satin vests emblazoned with the names of favorite bands. When things really got going, everyone would sway together and wave pennants and handkerchiefs in time with the music. They brought their own instruments too. Somebody had

Veteran's Park, Milwaukee, 1983.

made maracas out of a couple of Coke cans; someone else would improvise on a police whistle; and there were musical spoons as well.

It was here that I heard the Julida Boys for the first time. I had always wondered where Milwaukee fit into the picture. Although the city hosted the convention, all but one of the bands that played were from out of town. This would have been unthinkable in Buffalo, where there would have been ten local groups to pick from. In Milwaukee, however, polka music is divided into three broad styles. First, there is the Chicago style I've been talking about, also known as Polish-style or honky-style polka. Then there is the oom-pah or Dutchman style. And finally there is Slovenian—actually a blend of Austrian and Yugoslav influences—which predominates in Milwaukee. The first thing one notices about these three styles is the difference in their instrumentation. Oom-pah is perhaps most famous for its tuba. Slovenian is known and prized for its use of the banjo and two accordions. And Polish has moved into brass.

Despite the Slovenian style's dominance in Milwaukee, in the years since World War II it is the Polish Style that has experienced the largest growth in national popularity—perhaps because it is the most adaptive. Like oom-pah and Slovenian, Polish-style polka has roots that extend back into the Old World, to nineteenth-century Paris and ultimately to the Tatra Mountains of southern Poland, an area from which many Polish-Americans have come. In the course of its movement to the New World and into the second half of the twentieth century, however, the polka became an American music.

Amplification had a lot to do with this change. Volume alone, of course, means nothing; it is the quality of sound that is really important, and amplification is an ideal way to experiment with that quality. Anyone who has ever had to deal with a microphone knows that sound systems have a life all their own. They do not simply make the voice louder; they change its sound. A good sound system, then, gives the musician access to a whole new range of sounds. This is what makes a music modern. Modern music explores new ranges of feeling through new combinations of rhythm and sound, whether produced or treated electronically or not. And if music can do this through the use of a basic material that is itself "traditional"—through songs that recall the experience of the culture *before* electricity and cities—then all the better.

When, on the last day of the IPA and in the last slot of the afternoon, I heard the Julida Boys, they were something of a novelty. First of all, they weren't

Veteran's Park, Milwaukee, 1983.

all boys: right up there in front was a woman on one of the trumpets. Second, behind her stood a fellow playing tuba. It was the tuba that excited the most comment. Nobody had heard a tuba playing Chicago style before; it belonged to oom-pah, as did the major chord harmonies. Nonetheless, this big mellow sound was identifiably Polish. The urgency, the drive, and the power were all still there. I was impressed.

It was the memory of this sound that impelled me, some three months later, to climb into my car and head into the cold front that was bearing down on Milwaukee. I had braced for an autumn day, but even so it caught me off guard. My first stop was at Allan Bayle's house. Allan, who works in the product control section of a local factory, originally started and still manages the Julida Boys. Like everyone else in the group, Allan grew up on a Wisconsin farm; he had since moved into the ring of small towns northwest of Milwaukee and found a job in one of the medium-sized plants that came in the area in the 1970s. "We'll be going back out into the farm country tonight," he told me; the Boys were to play a wedding reception at Lisko's Tavern in a tiny village called Huillsboro. Before we went, we sat and talked. After a few minutes Roger Mertz the tuba player arrived to join our conversation, and then Janet

Noegel (trumpet) and her husband Mike (concertina and vocals).

This is where I got my next surprise. The bulk of the band is not Polish at all. Allan and Janet and Mike are German. Bobby Klesmith, who plays the drums, is said to have a little Polish in him, but only Jerry Halkoski, the accordionist, has any real relation to Polonia. The truth is, Allan told me, that the band started out playing oom-pah style. All the musicians but Jerry had grown up in the German farm belt that surrounds Milwaukee to the north, and all of them had begun by playing what folks up there call the Dutchman style.

It was in 1969, about five years after forming their band in high school, that the Julida Boys underwent their great change. Allan and a couple of the others were down in Milwaukee listening to music at a place now called the Schwabenhof when Alvin Styczynski came through town. Alvin is from Pulaski, the heart of Wisconsin's Polish-style polka belt. He's been around for forty years, a constant leader in the field, and he represents much of what is most exciting about the music. Alvin combines the musical vitality of the Polish style with a particularly theatrical performance. A polka dance demands a certain atmosphere, and the creation of this atmosphere is the job of the band

Veteran's Park, Milwaukee, 1986.

leader. He is the master of ceremonies, the presiding angel at all the festivities, and the court jester who leads the audience in its merrymaking. It is as much for his skill in these activities as for his musical abilities that Alvin is loved. Standing on top of a table in a flower-printed gray and black dinner jacket that is slightly too large, playing his concertina and singing his heart out, Alvin epitomizes the merry prankster and magical musician who is the abiding spirit at a polka dance.

All it took was one song by Alvin, Allan said, and they were hooked. In the week that followed, he took the whole group down there. Though they still played oom-pah on occasion and even prided themselves on their command of "modern" or rock tunes, the Julida Boys had been a Polish-style band ever since.

What we would see tonight, however, was something different: at a wedding reception like this one, it would be necessary to mix modern music with the polka. Unlike the IPA convention, where all the generations danced to the same music, in Huillsburo it was mostly mom and dad who danced the polkas, and they would be Dutchman polkas to boot. Polish style was felt to be too fast in this neighborhood; many of the younger generation couldn't even do the Polish hop. As a result, the band would play one of the evening's three sets in modern style alone. This wasn't

exactly what I was looking for, but the job was typical of the work a band would normally do in this part of the country.

By the time we got to Lisko's, it wasn't any warmer. The tavern, set at a crossroads in the middle of rolling farmland near the Kettle Moraine, has a dance hall in back. As soon as you walk in the door, you can see it's meant for business. Lisko's hall is nothing but a long, wide dance floor covered with a roof. Past the paper streamers and Chinese lanterns that hang from the exposed rafters is a ceiling that reminds you of a barn. There is a narrow bench nailed to the wall around three sides of the room, and the bar and bandstand are set back to leave as much of the floor as possible for the dancers. It is a space cleared for action.

Perhaps it was the cold that did it, but the action never quite got going that night. As the reception guests filtered in from the bar, they all remarked the chill. If there is anything that puts a damper on euphoria, it's being cold. The band seemed to catch it, too. They'd been telling me that a good polka dance depended on a kind of chemistry between the musicians and the crowd, that the subtle blendings of the music and the dancing related to the feeling of closeness and intimacy that comes from a real relation with an audience. But this crowd was "shy," and it wasn't till the third set that things got going. Then, just as the Boys started to break loose, there was a commotion on the floor, and about a third of the group broke off dancing, hurried to the cloakroom—their dates in one hand and their beepers in the other—and then rushed off for parts unknown. That's the risk you take, I suppose, when you play a reception for a member of the Auxiliary Fire Department in this neck of the woods. And so the evening ended.

It was not a propitious start, but I had high hopes for the next day. On Sunday the band had two engagements in Milwaukee itself, and at two halls renowned for their good dancing. The first was a benefit dance organized by the IPA in support of the organization's drive to build its Hall of Fame. From one in the afternoon until midnight, polka bands from as far away as Detroit would contribute their services at Kossins (pronounced "cousins") Music Land, out on South 27th Street in Franklin. After their hour there, the Julida Boys were due for an evening's work at Veteran's Park, a fabled tavern and dance hall at the end of the Mitchell Field runway on South 6th Street.

It promised to be an arduous afternoon. The IPA dance would be difficult because the band was scheduled to play for only an hour. This meant that to be successful, the band would have to go into full swing immediately, which is not an easy thing to do. At Veteran's Park, the problem would be different. Here they would have the pleasure of following none other than Alvin Styczynski. The anticipation of seeing Alvin, however, was accompanied by a slight but natural unease. If you're going to follow Styczynski, you have to be pretty good: when Alvin packs up for Pulaski, his fans pack up with him, and after last night, the band was a little worried that it might lose its audience again. This is, of course, the performer's nightmare. My heart goes out to the band that plays to an empty floor.

At Kossins, the prospects for a successful day didn't look too good. The crowd wasn't very big, and the long, low hall with fifty tables on each side felt rather empty. To make things worse, a *Milwaukee Journal* photographer had put up a big strobe at each corner of the floor and was waiting to blast away at anyone who ventured out to dance. The set went pretty well—

better than the night before, more "together"—and yet there was still something strained in the feeling of it all. Unlike Jimmy Meisel and the Music Explosion who preceded them, the Julida Boys seemed to be working too hard. The polka, a musician friend once told me, should be strenuous but not stressful. That is a crucial distinction, especially when one considers that most polka dancers are used to the most stressful kinds of work in their everyday lives. The thought of going four hundred miles to a polka dance after forty hours in a steel mill is tolerable only if there is a real prospect of coming home refreshed. Hard work and serious faces are no substitute for the exuberant liveliness of the original thing.

Instead of unwinding, however, the band got more uptight. Matters weren't helped at all when Jimmy Meisel, still full of energy after his set, came over and started playing too. Jimmy is one of those prankster musicians of the Polish style. He was a riot of rhythm, swinging at least three maracas and banging a tambourine on his belly. Jimmy drove the photographer crazy, and that didn't help the band much either. Perhaps, I thought, this was the difference between a Polish Polish-style polka band and a German Polish-style one. For all its good sound, the band was not especially theatrical. Perhaps this is what Jerry, the only Polish-American in the group, meant when he said that the real difference between the Julida Boys and other Polish bands was that the Boys hadn't grown up in Hamtramck—which is to say, in a "real" Polish neighborhood like Detroit's well-known Polonia. It was a relief when the set was over and we could leave for Veteran's Park.

Veteran's Park, set on a few acres of what used to be farmland, is a handbuilt, homey, sprawling sort of place whose character is profoundly shaped by that of its owner, Johnny Ignasiak. Although a Bohemian by birth, Johnny has, through a long-time association with the Polish community that dates back to before World War II, become closely identified with the music of the Polish style. Once you meet him, you can see immediately why he would be attracted to the music, for Johnny is also a great master of ceremonies and an inspired jester. People still talk of the time he went to the IPA wearing a Prussian helmet with a stuffed chicken perched on the spike and preceded by a goat on a leash. On this night, Johnny's latest work was displayed on a low roof outside the picture window by the bar: he had erected a Halloween display that included not only gigantic blinking pumpkins but live rabbits and guinea pigs as well.

Alvin Styczynski was just winding up his second set as I came through the door, and it was easy to feel what the band had been talking about. There seemed to be a volatile, lively feeling in the very air of the place. The noise was good. People were talking, laughing, and dancing as Alvin sang away up on his table. Two women I'd met at Kossins were also there, and one of them came rushing up right after the number: "You see what I mean about that inner rhythm? And isn't Alvin friendly? He makes you feel *so* good." I knew what she meant, and I could not help wondering whether the Julida Boys would make for good feeling too. They came in just as Alvin was finishing his last set. His final number is justly famous: jumping off the stage, he leads the audience in a long, wild chain dance through the hall, a progress that ends only when he lies down and plays the concertina over his head. It is pure crowd-pleasing virtuosity, and everyone in this crowd just hollered for more.

And more is what they got. With the Julida Boys' first number, it was clear that they had by no means been intimidated; instead, Alvin had inspired them too. As the band got going, people stayed on the floor. An accordion player named Eddie Pakula arrived to join in. When he did so, the sound got deeper and fuller. In a little while, another accordionist and a concertina player showed up; they had heard the Julida Boys over at Kossins and had been attracted, despite all the problems, by the group's special sound. When they joined in, things really started hopping. For the first time since the August convention, I felt the feeling— and from the faces around me, it was clear that I was not alone. Jerry did the vocals now, his face heavy with the deepest feeling. He was exploring the narrow edge of a pleasure so intense that it verged on pain. Eddie and Mike just stood there and played, beaming with all their might. A big guy in the audience wearing a red VFW baseball cap stood next to them and danced with his cane. Then, best touch of all, Alvin himself came back for a final vocal. It was simply too much. The dancing had become a transport of joy.

Suddenly the big man turned to me. He had heard me talking to Alvin during the break and had come to make sure I'd asked the right questions. "There's a lot of things you should understand about *that* guy," he said. "Have you asked him about his immigrant mother and his immigrant dad? You got to get him on that. He comes from the bottom up. Because it *starts* with an immigrant—it starts taking them stumps out. Working the land. I told you how many times he got nicked in the ribs? So did I when I was a kid." The man was a great talker. I asked him what he felt about the polka. "I know what the polka means," he said. "Happiness. It gives me—well, come here. D'ya feel that?" and he put my hand on his chest. "Where do these songs come from? They come out of the hills. Out of the feelings of a person. Listen to this song's tempo. It comes from *here*," and he pointed to his heart.

We stood there with our arms around each other's shoulders, and I could only nod in agreement when he surveyed the dancing hall and summed it up: "Where in the hell can you beat this? *This* is a wedding!"

Polka Joe Polakiewicz and Marcia Pawlak, Adam Mickiewicz (Mickie's) Hall, Buffalo, c. 1973.

6. Buffalo

In the twenty-odd years (1970–92) that we have been following polkas in Buffalo there have been a number of ups and downs in polka popularity, but the general trend is gently downward.[1] Certainly there are fewer polka taverns than there were twenty years ago. On the other hand, the hours of polka on the radio have increased, so that a fan can fill most of the weekend with polkas by switching from station to station. Stan Sluberski's polka hours on WBFO, the local National Public Radio FM station, are far and away the station's most popular program, as measured by "the ratings" and by listener contributions. There is still a big listening audience for polkas, but the problem is that as this audience ages and dances less, fewer young people are getting into the music. One theory is that they are not getting enough polka happiness as children to bring them back to the polka in their twenties and thirties after having passed through a teenage rock and pop phase. If present trends continue, polka bands and dances in Buffalo will fade out completely early in the twenty-first century.

The Polka Scene in Buffalo circa 1975

In the mid-1970s, when our research activity was at a peak, there was already a keen awareness among Buffalo polka people that conscious organizing efforts would have to be made to keep polka happiness alive. Just as the International Polka Association took shape in Chicago to find new ways for polkas to survive (see Chapter 3), Buffalo polka lovers grouped themselves into three organizations (with slightly overlapping memberships): the Polka Boosters Club, the Eddie Blazonczyk and the Versatones Fan Club, and the Happy Richie and the Royalaires Fan Club. For over a year much of our research effort was devoted to the Blazonczyk Club, presided over by Stan and Carrie Lewandowski. Photographing and interviewing, watching and dancing through many monthly meetings, we learned a lot about grassroots politics, patronage patterns, the steelworkers' union, foolproof recipes for feeding many people inexpensively, dancing partnerships, mock weddings, and—most important—the

symbiotic relationships between bands and fans. The Blazonczyk Club made big efforts to have live music at every monthly meeting: an established band could fulfill its sense of obligation to dedicated fans by playing there for its lowest possible fee; young bands just getting started could test their material; old-timers putting together an ad hoc group could revive the thrill of seeing people dance to their music.

Looking back from the 1990s to the mid-1970s, we see that there were more established bands for the fan and booster clubs to choose from and many more young "wedding bands" on their way to becoming "polka bands." The distinctions between "wedding," "polka," and "commercial" categories have probably always been fuzzy because any beginning band starts out doing weddings and other family gatherings for relatives and friends, may volunteer its services for parish lawn fetes in the summertime in the hope of becoming more widely known, and then may evolve in "polka" or "commercial" directions or pursue some combination of the two. Today there are fewer wedding bands and more disc jockeys playing tapes and records at weddings. Today most bands are either clearly committed to polkas or have "gone commercial" in earnest. In the mid-1970s many bands had the capacity to play weddings, polka dances, *and* commercial gigs; the tendency for a few bands to specialize entirely in "polkas, waltzes, and obereks" was just emerging.

This chapter focuses on the best-known of the Buffalo bands that moved toward full polka specialization in the last twenty years: the Dyna-Tones. A general description of the band scene in Buffalo circa 1975 and an interview with Larry Trojak, coleader of the band, will provide some context and orientation.

In the constant flux of wedding, polka, and commercial bands taking shape and disappearing in Buffalo's Polonia, a solid core of experienced polka bandsmen at any given moment keep eight or ten bands going with firmly established reputations.[2] Each of these is centered on a group of musicians who have played together for years; they have developed a distinctive style and following of fans who honor their continuing commitment to polka music and polka people. As a consequence, these bands play regularly, usually every

153

Blazonczyk Fan Club business meeting, Mickie's Hall, Buffalo, c. 1973.

Halloween decoration, Mickie's Hall, Buffalo, c. 1973.

Stan Lewandowski *(center),* Peace Bridge Exhibition Center, Buffalo, c. 1974.

Eddie Orzechowski, Mickie's Hall, Buffalo, c. 1973.

Donna Loomis *(left)* and friend, Mickie's Hall, Buffalo, c. 1973.

weekend at a dance, club, or wedding; they may even get out-of-town bookings occasionally. Their reputation enables them to make more money than newly formed groups, and a few may create the opportunity to record.

In 1975 about a dozen Buffalo bands were in this category. But as in every field, with only so much room at the top, competition was stiff. Local polka promoters Wally and Shirley Czaska of those years used to say that three or four bands on the bill would not attract more paying customers. The golden era of Eastern style (1940s and early 1950s) when legendary promoter "Big Ziggy" Zywicki brought the big polka and swing bands of Frank Wojnarowski, Bernie Witkowski, Gene Wisneiwski, Walt Solek, and Ray Henry to town, is just a memory. Yet the leading polka bands could be arranged along an "Eastern" to "Chicago" continuum.

The massive shift from Eastern to Chicago style began in Buffalo in the early 1960s; by 1975, 90 percent of the polkas to be heard in greater Buffalo were in the Chicago tradition. The best-established bands, listed in an order that is generally from east to west, began with the orchestras of Eddie Olinski and Joe Macielag, which represented the last bastions of Eastern strength in the city. Eddie O.'s carefully arranged ten pieces deserved the name of orchestra, and true

Donna Loomis *(center)* at mock wedding, Mickie's Hall, Buffalo, c. 1973.

to the Eastern tradition of blending polkas and swing, they were also the foremost proponents of the Glenn Miller style in the area. Joe Macielag premiered his Melody Bells Orchestra on Christmas day 1954, and in 1960 it was featured in the new television program *Pic-a-Polka Hour* over WGR in Buffalo. Frank Wojna-rowski fronted the band the first few years, and the program was enormously popular; in the Buffalo area it became the showcase for Polonia's musical talents on Sunday television. The TV show went off the air in 1965, but the Macielag band still plays on in 1992, retaining the Pic-a-Polka identity.

The G-Notes of 1975 might be described as semi-Eastern (fast tempos), and the Krew Brothers as semi-Chicago in style (faster then the true Chicago beat). Both bands justifiably took pride in their pro-fessionalism, and like Eastern gentlemen, each group referred to the other as "the best band in Buffalo." The G-Notes' trumpet player, Jerry Miesowicz, could triple-tongue with the best and play two trumpets at once! His brother Len did the drumming. Tenor saxo-phonist John Karas was also an impressive soloist, and his brother Tom arranged and played accordion. Gino Kurdziel was a very genial emcee and played bass. The Krew Brothers consisted of six brothers whose real name was Krupski, led by Tony, the oldest. Like most

Donna Loomis and friend at the bar in Mickie's Hall, Buffalo, c. 1973.

Mock wedding at Mickie's Hall, Buffalo, c. 1973.

Blazonczyk Fan Club members, Mickie's Hall, Buffalo, c. 1973.

Nowicki and Ed Grabski made the Jacks a force to reckon with.

The Modernaires, the Dyna-Tones, the Polecats, Happy Richie and the Royalaires, Big Steve and the Bellares, the Hi-Notes, and "America's Polka Sweethearts" Wanda and Stephanie were all solidly in the Chicago tradition. The Hi-Notes were probably closest to the original Li'l Wally sound, but Big Steve and the Bellares were taking credit for being the first Chicago band in the area. The Polecats gave their "honky" stylings a few special twists, and Bobby Vinton paid them the compliment of borrowing a song of theirs, "Proud to be Polish Polka," for his stage show.

Happy Richie (Bojczuk) and the Royalaires were probably the heaviest, loudest polka band in Buffalo and the only local group at that time with a formally organized fan club. The Royalaires always gave their all, and the addition of two bell-shaking women out front increased the intensity still another notch. The Modernaires had been together for six years by 1975, getting better every year, and were so consistently good that it was easy to take them for granted. Most fans would have placed them very near the top of the list.

The mother-and-daughter team of Wanda and Stephanie Pietrzak, though not quite a band all by themselves, were certainly Buffalo's greatest polka stars in the eyes of the rest of the country. In fact, their work outside the area limited their Buffalo appearances in the early 1970s. They twice won the International Polka Association's annual award for "best female vocalists," and their versions of old favorites plus original compositions such as "Lover, Oh Lover" were the high point of many a "polkabration." Their records (like all polka records) give only a hint of their power "live and in person."

Other groups in mid-1970s Buffalo were the energetic Silvertones, who made a lot of music with two saxophones, Chordovox accordion, and drums; the Varitones and the Associates, who were working hard to be first rate; the Hotshots (kids not even into their teens yet) and the Polka Fathers (concertina players in their fifties), who were active and playing for the Blazonczyk Club meetings.

polka bands, they had an "English" book, and theirs included spirited African-American soul tunes, rock classics, and some good Latin numbers. Both these bands made good records and enjoyed growing national reputations.

The Jumping Jacks, once a leading Eastern-style band, in 1975 were establishing themselves in the Chicago idiom. One of their best numbers, "Let's Play a Polka by a Good Old Buffalo Band," mimicked the styles of the best-known groups doing their best known-songs. The energy and wit of leaders Bob

Bride and guest, Buffalo, c. 1973.

The bar at Erie Days Polka Festival, Erie, Pennsylvania, c. 1973.

Jerry Podlewski and Susanne Boruszewski at lawn fete raffle, Buffalo, 1973.

Blazonczyk Fan Club banner, Mickie's Hall, Buffalo, 1972.

Blazonczyk Fan Club dance, Buffalo, c. 1973.

One reason there were many more bands then was that young musicians were still being trained in the music-store schools—Edwin's on Broadway, Dick's on Clinton—and in smaller music studios such as Johnny Johnson's and Dave Gawronski's, which specialized in turning out competent young musicians swiftly. The stores and studios encouraged youngsters to band together, supplied them with the basic "book," and pointed them in a performing direction as quickly as possible so that parents paying for the lessons could share the pride of public performance and some early return on their investment.

It was in this era of music stores, studios, and parents working together to give the children a chance to create polka happiness for themselves and others at an early age that the earliest version of the Dyna-Tones took shape. By the mid-1970s the band had achieved

the status of Buffalo's best in the Chicago-style spirit of being loose, a little crazy, forgetting that you have to go to work on Monday.

A Talk with Larry Trojak

Bill Falkowski was a graduate student when he interviewed Larry Trojak of the Dyna-Tones in 1981. We thank Bill and include most of that interview here as a discussion between two young men of Polonia recalling the character of the old neighborhood and trying to figure out what keeps them there. Many of this book's underlying social themes related to Am-Pol identity, interaction with mainstream culture, and the disappearance of ethnic communities are highlighted here as they affect Larry's life choices.

Wally Czaska *(left)* and Charles Keil, Buffalo, c. 1973.

BF: What's Polonia and how do you see yourself fitting into it?

LT: It's just the neighborhood that I've grown up in. I'd like to make some kind of contribution to keeping it the way it is. I hate to see a lot of the small businesses closing down on Broadway. Growing up, I knew the guy at this store, at that store. Seems like they've all gone the way of the wind. I remember this one place—Victoria's Restaurant. It was a converted house, just like any home in the neighborhood. It had the best food in the world. But the pace of life just seems to have gotten faster everywhere. People just don't take the time to sit down and enjoy that kind of meal anymore. I don't mind seeing a fast food place going up, but not at the expense of losing a greasy spoon place or any type of place that you can go in on a Friday and enjoy a fish fry.

There used to be a small grocery store and a deli on just about every block. But supermarkets have done away with them. The small family business just seems to be losing out to the big buck everywhere you go. So, being part of the neighborhood and not wanting to see it lose its atmosphere, I try to support neighborhood businesses even if things might cost a little more.

BF: What do you mean by the atmosphere of the neighborhood?

LT: It's the people. Polish people are basically happy-go-lucky. They seem to be able to adapt to just about anything. They can get by in tough times. My next-door neighbor is always whistling while he's shoveling snow. I think that it's a good trait to have. I try not to let things get me down. People being out of work, the world situation—all that contributes to making things seem pretty grim. The price of gas is enough to ruin your whole day. But you cope. Polish people just seem to be better at coping with hard times than other people. Things have never been easy, so you have to expect to cope with problems in your everyday life.

BF: What was it like growing up in the neighborhood?

LT: I wasn't very aware of the neighborhood when I was growing up. It's there, and it's the only world I knew. My parents lived on Sears Street when I was born, and then we moved into an apartment above a cleaner's shop on Broadway. My mother worked at the cleaner's downstairs. My father worked at the railroad all his life. The place he worked when he started out went bankrupt, and now he's working for Conrail. He was really fortunate getting that job. He had twenty-six years of seniority working for the other railroad line when he was fifty-eight years old. That makes it awfully tough getting another job. But some friends managed to get him in at Conrail.

BF: What about your grandparents?

LT: I never really had a chance to get to know them. My father's parents died before I was born. Same with my grandmother on my mother's side. I only saw my grandfather on her side when I was very young, and then he died too.

Polish Falcons' lawn fete, Depew, New York, c. 1973.

All I remember about him is that he was old, spoke Polish, and always wore a white shirt with suspenders along with a straw hat.

Most of our other relatives lived out in the suburbs, so we never really had that much contact with them. I spent most of my time with friends—neighborhood buddies. They were all Polish. I went to St. John Kanty's grammar school. Out of my graduating class the most non-Polish guy was named Ed Perry. Still, both his mother and father were Polish! Either somewhere along the line somebody in the family married a Perry or they changed their name.

I enjoyed going to school. I'm opposed to the way things are with kids in public schools, constantly changing classes during the day. One nun taught everything at Kanty's. We had different nuns from grade to grade, but it was always the same crew of kids being together. I always used to come home for lunch because I lived less than a block away from the school. You really got close to everybody in your class, a lot closer than I got with kids when I went to public high school. At Kanty's it was like one big family. We developed a really close camaraderie with each other. I really, really hated to see it end. That doesn't sound too maudlin, does it?

BF: High school was really different from what you were used to at Kanty's?

LT: Yeah, it was different just on the basis of changing classes and being with people of different backgrounds—

being with blacks for the first time. I never really thought about race before I went to high school. I think my generation is different from my parents' generation. I think most older people look at the question in terms that black people are equal as long as they don't take any food out of their mouths. I'd like to say that all Polish people get along with blacks really well, but I don't know if I can honestly say that. Too many people use the word "nigger" like a household word, which makes me feel uncomfortable.

There were people in high school from other backgrounds too. There was a lot of rowdyism that I was never exposed to previously. It was different, but I guess it prepared me for what was waiting out there in the real world. Fraternities were a big thing in high school. I don't know why they called them fraternities; they were really gangs. Their existence revolved around who they could pick fights with. These guys would hit on one guy because he was black and another because he was Italian or Irish. I never got involved in any of that.

I was really into the polka, and other people in school used to laugh about it. The polka has always had some kind of bad reputation. Most people have never really understood it. I never backed away from my interest in the polka. People knew that I was really into it. Same with my name. I could have changed it to something American, but I never saw any reason to do that. There were always jokes about "dumb polacks," but I never let them bother me. I always figured that

Happy Richie at Weimer's Grove, New York, c. 1973.

getting upset about stupid jokes would just be an admission of ignorance. I knew that they weren't true. If other people thought they were, they were the dumb ones.

BF: How did you get interested in the polka?

LT: My folks were really into polkas. My father was a trumpet player with a couple of bands in his day. I never really thought of it as polka music—it was just the music my parents listened to. I started playing drums when I was about thirteen years old. I took lessons from a guy named Skip Spychaj, who used to play with Art Kubera's Orchestra. I used to go right to his house for the lessons. He lived about a block away.

Then I became a drummer with your regular wedding combo band back in about 1965. The Beatles were popular back then. I liked their music, but not for playing it myself; all I was ever interested in was polkas. I never wanted to play in a rock-and-roll band. The first band I played in was called Dave Kolata and the Debonaires. Whitey Ryniec was in the band along with Roger Nowaczyk—later they were both in the Dyna-Tones. Whitey and I wanted to do more polkas, but Dave Kolata was just interested in doing commercial stuff. So Whitey and I left the group and we started our own band called the Casinos.

This was right around the time when I first saw Eddie Blazonczyk. My parents took me to the 1965 International Polka Association convention at the Thruway Mall grounds in Cheektowaga.[3] I had heard him before on records and on the radio, but it just wasn't the same as actually being there and listening to him live. There was a super-huge tent filled with thousands of people from all over the country listening and dancing to bands from all over the country and some local bands too. It was a feeling and a half. It's hard to describe it in words. Whitey was there too and when we saw Blazonczyk, we decided that we wanted to get our own group together with a couple of horns and pattern ourselves after that kind of sound. Whitey and I had been the closest of friends all through the time we were growing up. We lived near each other, went to Kanty's together, and were always playing together from morning to night when we were younger. And we both loved polka music.

BF: So, how did you guys actually go about getting the band started?

LT: The guys we got into the band were taking lessons at Johnson's Music School or at Edwin's Music Store in the neighborhood. Johnny Johnson played accordion with the New Yorkers and had different teachers giving instructions on individual instruments, and there were combo lessons, too. His real name was Banaszak. I guess he changed it for professional reasons. He did a lot of solo things, and it was easier to get that kind of job if you had an American name. I remember

Wanda Pietrzak, Strand Ballroom, Buffalo, c. 1973.

he used to play in a group on *Dialing for Dollars* on TV. He also played Promo the Robot on the kid's show, *Rocketship 7*. Over at Edwin's you had Edwin's sons giving instructions.[4] There was Jimmy Grzankowski who used to play drums with the New Yorkers and his brother, Greg, who played with the Bellares. There were other guys that taught too.

We got Jan Cyman and Whitey on trumpet, Joe Grenda on accordion, Rick Walczak on bass, and I played drums. Then I met Scrubby Seweryniak at Chopin's, and he joined up.[5] He played concertina, and there weren't too many good concertina players around. There was also Richie Kurdziel with the Hi-Notes, and both he and Scrubby took lessons from the same guy in the neighborhood.

Different guys have come and gone with the group over time, but Scrubby and I have always been together except when I was in the Air Force. Scrubby and I are both really close to our families, and we both see our efforts in terms of being a polka band, nothing else. Some guys have left because they've gotten jobs in other parts of the country. Whitey is playing full time with Marion Lush out of Chicago. Jan Cyman has his own group, the Musicalaires, out of Pennsylvania.

During the summers, we used to play outside the Broadway Market. The stores would pull their stuff out and have a sidewalk sale. We played for free at these affairs and at lawn fetes to help raise money for neighborhood parishes. Eventu-

ally, we'd start getting called up for bookings. We'd do mostly weddings. Then we started playing in places like Chopin's and the Warsaw Inn. We were playing all sorts of music—slow American pieces, rock-and-roll—all kinds of crap. We played lots of "Spanish Eyes." Oh boy! People would always want to hear that, and we got sick of it. Then there were weddings where we didn't play any polkas at all. Sometimes we got hired for Italian weddings or Irish weddings. They just wanted some music.

To cut our first album, we changed our band's name to the Dyna-Tones because a group that called themselves the Casinos was already recording on the label we were going to record on. We took the name Dyna-Tones from a group that had recorded on Li'l Wally's label Jay Jay: Leon Kozicki, the president of the International Polka Association, had had a group called the Dyna-Tones. So, that was the tradition.

We recorded on the Bel-Aire label that Eddie Blazonczyk runs out of Chicago. That was back in 1969. I brought the album into school. People were really surprised. It wasn't anything like they expected. Even the black guys liked it. They said it had a lot of kick to it. Most people get the idea that the polka is some old guy that squeezes on an accordion—oom-pah-pah silly songs. Stuff like "I don't want her. You can have her; she's too fat for me." A lot of the lyrics are still like that, but the music can still have a lot of push to it.

Stephanie Pietrzak, Strand Ballroom, Buffalo, c. 1973.

We were playing at Chopin's and at the Warsaw Inn in the neighborhood on a more or less regular basis. We had around four gigs a month at that time, including weddings. Our first really big gig was at the Strand Ballroom in Kaisertown, which is a Polish section just south of the East Side. My father taped it, and I still have the tape from it. I guess there were about three or four hundred people there, and we played with a couple of other local bands.

BF: So what happened after you finished high school?

LT: I was pretty disoriented as to what I was going to do. I didn't know if I wanted to stay with the band and work in a factory or go to college. I wound up joining the Air Force and spent four years in the service. I didn't think too much about Vietnam at the time. I figured that if I joined the Air Force, and if I got sent to Vietnam, I would just be working at air bases without having to worry about getting into the thick of the fighting. I didn't think it was right for us to be in Vietnam, but I wasn't anti-American. It just didn't seem right for us to be over there. People had a right to protest, but I didn't see any reason to be burning flags either.

In the Air Force, I got some training as a weather observer. I spent time all over in different parts of the country and over a year in Korea. I loved it there. It was like one big party. Everything was cheap, and you could have a really good time. I was one of the few guys who spent a lot of time looking into Korean culture. My closest friends and I would be looking into temples while other guys were getting screwed up all the time.

The heritage of the Korean people is probably more drilled into them than it is with us. Here on the East Side, a kid might be growing up and getting farther and farther away from his heritage. I don't think I knew I was Polish until I got into high school. Whatever I was, I had just taken it as the way things were. In high school, I could see that my experiences were different from other kids'.

Growing up, my mother would swear at me in Polish. There was always *golabki,* kielbasa, and other Polish foods to eat.[6] At Christmas, my mother would take out a little manger and call it *zlobek* [manger]. I stopped going to church after grade school. My parents just pretty much let me go my own way. After I stopped going, they didn't go too much them-selves. We all have the faith, but going to church just isn't all that big a part of it. There were always special occasions like Good Friday when you kept absolutely silent between noon and three. On Holy Saturday we'd take our basket full of food to get blessed for Easter. There was always the sharing of the *oplatek* [ritual wafer] on Christmas Eve with the special *Wigilia* supper and then Midnight Mass.[7]

We still share the holidays together, but we don't observe the traditions like we used to. We're still close, and I go over

Larry and Karen Trojak with Karen's cousin *(left)*, IPA Festival, Rosemont, Illinois, 1983.

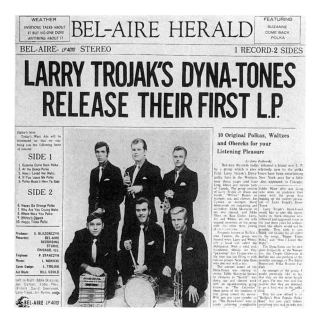

The Dyna-Tones' first album.

to my parents' house during the week a lot, and they come to see us play. But we don't really make that much of a thing about being Polish.

BF: How did you go without the polka while you were in the Air Force?

LT: I was getting tapes from my father every week; he used to record the polka show for me. The guys I was with had never been exposed to the polka, but once they heard it, they learned to like it. They joked a lot about it at first, about me playing in a polka band, but after a while they learned to appreciate it, especially if they were musicians themselves. They were able to really get into the trumpet harmonies. I used to spend the weekends in Chicago to catch the polka music. The guys saw me going to Chicago and saw the way I was coming back from Chicago—kind of wiped out—and they wanted to check it out for themselves. So we went to a really big dance they had there one weekend with eight bands performing. They were really blown away by it all. So, it's easy to learn to appreciate the polka once you've given yourself a chance to be exposed to it. I didn't have to push it on people.

When I got out of the service, I moved back with my parents. The band was still playing. I was lucky to get back into it. The guy who had taken my place wasn't working out, so he moved on, and I moved back in.

Nowadays, I work hauling newspapers for the *Buffalo News.* They just cut our hours down. It's not too bad for me because I can make some extra bucks playing in the band. But for other guys with families and kids, with all kinds of financial responsibilities, it's really rough.

I'm not really happy with the life I'm living. Sure, I have aspirations, ambitions, a goal in life. I'd like to play music full time. I'd like to do away with work altogether. I've thought about going to college, about throwing away four years of training as a weather observer in the Air Force to be driving a truck. It's not really hard work, but I don't enjoy it, either. It isn't something that I want to do the rest of my life. But jobs aren't that easy to come by, and you have to work to pay the bills. Driving the truck isn't too bad because I get to travel all over the area. I'm not in the same spot all day long. I've never wanted to work in an office or on an assembly line where your purpose in life is bolting manifolds on motors as they pass you by. I know guys in the United Auto Workers, and even though they make decent bucks, I'm not the kind of person who would want to be doing that kind of work all day, no matter how good the pay might be. I'd rather enjoy what

The Dyna-Tones at Mickie's Hall, Buffalo, 1972. *Left to right:* Bob Wroblewski, John Kilian, Roger Nowaczyk, Scrubby Seweryniak, Bill Barnas.

I'm doing. Human beings aren't meant to be cooped up in one place for all that time.

BF: What does "making it" mean to you?

LT: "Making it" is being in the best damn polka band in the world. Making it would mean traveling thirty weeks out of the year, playing three nights a week and making good bucks. I'm not interested in getting a house in the suburbs. I don't foresee getting married. I'm not the marrying kind. I can't settle down. I like my freedom too much. Very few women would want to put up with a guy whose great goal in life is to play polkas, traveling thirty weeks out of the year. I wouldn't want to put any woman through that.

I love traveling, meeting people. Maybe it's a little bit of

an ego thing. In Buffalo we play a lot, so it's not all that special a thing for people to come and see us. But if you travel someplace maybe only once or twice a year, people will come up to us like it was an honor to talk to us. And when we play out of town, we really play our hearts out for the people. We owe it to them and we love doing it. And they love it too. So, it makes us feel like we're really doing something, making a contribution to peoples' lives.

BF: So you don't see a move to the suburbs as being indicative of "making it"?

LT: I guess a lot of people move out because of the status thing, but I've always loved the city. For a lot of people, moving out into the suburbs was like they made it in life. People were just brought up that way. Parents would tell their kids, "You're going to have it better than we had it."

My brother is married and lives out in Texas. He was stationed out there when he was in the Air Force. He used to come home on leave, and he met a Polish woman who used to be a regular when we played at dances and gin mills in the neighborhood. So he married her and got himself a job out there as a systems analyst with some insurance company. He hates Buffalo, and he hates the polka with a passion. I don't know why. I guess he just hates the weather here. And he used to play accordion with a wedding combo when he was younger.

For me, there's just something about the city that I like. People seem closer here—aside from the fact that the houses are so close together that you can hear the guy in the next house sneeze. I have a neighbor who is around seventy years old. He just bought a snowblower, and he goes out of his way to do the sidewalks on both sides of the street. The people around here are mostly older people. They're the nicest people in the world—except for one across the street; she had the nerve to tell me the other day that I couldn't park in a particular spot because her family had three cars and needed the space. It's a one-way street with alternate parking and people have to battle for space. But aside from those kinds of hassles, it's a perfect place to live.

BF: Do you see yourself living here ten years from now?

LT: Yeah. People are beginning to realize that it's a good deal to live here. The prices for apartments are really high out in the suburbs and in other parts of the city. Here, you can get a really nice place for a hundred dollars a month. So people are going to be coming back.

I live a basically quiet life these days. I work, come home and read, watch TV, and listen to music. I don't go out as much as I used to. I used to go to bars in the neighborhood to drink a lot and just to be with friends. But I've given up drinking for over a year now. I didn't feel that I was handling it right, so I've given it up completely. I'm the type of person who doesn't like to do anything halfway.

I've just recently started to go to plays. The first play I ever saw—just a week ago—was *Elegy for Stanley Gorski*.[8] It was about a guy in a union who was going through hard times. I guess it was set back in the 1950s, but it could have been taking place today. There's people in a rut because of the economy, and they're looking for ways to entertain themselves.

I just put up a notice at work on the bulletin board about getting up guys for a league at Corpus Christi Bowling Lanes. Thirty-six guys signed up. There were even black guys who signed up. Yeah, of course I like bowling—hey, everybody knows we like bowling. I like all kinds of sports. I'm going to try out for the Broadway Grill Softball team this spring. And I've been running for over a year now. I enjoy running races with myself, trying to better my time. I try to do about six miles a day.

I like all kinds of music, too. I've always liked to go see the Philharmonic. I don't like disco at all, though. The music is too monotonous. It's just a beat with all kinds of gadgetry. I never go to discos. I've seen disco shows on TV where the people look altogether phoney, like they just went out and bought all new clothes and had their hair styled. I guess they think "Hey, tonight I'm just going to be super." I like country-and-western music, any kind of music but disco. It's just not down to earth. And I think reading is one of the greatest things in the world. I used to read a lot while I was in school, but then I got involved in just hanging out a lot. I don't know how I got by without reading for such a long time. I like to read fiction—stories about life, about different people. I like Kurt Vonnegut. I just finished reading *The World according to Garp*. And I've read Kafka too. It's sort of an escape. I enjoy imagining myself in the different situations in the stories.

I've had cable TV for a while now. I like to watch old stuff—old reruns of *M.A.S.H.*, *Barney Miller*. I especially like to watch *Nova* on public TV. I've always been interested in scientific things, with ecology. I belong to the Sierra Club and a Save the Whales group.

BF: Do you consider yourself "cultured"?

LT: Well, I guess that depends on what you mean by "cultured." Yeah, I'm cultured, but I'm not a culture vulture or a culture snob. I can appreciate all kinds of music, literature.

BF: Is the polka "cultured"?

LT: I've never considered the polka cultured. I just consider it as music.

BF: How does Chopin fit into your life?

LT: Well, Chopin's Clubrooms are just around the corner from the Broadway Grill. They've been having live polka music there lately. But seriously, I do listen to classical music and enjoy it a lot. I've never really gotten into Chopin that much though. I guess I've never been exposed to it that much.

BF: Is the polka as "cultured" as Chopin's polonaises?

LT: Yes and no. No. Yes. That's a difficult question. The polka is different. What do you mean by culture? That's the whole thing. I'm going to commit myself here. The polka is just as cultured as Chopin's polonaises. I guess you have to ask if the music contributes anything to your knowledge and understanding of life, of your ethnic background. The polka does make that contribution. If people joke about the polka, it's just because they have the wrong idea about it. They've never been exposed to it. You can't really blame people for that kind of attitude. They just don't know any better.

BF: What makes the polka so special to you?

LT: It brings people together. Every band has its bunch of regulars. Reunions are big. People come to see friends they haven't seen for a while. And people will go see groups that come in from out of town, that you can't see every week. So there's that mingling aspect that's important.

BF: What about the dancing?

LT: Well, I leave that fancy shit to the experts. I've never really been a big dancer. It helps us play when a lot of people are dancing. I can time my drumming by watching the people out on the dance floor—whether we're dragging too much or pushing too hard.

BF: Do you see the polka dying out?

LT: People in the neighborhood don't seem to support the polka like they used to. I suppose they listen to the polka shows on the radio, and that's part of their lives. I don't think it will ever get to the point where people will just forget about the polka and never come out to hear live music. Maybe people won't attend on a weekly basis, but they'll come out to the bigger dances where you have a few bands playing.

I don't think the polka will be so much a way of life with kids growing up in the suburbs now. They're exposed to so many other types of music. There are a lot of dances out in the suburbs. But the polka came out of the East Side. That's where its roots are. A lot more places are having live polka music on the East Side now on a weekly basis. For a few years, the Broadway Grill was the only place to go. Now, you can go to the Front Page; the Warsaw Inn just started having live polka on Saturday nights; and Chopin's has polka again on Friday nights. So now there's more of an opportunity to be exposed to it, and a lot of people are coming out to check it out for the first time.

Other groups are into doing American numbers along with their polkas. But we're a polka band. We used to do American numbers at weddings. We just never played "Tony Orlando and Dawn" numbers that well. Even if a Holiday Inn called us and wanted to book us three nights a week for big bucks to play that kind of stuff, we wouldn't do it. We take our polka music real serious. A lot of other bands seem to think that people want to hear that American stuff, but it seems to me that people just grumble under their breath when they hear it. You can go to a hundred other places to hear that stuff.

People that come to see us play now aren't just from the neighborhood. A lot of them come from the suburbs. It isn't so much like when my father was playing—when all the parishioners from a particular church would turn out. I suppose it's just that a lot of people have moved out into the suburbs and the people that are left in the neighborhood are mostly older and don't go out that much.

People do turn out in droves on Dyngus Day, but even Dyngus Day isn't exactly what it used to be.[9] It's nice to see Broadway filled with people at night. But every place is so crowded and people don't know each other like with the regular crowd. It makes it difficult to enjoy the music, to dance. The spirit isn't there. It's really become commercial. The people who come you won't see again until next Dyngus Day. Most of the people there will have no idea what it's all about. This year they'll have polka bands at the mall in Cheektowaga, and more and more places in the neighborhood are sponsoring affairs this year. We'll be playing at the Broadway Grill. We've been playing there regular for the past several years, and it's like our home. It's where we made our friends over the years.

BF: What is there about you that makes you "ethnic"?

LT: The fact that my grandparents came from Poland does it. It's the food I eat. I play in a polka band. I live in a Polish neighborhood. When people ask me what my ethnic background is, I say Polish. The very fact that you're here in America makes you American. I think it's picky saying that you're Polish-American. If you really want to get technical about it, the only real Americans are American Indians. I just don't put that much emphasis on being Polish. I guess it's just not our *shtick*. I'm proud that I'm Polish. If people ask me, I tell them.

The Irish guys at work are different. They seem to go out of their way to advertise that they're Irish. They're always wearing green. I don't go around wearing red and white and saying *Dzien Dobry* [good day] to people. The Polish guys at work don't go around talking about what a great guy Pulaski was.

BF: How do you relate to figures like Pulaski and Kosciuszko?

LT: Well, they were important in history, but I'm not a historian. I probably take more pride in my parents. They worked their asses off to raise me. I'd love to go to Poland. Maybe sometime we can get some sort of package to go play there at the World Polka Festival instead of doing a Caribbean cruise. I'd really like to explore the music there. . . .

One time we went to a Mazowsze concert; they're a folk song-and-dance ensemble from Poland. Afterwards, we went to a hall in the neighborhood that was having a reception for them. We were really turned on by the performance. We went to the reception, but they wouldn't let us in. The guy who was running the thing gave us a song and dance about how we just wanted to get in on the party and booze it up. We were really interested in talking to the performers, but we weren't allowed. So I sent a letter to the editor at the *Buffalo Evening News*, and the night the letter appeared in the paper, I got a call from the president of the Polish organization that ran the affair. He was very apologetic, and I've been getting the group's newsletter to this day, although I don't subscribe.

BF: Who are the big wheels in this neighborhood?

LT: Certain businessmen have pull. For some reason, they took the Pulaski Day parade from us. They took it out of the neighborhood, and now they have it downtown. I guess it was downtown politics. We made a real effort to keep it in the neighborhood. We signed petitions and were even talking about having our own parade down Broadway. When the parade was in the neighborhood, the parishes would get involved. The bars would have their social clubs represented. We used to make up a float from the Broadway Grill. It doesn't make any sense to have the parade downtown. Not that many people show up for it or take part in it. Having the parade downtown instead of in the neighborhood would be like having the St. Patrick's Day Parade down Jefferson Avenue in the black community. And they decided on putting a statue of Pulaski downtown. Something like that should be in the neighborhood. . . .

BF: Would you play at a benefit for a politician?

LT: Politics doesn't get involved with our playing. We play because we like to and to make some bucks. We'll always play because we like it. We wouldn't see our playing as supporting a candidate. Polish politicians probably aren't too much different from other politicians. I'm sure some of them care about the neighborhood. But if they're anything like most politicians, they're primarily looking out for themselves.

BF: You made mention of the black community. How are Polish folk different from black folk?

LT: Say what? I've never had that much contact with blacks as far as life in the neighborhood is concerned. Fillmore Avenue is sort of the dividing line. There are a few Polish people who live past Fillmore—the diehards, the people who grew up there and won't move out no matter what. I guess people moved out like a chain reaction. One guy would sell his house and a couple of black families would move in where only one family was living before. And the value of your property goes down. Nobody wants the value of their property to go down. You don't really have control over that, so there's nothing else to do but move out.

I think blacks have a lot of pride in being black. Polish people just don't seem to make such a big deal of being Polish. The civil rights movement back in the 1960s brought about a greater sense of pride about being black. And rightly so.

BF: What are you most proud of in your life?

LT: Our album *Chapter VII*. It took a lot of work. The album tells the story of Christ. It's a concept album. We were interested in doing something different than just a bunch of songs. I listen to the album a lot. Other albums we've recorded I don't listen to at all.

One polka disc jockey won't play it. Maybe some people feel that religion doesn't mix with polkas. I know a lot of people who weren't crazy about the idea of a polka Mass until they went to one. Perhaps people who don't like the idea see the polka as being limited to happy snappy music with lyrics about a guy in a bar getting shit-faced. A lot of it is this way; there's nothing really wrong with that aspect of it. But it can be about a lot of different sides of life.

Postscript: Larry did get married a few years ago but stuck it out with Scrubby and the Dyna-Tones as they disbanded and reformed several times during the 1980s. In 1989, after graduating from college, he moved to Minnesota near his wife's family, where he runs his own advertising firm. We miss him in Buffalo.

To the Grill, to the Grill, to the Broadway Grill

The following recollections of an afternoon with the Dyna-Tones at the Broadway Grill will give readers

Scrubby Seweryniak *(right)* and Jerry Podlewski, Erie Days, c. 1973.

a feeling for the band's performance style, as well as a sense of the complex relationship between the local community, the band, and an evolving polka culture.[10]

Because folklorists and anthropologists are always collecting information after the fact, arriving on the scene after the scene has been established and reporting on it days, months, or years after the curtain has come down on a specific drama, both our works and the creations of the people we write about seem old, a residue, something left over, "folklore." This is unfortunate, because the very essence of the folk process is spur-of-the-moment group creativity, the re-creation and invention of culture in present time. The past tense may be true to the reality of the writer and the alienated labor of turning improvised music or spontaneous banter into scholarship, but it is a continuous distortion of unique, once-in-a-lifetime happenings into typical, patterned what-happeneds.

The last set of a certain Sunday evening in March 1977 will never be repeated. The Dyna-Tones rehearsal described below could happen only once. The phono-

graph record is where folk and folklorist can meet, but its frozen, perfected, repeatable sound is like our tales, texts, and articles: an artifact, outside the creative process, with a strange life of its own. The difference between live and recorded performance has been noted in other chapters; here, the distinction is maintained in order to talk about live and recorded performances as they function within—and express—the creative life of a single band.

The Dyna-Tones had been playing most Sunday afternoons at the Broadway Grill since September 1976, after the big summer polka season ended. The Grill had been opened by Hank Mazurek (also a well-known clarinetist) and his wife, Pat, during the summer with the hope that polka people would make it their partying place. They did. On Sunday afternoons the bar and the back room were filled with people having a good time.[11]

This particular Sunday in March was an especially good time; it was the first warm and sunny Sunday of spring and some of the Dynasticks from Detroit were in attendance, as well as an unusual number of Krupski brothers. The Dynasticks were known as a musician's band; they did things that other bands didn't. As one of the Dyna-Tones put it, "Some of those guys take their instruments home and practice all day and into the night." And if the Dyna-Tones wanted to think of themselves as Buffalo's "No. 1 Polka Band," the Krew Brothers were still the top local rivals, the band to "beat." So the sun was out, the crowd was up, the musicians were in, and by the last of four sets the atmosphere was both mellow and charged.

The set opened with songs that had been put together in recent rehearsals for a recording session coming up in April: "Rosalinda," a real oldie with quaint lyrics, and "Over and Over Again," a country-and-western borrowing. Scrubby Seweryniak was a little worried about our taping these songs in rehearsal, but the Dyna-Tones wouldn't have played fresh, unrecorded tunes with a highly attentive Detroit band in attendance if there hadn't been some code of honor at work to keep the music safe from borrowers. Both polkas were perfectly executed—new songs requiring full concentration will often sparkle more than old songs that play themselves—and the tiny dance floor was packed with couples getting a feel for the new phrases.

After a solid "Nickel City Oberek" there was a request for "Goral Polka." On the band's last album, that number had featured the fiddle of Canadian Stas Malkiewicz, especially in the opening refrain. How to get it rolling now, with Stas in Toronto? Unaccompanied concertina was the answer. When you hear the concertina played well by itself, it stirs opposing feelings: first, a sense of a pumping heart, steady ebb and flow, it's strong and reliable, there's some melody there, there's harmony too and a strong beat implied underneath; second, a sense of uncertainty, insecurity, as all the notes fade in and fade out with the shifting air of the bellows. Actually, the sound is too thin and reedy to go on for very long all by itself. The heart cries for support, for a bass and drums to thump the beat and drone the harmony, for horns that will punch out the melody a concertina can only sug-

gest. So, when the full band finally comes in, it's a real lift.

Two new tunes, then an old one with a new and uncertain beginning, and finally—wham, a full thrust everyone knows and can dance to, anticipating every beat and phrase without a worry in the world. Somewhere early in "Goral Polka," the back room at the Broadway Grill in Buffalo, New York, became a separate world in which everybody would love and enjoy everybody else equally and effortlessly. No stars, no show, no entertainers and entertained—just everyone having a good time.

And oh, so silly: the silliness bug jumps from person to person, but it seems to bite Scrubby most often. People are sitting down after whirling through the "Goral Polka" when Scrubby looks off into nowhere for a reflection of his silly smile, then turns and whispers "Ee-yi, ee-yi, eeyi-o" into the microphone. The crowd responds immediately with an echo. Pause. Scrubby tries it again in another voice and gets a reply that is twice as big. It's as if he's doing a mood and unity check. As he repeats the calls in still other voices, the responses come in loud, and it is clear that all systems are go. With the piece so perfectly prepared for, the actual singing and playing of "Ee-yi, Ee-yi, Eeyi-o! Polka" is almost an anticlimax. The song concludes with Scrubby shaking out the concertina in a long coil of bellows spilling over his lap in hills and valleys. What had been a little squeezebox becomes a great organ stretching between one arm and the other at the final note. Scrubby's concertina has the look of an exhausted library shelf. This is, he seems to be saying, surely the end.

"It's so hot in here, we'll do a Christmas song," says Scrubby. Drummer Larry Trojak grabs his microphone to add, "It's Christmas all year long at the Broadway Grill." Roger Nowaczyk, the clarinetist, makes a crack about Santa Clawed, and suddenly everyone is chanting very quickly to the tune of the Lone Ranger theme song:

> **Tothegrill tothegrill tothe Broad way grill**
> **Tothegrill tothegrill tothe Broad way grill**
> **Tothegrill tothegrill tothe Broad way grill**

Tothe grilllllll
Tothe BroadwayGrill
Tothebroadwaybroadwaybroadwaybroadway-
    broadwaybroadway
Broadwaygrill
Tothebroadwaybroadwaybroadwaybroadway-
    broadwaybroadway
Broadwaygrill
Tothegrill tothegrill tothe Broad way grill
Tothegrill tothegrill tothe Broad way grill
Tothegrill tothegrill tothe Broad way grill
Tothegrilllllll
Tothe BroadwayGrill!

There is a big cheer and then Roger says, "Take me home in a coffin."

From here on the set is as much collectively improvised comedy as it is music and dance. Every polka band talks it up a little between numbers. There are requests to acknowledge and dedications to do, and Scrubby is always looking for extra *bon mots*, "good words," words to make you feel good. But when spirits are really high, everyone gets into the act. Scrubby still carries the conversation along, backed up by Larry, but all the band members have something to say, and people at the tables are ready to pounce on any line with a comment—usually one that seems to put down a musician or the whole band in the friendly spirit of the banter.

Scrubby is serious about the Christmas song, and soon the floor is packed with people bouncing around to "Tuning Up the Fiddles Now." It ends with Scrubby wishing "Merry Christmas everybody!"

"We thought we'd celebrate a little early this year," adds Larry. "Boy I wish we could go outside and play in the snow. Where did all the snow go anyway? It was here a minute ago."

"Do you want another blizzard?" says someone at a table.

"Yeah, I wanna nother blizzard."

"I survived the Blizzard of '77," Scrubby affirms in his news commentator's voice.

In an old-timer's voice, Larry echoes, "I survived the Blizzard of '77."

"I was stranded at the Broadway Grill, and boy did I have a good time," says Roger. There is some band discussion off-mike and then a big laugh. Resentful fans shout, "What's the joke?" "You can tell us." "Keep it clean." Negative motions from the band: "You don't want to hear it."

"I survived the Blizzard of '77 at the Broadway Grill and have the ulcer to prove it," offers Scrubby. It is clearly not what the band was laughing about. After a pause, Scrubby begins again: "Now we'd like to feature someone who seldom sings."

A voice from the crowd ventures, "That must be Scrubby!"

Scrubby looks hurt and annoyed. "No, no, it's our trumpet player John Kilian with his version of 'Thinking of You Polka.'"

John gives a big grin and says "Thankyou" in good clipped Jimmy Carter style. There is some kidding about John's forgetting the words and a few more "thankyou's" from John. In fact, he does seem to be having trouble remembering the lyric. But with a little prompting from band members and Larry's clicking sticks counting off, the song is under way. It's the same tune that the New Brass does as "Streaking with You"—"I'm full of happiness and cheer, streaking with you and drinking beer"—and John's version has some very salty lines. But no one seems to notice; they're too busy dancing and drinking.

"That was the golden voice of polkas—John Kilian," says Scrubby. "He'll be signing autographs later— way later. *Way* later. Didn't he do a great job?" Some catcalls drift up from the tables.

"It's polka time again, and this time we'd like to feature Roger on the vocal doing 'Lovesick Polka.'" This turns out to be a vocal duet, Roger and Bill Barnas, the bass player. Somebody from the Dynasticks is sitting in at the keyboard and adding those downward sweeps that you hear on records at the beginning of every "push" chorus (it's an echo of the older polka style that can be dubbed in without adding an extra musician). "That's Paderewski on the piano," says Scrubby after a particularly nice swoop down the keys.

"Well, it's that time again. Just one more tune. Did everyone have a good time?" A big chorus of "boo" and "no" from the audience: "boo" because the band is stopping, and "no" for the same reason and just to be teasing the band.

"Well, too damn bad," says Scrubby. "So it was a rotten time." Roger adds a clarinet obligato to Scrubby's griping. "We hope you'll come back next week for an even rottener time next Sunday. This crowd was too loud anyway. Wouldn't shut up. We can hardly hear ourselves think up here. So of course you had a *rotten* time. I'll tell you what. I'll just wear these clothes to be sure that everybody has a real rotten time next week. So you had a *rotten* afternoon?" Band members: "Good. Good." "No, bad, bad." "Good!" Eventually Scrubby introduces the final tune: "This will be on our next album, 'Down at the Friendly Tavern'; we'll send this out especially for all the members of the Polka Booster Club that are here today, oh, and I see the 'Little Mayor of Black Rock' coming in a little late." "Or is it the 'Black Mayor of Little Rock?' " says another band member. A very small man who must be from the other Polish section of town is tipping his hat to the band from the passageway that leads to the bar up front. "Didn't we see you in *The Wizard of Oz* last week—as a munchkin?"

Halfway through "Friendly Tavern," there's a refrain: "No need to ask us where. Down at the friendly tavern, everyone's happy there." And already people are getting the idea that a shouted "Where?" sounds funny after the line stating "no need" for such a stupid question. By summer-time hundreds of fans will be shouting "Where!" if the tune catches on.

At the end of the song there are cries of "More, more" from the tables. "One more." "Come on, you guys!" Scrubby sings "Good Night, Sweetheart" very slowly, but the tables are unhappy. "Oh, drinks!" he sighs as Hank's wife appears with a tray of drinks for the band members.

"OK, one more!" says Scrubby very very quickly. "We'd like to do 'Oj Dana' featuring Larry Trojak, the gentleman on my right," and peers over his shoulder as if Larry might somehow not be sitting behind his drums waiting to see what comes next. Scrubby makes this announcement by using the microphones inside the concertina, talking loudly with his mouth pressed against the keyboard; the effect is ghostly. Then, grabbing the regular microphone, he announces, "Back to reality!" The sound is crisp and neat. Larry clicks off the tempo immediately, and the band goes full tilt, knowing this indeed is the last number. "Oj Dana" is a call-and-response tune that all the bands do; Larry sings the calls, "Oj dana dana, oj dana," and Scrubby leads the community responses, "Oj da-na!" Because everyone will be shouting back anyway, Scrubby can fool with his timing and his voice quality, coming in late with a very drunken slurred voice that threatens to mess up the whole song, or with a woman's voice, "Oj danaaa," adding another person to the crowd with each gusty response.

Every polka ends very precisely. Nothing hangs over. For the drummer this means grabbing any and all ringing cymbals immediately; the bass player makes sure all strings are muffled; the horn players drop their horns. It creates the effect of a community exhale. After a good number you will often hear nothing but a big "sigh" or "whew" sound from the dancers and the band. No musical sounds fading away, no applause, no stomping, just a big release of air and shuffle of feet before the hum of conversation and partying takes over. With the final song of the event, the effect is even more startling and more lasting. The everyday bar scene gradually takes over, and "polka happiness" recedes into memory.

At a Dyna-Tones Rehearsal

Twenty minutes with a band in a recording studio can reveal more about most styles than weeks and months of listening to the finished records. You also learn much more about the music in a studio than from live public performances. Records and performances are always complete, maintain the illusion of perfection, are never interrupted, and contain no self-criticism. At the studio, by contrast, every note, phrase, instrument, blend, tempo, texture, and dynamic is open to inspection. Mistakes are exposed, weaknesses discussed, and strengths heightened. The norms that underpin a style are defined quite systematically and with great sub-

Larry Trojak (drums) and Scrubby Seweryniak (accordion), USPA Convention, Niagara
Falls, 1976.

tlety. Take, for example, the way a black soul singer's "ecstatic melisma" (stretching one word, syllable, or vowel over many notes) is under perfect control as he or she puts a song on tape in the studio:

The lead singer of a rhythm-and-blues vocal group embellishes the melody in a very different manner on each of the first five run-throughs or takes, and the best of these versions is selected; after listening to it once, the singer proceeds to sing in unison with himself the second time it is played back (multiple-track tape again), matching each involved inflection with perfect split-second precision, thereby increasing the power of the piece immeasurably.[12]

A few hours with the Dyna-Tones in June 1977, as they prepare for a recording session, reveals even more than the session itself. In the back room at the Broadway Grill, where the Dyna-Tones have been playing most Sunday afternoons from four to eight o'clock, Larry Trojak and David "Scrubby" Seweryniak (the two original members of the band) are talking about how being a polka musician affects the rest of one's life. They discuss various turnovers in the band's personnel as present members wander in. Most of the stories about musicians who have left or were asked to leave are well known, probably a recurrent topic of conversation on those long weekend trips and a way of keeping the present personnel together. As the musicians arrive and become aware that an interview is being taped, they begin joking about the dropouts: "Wasn't he voted out because he refused to take a bath?" "No, it was after he broke his wife's arm that we had to let him go, 'cause we do have a certain reputation to uphold, you know." "Do you suppose that guy will *ever* pay back the $600 he owes the band?" "He still owes everybody in Buffalo, he won't pay us back," and so forth, as the instruments are unpacked.

Nobody wastes much breath warming up—or time tuning up. No one really calls the rehearsal to order. When everyone has gotten his drink and checked out the hockey game on the TV up front at the bar, Scrubby suggests they review "Down at the Friendly Tavern," a number worked out at a previous rehearsal. Larry counts off, clicks his sticks twice, and the song

is under way, but only concertina, bass, and drums are playing. The two trumpets are in for a section, then out again, and now nothing takes their place as the bass, concertina, and drums drone and thump along. It's a good bottom half of a polka band, but something is really missing—the vocal. Pow, the trumpets are back in with a flashier melodic line, only to disappear again; the lack of a vocal is very conspicuous by this time. Scrubby calls specific notes to Bill Barnas as they go along: "G, G, D." In the tight structure of most polkas there can really be only one best bass note at every moment in the progression. Scrubby and Bill are listening for the solidest possible bass notes to sustain and blend with the concertina chords.

All Bill's notes combine enough "overamplified throb" and "out-of-tune edge" to thrill and distract. But how is the bass line being perfected? The whole "out-of-tune" question is fascinating but is not a question at all for most polka musicians. They recognize that Ray Henry's great sound of the late 1940s featured a terrifically out-of-tune clarinet player known as "the nightingale," but no one tries to explain, replicate, or justify it; that's just the way Ray Henry's great sound was. Similarly, the classic Chicago-style band, together for over twenty years as the AmPol Aires, relies on a string bassist whose notes are often a full half-tone or more "out of whack" for reasons that no one has bothered to articulate. But all knowledgeable listeners will agree that the peculiar quality of Ray Henry's sound and the strong bottom of the AmPol Aires' music are both exactly right: just what everyone wants to hear from those particular bands.

The question of tone quality is even more mysterious. During a break, Bill says that the selection of bass notes may not be finally made until a week or so before the two-day recording session, when he will have to transfer his electric bass lines to the string bass he will use in the studio. The heavy semipitched throb of the electric bass in performance and in rehearsal is, somehow, better maintained by a string bass in the studio. Or is it possible that the electric bass is simply an approximation of the studio-boosted and studio-balanced string bass?

But that question is not at issue in this first runthrough of "Down at the Friendly Tavern." Here, the band's goal seems to be to solidify the rhythmic and harmonic foundations of the song while reviewing the brass parts. A second runthrough, this time with the vocal, sounds good but leads to a lot of discussion about restructuring the whole thing. Roger, the clarinetist, says, "This sounds like a tenor song; do you think I should play tenor on the riff?"

What is the "riff"? In jazz parlance it usually means a single phrase repeated over and over again, usually by a few instruments backing up a soloist or vocalist, but "riffs" of that kind aren't a part of polka style. As Roger tries his part on tenor, he seems to be working with the flashy trumpet refrain. It is common for a polka to have a section, also called the "push part," when the trumpets take off to play their trickiest turns, and the drummer shifts his right hand from snare drum to big cymbals in order to push the beat along. There is some discussion about dropping the present "riff" altogether. Then Larry says to John Kilian, one of the trumpet players: "Didn't you have a riff on tape that would fit in here?" John spends a few minutes trying different sides of a few cassettes in the tape player, hoping to locate it. No luck. Larry sings another riff in nonsense syllables. No one is enthusiastic. "Is there a way to hit some octaves in there? Maybe that would give it a lift." More discussion of whether or not to seek out a new riff altogether or try to improve the present one. A riff, therefore, can be taken out, invented, revised, replaced with a completely different riff at the drop of a note. A riff seems to be an oppositional element in the song structure, something that will contrast sharply with the song itself and yet still fit in.

The issue remains unresolved as Scrubby starts teaching Bob Wroblewski, the other trumpet player, the melody line of the next song, and the band moves on to "Rosalinda," a waltz by the Slovenian-American stylist supreme, Frankie Yankovic, and now about to become a Polish-American polka. Scrubby is going through it on the concertina and checking himself quickly against a taped version he made weeks or months before. The tape recorder is clearly in use as a memory bank, a place to deposit songs until the time comes to arrange them. While Scrubby consolidates his part, the rest of the band members try out bits and pieces of it but spend most of the time talking about the possible overall contours of the tune.

Six people are all playing and talking through the options simultaneously, and it's hard to tell how the song is actually taking shape or who is shaping what. The trumpet players seem most concerned with checking the concertina key and the melodic range. Larry is full of suggestions about sequence for the different sections, possible modulations and key shifts—normally none of a drummer's business. Bill plays along with Scrubby to pick up the bass line and at the same time argues with Larry about the best sequence. Roger sips his drink, listens, comments on sequence possibilities, and talks up the idea of everyone pitching in for a weekend hayride. Clearly, no one person is composing and arranging this song. On the other hand, it is not clear how the group does it either, since everyone seems to be working on two fronts at once.

Suddenly, Bob is bending over Scrubby with his trumpet and adding a simple melody line to the concertina. A minute later he is doing it with John, who finds a nice harmony for it, and in a little less than three minutes one element—the two-trumpet version of the basic vocal or melody line—is in place. Bill and Roger are quick to point out that some of the trumpet harmony is too low; John says he'll put those parts up an octave. The two trumpets try it with the bass and concertina. It sounds powerful. Over against the wall Roger plays along on tenor to hear whether he has something to add. He does, so they do it again. Larry adds the drum part. It sounds not just powerful but perfect, something that could have taken hours—not five minutes—to achieve.

Elated by the sound of quick success, Bob and John set to work immediately to figure out a trumpet "riff" or "push part," starting with three climbing phrases that John remembers from a riff he put on tape but again cannot find. Roger asks, "Doesn't it sound like a 'breaker' somebody used to use?" (A "breaker" is the bit of flashy music with which bands announce the end of a set and intermission.) The "compositional" process is now even harder to follow. John has the basic idea, but Bob has to crystallize his part before John can put in a harmony line. So John helps Bob shape the convoluted melody, and then Bob helps John fit the harmony to it. Most of the time it takes, fifteen minutes or so, to put the riff in shape is wordless; John and Bob face each other, bent over, elbows on knees, and play very tricky phrases back and forth at half speed, then together at full speed. Occasionally, one musician sings a phrase to the other or moves the trumpet away from his lips far enough to mutter "again" or "from the top."

Meanwhile, other band members go to get drinks and return to discuss structure some more. Larry: "The only thing I can see bad about that would be a real strong vocal in that upper key, and then when he goes down it's going to be kind of a—" Scrubby: "Yeah, I'd rather go down first, start off in the lower key and then go up." Bill: "All right, let's go with that." With this decision to go from a lower to a higher key within the vocal section, it seems that the trumpets will have to transpose their riff into still a third key. Having just put all that concerted energy and empathy into mastering a long string of complicated and harmonized phrases, Bob and John get the message: "It's got to go out of D; try it in A." But they don't seem surprised or bothered, and indeed it just takes a minute or two to find the range and put the whole thing into A. Even more amazing, a few minutes later they are trying it in G, just to check the range and timbre. How is all this instant transposing of very difficult lines—just learned by ear minutes before—even possible, much less easy?

Now the trumpeters are busy making final adjustments in the riff. Bob suggests putting a few fifths into the harmony line; they try it, and everyone nods. John: "Hey, that should go well in there." Bob: "Doesn't it? It just puts a fifth in there instead of all those firsts and thirds." John: "Try it with the bottom." Larry: "Try it on the box." They do it with the concertina alternating single bass notes and chords underneath. Larry: "I think it's kind of nice really, with the box." John: "It fits in the chords." Bob: "Yeah it fits, it's not that noticeable but at least it feels good." John to Scrubby: "Did you hear how the harmony switched?" Scrubby: "It's hard to hear really." Bob:

"But it breaks the monotony a little. I don't think anybody else can hear it but us. It just puts different parts of the chord in." Scrubby: "Why don't we try it from the chord change where you guys go up to A for the vocal part? I'll take my solo in D, then you guys go down to G for the push part."

They try it once, and then again from the "stop," a nice big empty space that comes right after the trumpets finish their version of the vocal line and just before Scrubby sings. When they do it for dancers, there will be a wonderful moment in which all you hear is the swish and stomp of dancing feet.

Overall, it sounds great to us—a song recomposed and arranged in half an hour—but everyone feels the trumpets need a lot more work, so there is a break for the others while Bob and John check each phrase and look for improvements. Learning definitions of terms like "breaker," "push part," and "stop" with Scrubby and Bill, we go over the ways of picking up different instruments in the studio, what to do for the string bass, how to keep the trumpets bright. There is so much concern for getting things right, for achieving the best possible version of each phrase in every number, that Bob's doubts—"I don't think anybody else can hear it but us"—have a certain force.

The Dyna-Tones on Record

The cover of the album *Down at the Friendly Tavern* has a color photo of the Dyna-Tones and their fans assembled in front of the Broadway Grill.[13] In the photo, everything looks normal, familial, communal. But inside the album some strange things are happening. Even though these are the same musicians (minus one) who recorded the preceding *Six Million Dollar Band* LP, the feeling of the two albums is very different. *Six Million Dollar Band* was a boost, utilizing Beethoven's Ninth Symphony for the themes that open side one, reaching back to Poland for the *gorale* violin sounds and the Polish vocals that open side two. It was an expansive album, very upbeat.[14]

The *Friendly Tavern* collection seems to go "down and inside" with a lot of heartbreak borrowings from

The Dyna-Tones and "friendly tavern" fans: Stas Malkiewicz (violin), Scrubby Seweryniak (concertina), John Kilian (trumpet), Larry Trojak (drums), Bill Barnas (bass), Bob Wroblewski (trumpet), Roger Nowaczyk (clarinet).

country-and-western, vocals in English, a desperate feeling, and a sense of time-out-of-joint. Maybe it really is just a time difference. The first album celebrated the addition of Canadian Stas Malkiewicz's violin, the bicentennial spirit of '76, and the discovery of new music being made with old forms. *Friendly Tavern*, a year later, takes locality as its theme, and any evocation of Polish Broadway in Buffalo has to register some of the feeling of factories closing, stores boarded up, and only temporary happiness at the bar.

Side one certainly tries to be cheerful. "Chitty Chitty Breakdown Polka," as arranged by trumpeters Wroblewski and Kilian, runs circles around the Disney movie theme. "Happy Bachelor" is happy enough. The country-and-western borrowings—Buck Owens's "Over and Over Again" polkafied, and Merle Haggard's "Today I Started Loving You Again" done as an honest "cover" with piano, violin, and guitar straight from Nashville—are both friendly and warm.

On side two, the Dyna-Tones seem to be reaching for feelings that other bands might fear, letting the music develop in ways that some might reject as too risky. Though we had heard "Rosalinda" being assembled, we found some things still surprising—even baffling. The beat gets reversed somewhere in the eleventh or twelfth measure of the vocal. They sing a long line, "How can you hinder this great romance? You see I love you, love you so, you mustn't answer 'No.'" In the midst of this hindered romance the Dyna-Tones may have reinvented Gerard Manley Hopkins's "sprung rhythm." Is a beat added? Or subtracted? All of a sudden you find yourself dancing against the usual pulse. If you stick to your step, it comes out OK at the end of the second vocal section, where the same fast-talking long line of the lyric somehow restores the balance and "one" is where it ought to be. As the trumpets take it out at the end, though, the echoed vocal line leaves you stomping on the wrong foot again.

"Rosalinda" is followed by Larry Trojak singing his own lyrics to Kris Kristofferson's tune "We're but a Moment," as a polka. Here the long line is not compressed to the point of altering the beat but rather paced out over the beat. The effect of an idea like "wondering how we ever could have thought that we were more than just a moment in this mystery called time" expressed inside polka process is very disturbing. Lines about passing time and changing perceptions serve to heighten the tension between polka experience, lived in the present, and life in the past tense.

> Hours turn into days turn into weeks.
> We're at its mercy still we try
> [a pause for two "pushed" concertina chords here]
> To hold it back, say it's not so,
> Convince ourselves we're more than that,
> Wondering how we got this far
> And wondering how we ever could
> Have thought that we were more
> Than just a moment
> In this mystery called time.

This juxtaposition of existential wonderment and polka time works on the record, even if it probably gets lost in the shuffle at any actual polka dance.

The mood of sadness and uncertainty is sustained in the album's two new songs, "Let's Put It Back Together Waltz" and "Some Broken Hearts Never Mend Polka." In both, the Dyna-Tones are playing with time, compressing it when it suits them. It doesn't matter whether country-and-western originals provide models for these compressions, or whether measures or beats get lost. The point is that the feeling of expectations breaking down is present in all four of these songs. In the waltz, pauses are missing where the melodic line leads you to expect them. In "Some Broken Hearts," the title refrain is a song within a song which interrupts the narrative: "The first thing in the morning that I do is start with singing 'Some Broken Hearts' . . ." and later, "In the middle of love's embrace, I see your face, 'Some Broken Hearts' . . ." Roger Nowaczyk overdubs some beautiful clarinet duets for this tune; a double-stopped violin solo and straightforward trumpet duets with drum-punctuated

modulations take it out. With a surging beat behind the last selection, a Frank Wojnarowski standard called "I Would Marry You Polka" sung in Polish, the feeling of normal polka happiness returns. But in that four-song sequence of troubled lyrics and troubled structures, the Dyna-Tones seem to be trying to reflect troubled times. There is an undercurrent of tragic feeling. Workaday heroes and heroines describe their struggle against long odds to keep relationships from falling apart. The pain of daily life surfaces in these songs more clearly than it does in most polka music.

Side two of *Friendly Tavern* foreshadows the first "concept album" in polkas and the first effort to go beyond the eclectic "polka Mass" idea to a unified expression of Polish-American Christian spirit: the Dyna-Tones' *Chapter VII*.[15] This album changes the whole definition of "polka music" in many ways that have yet to develop, but the title itself is emblematic. Calling it *Chapter VII* suddenly turns the first six albums of the Dyna-Tones into phases of development, stages of a pilgrimage. Telling the Christ story in polka music for polka people brings the sacred themes into what had been a very secular world. It begins to reverse the "polka Mass" process of bringing the music into the church for the revitalization of Polish Catholicism.

What is Polish-American Christianity? What is the message or concept of this concept album? What is special here—though this may seem both too subtle and too simple an answer—is the extreme normality of failure, the unoriginality of sin. The message is, "We blew it and are continuing to make a mess of things." The spoken portions that begin and end the album spell out our failure in plain language. From the "Epilogue":

> The writings become clearer now,
> Immensely clear, and yet somehow
> We fail to recognize the signs
> Of what He called "the troubled times."
> How much more wrong will He allow?

And from the "Prologue":

> What fools we must appear to be
> To one as glorious as He.
> He offered to supply our needs;

We chose to bite the hand that feeds.
We truly are a mystery.
So sit back now and hear again
The story from a time back then
When for our sins He came to be
A man as much as you or me.

After the spoken word, the happy polka sound and the story of "The Birth" come as a relief and a shock. The three kings have their burdens lifted—"When the star showed our way / And our faith was defended / Our worries were part of the past"—and then dance their way to the manger with everyone else. The shepherds show no fear of transparent angels and are told, "We bring news of great joy / And although you see through us / There's something that you have to hear." A democratic Christmas polka party at which kings and shepherds mingle, where they "welcomed salvation home," is just the way it must have been. In Polish parishes, people go to church on Christmas eve and bring home some straw from the manger. That's what a manger holds: straw for the animals. If it was good enough for Christ, it's good enough for us too.

The next part, "He Told Them," sustains the joyful polka mood as Christ, age twelve, goes to the temple: "He told of life, He spoke of love, . . . and they knew this was no ordinary boy." Scrubby and Larry do a high tenor duet on the chorus, using the sweeter-than-sweet sound that Blazonczyk and Gomulka have perfected over the years. In this context it gives the feeling of two altar boys assisting at a first communion and reminds us of Christ's youthful glow as well.

"John the Baptist" is a ¾ oberek and an inspired pairing of word message with dance process. The heavy "industrial-strength waltz" feeling of the oberek is just right for a path-blazing John the Baptist. The first stanza of the lyric summarizes Polish-American family feeling as the basis for good actions in a treacherous world:

They were old, so they thought,
Too old to be thinking, "A Son."
But they fit in God's plan and gave
Birth to the one they called John.
Everything they could ask for,

He loved them till their dying day;
Then he knew Christ was coming and knew
That he must pave His way.

And the fourth stanza finds John defending family integrity at the cost of his life:

The Baptist cursed Herod
for marrying his own brother's wife.
Daughter Salome saw this
and asked for this righteous man's life.
On a platter of silver, even Salome
must have been awed.
But his work was all done: he made
way for the one Lamb of God.

The conclusion of side one, an instrumental polka called "Wedding at Cana," sustains the family feeling. Polish weddings are legendary for many reasons, among them that a wedding brings religious feeling, family, and the polka party together in one place. It was at the Cana wedding that Christ ordered the servants to fill six pots with water and then changed it into wine. From John 2:9–11: "When the ruler of the feast had tasted the water that was made wine, and knew not whence it was (but the servants which drew the water knew), the governor of the feast called to the bridegroom, and saith unto him, Every man at the beginning doth set forth good wine; and when men have well drunk, that which is worse; but thou hast kept the good wine until now. This beginning of miracles did Jesus in Cana of Galilee, and manifested forth his glory, and his disciples believed on him." Christ's act—keeping the party going strong at his mother's request—was a very Polish-American thing to do, a good "beginning of miracles," a foreshadowing of Christ's sacrifice and the communal blood that we drink—and an appropriate closing number for the album's first side.

Side two opens with "Matthew 14," a polka accompaniment for the story of the miracles, told in a way that interprets Christ's actions as a normal response to needy people: "They wanted just to hear Him speak and feel His company," so he divided the loaves and fishes. Similarly:

He walked the sea if just to ease their fears,
But they could not believe their eyes
and not believe their ears
Till Peter tried; his faith wasn't too strong.
Christ rescued him without a word
and proved that they were wrong.

The plain language of these stanzas makes the miracles seem like everyday events, favors you do for people, a matter of helping out. And people, in turn, do the best they can, which is not very much. Peter tried, but like a lot of us, he lacked sufficient faith.

Peter is the key figure in "Waltz Trilogy: The Last Supper, Prayers at Gethsemane, The Betrayal." These themes are given a very effective musical setting by leaving out the drums and trumpets and slowing the tempo so that any suggestion of a dance context disappears. A listening intermission in the dance of life: full piano sound, concertina arpeggios, and clarinet interludes underpin these moments of reflection on forgiveness and foreknowledge of the crucifixion. We can feel Christ's loneliness in the suspension of time. The betrayal by Judas and the failure of Peter— " 'Rock Peter' / as true as you be / before three crows you'll claim / that you don't know me"—unfold naturally, predictably, in slow motion. Before and after any miracles, this is how human beings are: "They slept while I knelt here / in undaunted prayer / They slept thrice and acted / as if they don't care." Judas takes the money. Peter tries to make up for lapsed vigilance or lost commitment with violence.

> "Unhand Him," shouts Peter;
> his sword finds an ear.
> Then good Jesus heals it
> and says, "Show no fear.
> Live not by the sword
> for you'll die the same way.
> Twelve legions of angels
> would come if I say."

"No fights" is Christ's message to the people and still the watchword at polka events today. "Thousands of people at the convention last year, and not a single fight"—the seal of approval, a final proof of polka happiness.

The juxtaposition of Christ's words and the appraisal of polka dances may seem strange or in poor taste, but we must not overlook the humor, even delight, in mixing Christ's passion with the secular polka world. It is hard to ask someone, "Would you like to hear 'John the Baptist Oberek' or 'The Crucifixion Polka'?" without smiling at the same time. The intent here is not disrespectful but fits with the "good news" of salvation, the feeling that Christ's story belongs to everyone all the time everywhere. Whatever the truth is about Christ or Christianity, the story is part of the world and takes on meaning according to context. In Polonia, the injunction "Live not by the sword" stands for a long tradition of politeness in the face of insult, patience in circumstances of prevailing injustice.[16]

The music for "The Crucifixion" is the most memorable polka on the record. The key is minor and the feeling very Russian; more than that, it is Russian Jewish, like *hora* that are played at Jewish weddings. Clarinetist Nowaczyk improvises beautifully behind the vocals and adds a wild triplet figure behind the trumpet push part, which builds to a climactic pause before the last chorus, when thunder rolls and the narrator speaks: "Father, into your hands I commend my spirit." It is a rebirth of music from the spirit of tragedy, for the music echoes the persecution of Poles by Russians and Germans, as well as the suffering of Jews at the hands of Poles, Russians, and Germans.

> The King of Jews is crucified,
> His banner is above.
> "Father, they know not what they do;
> forgive them with Your love."
> One believer said, "Take me with You."
> Darkness came. Mankind could start anew.

"The Resurrection" is a happy snappy polka which, aside from the satisfying "Alleluja" that closes each stanza, does not really stay in the mind. After the slow, melancholy waltz of betrayal and the urgency of the crucifixion music, the message here is less convincing.

Finally, the "Epilogue" asks us to pray and keep the

Scrubby Seweryniak, IPA Festival, Rosemont, Illinois, 1983.

faith, but the music has stopped and with it the magic of feeling the old story given new life in a way that was singularly appropriate to the lives and times of Polish-Americans during the year when *Solidarnošc* held out so much hope for a genuine Christian socialism.

Somehow playing this music at regular dances or asking people to dance to it at special events is inappropriate. At one live performance at the Polish community center, staged as a concert in sympathy with Solidarity, the music felt exactly right, because it was the Polish workers who pulled the Church into that struggle. But although disc jockeys around the country may play parts of *Chapter VII* at Easter each year, to date there are really no other contexts for this extraordinary album.

Live Wire (1982) is the eighth chapter in the partnership between Larry Trojak and Dave "Scrubby" Seweryniak of the Dyna-Tones, a partnership that owes something to the Apollonian/Dionysian dialectic that underlies any vital people's music.[17] The tensions that characterize these very different ways of being stem from the nature of humanity itself. As *homo sapiens*, the being that knows, we remember and name our pleasures and pains; we can see death coming long be-

IPA Festival, Rosemont, Illinois, 1983.

fore it arrives. Broadly speaking, there seem to be two forms of relief from this burden of knowing. One is to have clearer ideas about things, to order the world according to plans, to write a book, to perfect a recording, to project a dream or a myth so compelling that people can share belief in it and feel that the ideal is more real than their own mortality. This is the Apollonian solution. The other release is to "get down," go with the flow, fill the senses, drink firewater, pull the smoke into your lungs, feel the feathers on the wings of death's angels, follow the urge to merge with everyone and everything to a point of trance-dance exhaustion. This is the Dionysian solution.

How such diametrically opposed forces can be reconciled in Greek tragedy or in the Chicago-style polka party is a great mystery.[18] It is too simple to say that Larry Trojak is an Apollonian planner-perfectionist and Scrubby Seweryniak the force for Dioynsian reveling; they both contain these two forces. It is the balancing of the two that is familiar to every polka participant: the question is, for example, how to be drunk enough to lose your inhibitions but conscious enough to coordinate at high speed with your partner and in relation to contiguous dancing couples. To any outsider who looks at this process with and from an analytic, alien perspective, the Dionysian aspect of any live

polka scene will appear dominant, if not overwhelming. To an observer with a notebook, tape recorder, and camera, the party seems out of control, a swirl of confusion. The dance maneuvers look effortless, but as soon as the outsider puts down the equipment in order to dance, the control required becomes formidable. For every participant, the unscripted drama requires various kinds of control and concentration: these are highlighted in the dance but are also involved in decisions about where to sit and with whom to gossip, the whole patterning of an evening's interactions. The Apollonian principles, then, are often invisible but still central to the structure of the performance and the party.

Similarly, the musicians have to be "wild and crazy guys" while keeping tight control of techniques, tempos, dedications, announcements, requests, and the sequencing of songs. Scrubby, the sad clown singing happily with a little bit of hurt in his voice, has to devote a great deal of attention to the demands of a concertina whose pitches shift with the in-and-out motions of the bellows as his right hand doubles a clarinet part and his left hand doubles or fills out the bass. Sipping his drink between songs, or with a cigarette between his toes, Scrubby always appears relaxed, open, full of cheer and impish good humor just be-

Scrubby Seweryniak, IPA Festival, Milwaukee, 1976.

neath the generally impassive expression on his face. But as a vocalist with words to remember and express, as the unifying instrumentalist holding top and bottom together, and as the master of ceremonies who calls the tunes and anticipates the needs of the people, Scrubby personifies the ordering spirit of Apollo working on his Dionysian soul at all times.

The polka party is a Dionysian ritual, a collective bonding through song, dance, drink, humor, and many little rites of conviviality. But it has acquired form over the years, and this audiovisual orderliness is also Apollonian, a dream of how life should be more of the time. In the live event, control and perfection of a kind are just as important as in the recording studio, and in either context the goal is always fusion, balance, of form and energy.

It was probably the separateness of the recorded and live polka traditions that highlighted Trojak as an Apollonian planner-perfectionist in recordmaking and Seweryniak as the Dionysian energizer of live performance. It was even easier to see the Apollonian spirit in Trojak after he stopped drinking and started running. And once he was going to college, writing

candid and critical reviews of polka records for the new *Polish-American Voice*, and working toward a career as a writer, it was easy to look back at all his effort to perfect the albums as a continuous development. But for a decade of Dyna-Tones' performances, Larry was a drinker and a drummer, providing the loose beat, the wild fills, the cymbal crashes. The Dionysian pulse of the music was in his hands.

The stereotype of Scrubby as the Bacchic reveler doesn't hold up to inspection long, either. The concertina requires all that control, calculation, and discipline of the energy pressed into buttons, the air squeezed into bellows, the exact opposite kinesics of drumming, where arms and sticks move around the set striking freely. And for many years Scrubby was doing all of the booking for the band, working out logistics of weekend tours, bargaining with patrons, planning the travel and accommodations—a mountain of detail work in which no one could revel. Because the Dionysian and Apollonian are fused in personalities, fused again in the meshing of those personalities with the characteristics of the instruments they play, fused yet again in the band and finally in polka happiness, the dialectic almost disappears. Nevertheless, the struggle to resolve the Apollonian/Dionysian tensions between Larry and Scrubby were the most important element in the band's exciting evolution through its last four albums—and also the reason that their long partnership dissolved and reformed a number of times.

The same dialectic has worked on a macrocosmic level in the evolution of Polish-American and other polka styles (and in the blues as well) over the decades.[19] It is the sign of stylistic vitality. Wherever culture is taking shape and a style is being forged within a social group, Dionysian feeling and Apollonian form will be struggling for supremacy. Many books have been written about feeling and form, but the general refusal to take ethnic working-class music and culture seriously as generators of artistic products has kept this interchange hidden, both in the broad area of stylistic evolution and in the day-to-day musicmaking negotiations of specific bands. Perhaps every band working in a vital style contains these tensions, but the Dyna-Tones are special in having resolved them differently in each of their last four albums. *Live Wire* records some of their most requested tunes, played before a live audience of about five hundred at a Veterans of Foreign Wars hall in Lackawanna, New York, and the result is a celebration and documentation of Polish-American polka processes at a particular time. This live "Chapter VIII" has a different and disturbing sound that illumines all the albums before it as stages of evolving polka style.

In this LP and in other live Dyna-Tones performances of the late 1980s, the opposing forces often seem locked in each other's grip, like evenly matched wrestlers rather than dancing partners. The sound is too essential, too controlled, and at the same time too excessive and too desperate. Without Nowaczyk's improvising clarinet or a wailing violin, there is no life in the instrumental upper register. The two trumpets execute their lines flawlessly, clearly, without a single deviation in the entire album: there are no buzzed tones, no spontaneous bursts, no high notes held over a shifting chord pattern, no solos, no freedom, no mistakes, no personality—just two disciplined interchangeable parts locked together to serve their essential

purpose in the music. In fairness, one must remember that the two-trumpet sound in Chicago-style polka music has always been powerful because of the tight unison perfection effect. But the general exuberance of the *Live Wire* album highlights the fact that these players are in chains almost as tight as the ones that tie the first and second violinists of a symphony orchestra to their chairs, desks, and notations.

In the bottom part of the Dyna-Tones sound there was a major transformation when Dave "Nigel" Kurdziel replaced Al Parker on bass and Al Piatkowski became the sixth man, his accordion or concertina reinforcing Scrubby's squeezebox. Nigel's high volume and frequent use of throbbing double stops or double-time eighth notes on one pitch to push the band along also pushes the Dyna-Tones closer to the rock norms of playing at the crowd rather than to or for them. The second concertina or accordion adds to the drone and throb effect, as if still more power must be used to involve people in the party and the dancing. The clear, controlled trumpets on one side and the excessive undertow of Rickenbacker bass combined with squeezeboxes on the other side bracket the voices of Scrubby and Larry, which seem much bigger on this album because the crowd voices are present, at a lower volume and coming in from a distance. The big voices recall Li'l Wally trying to carry the band and the party on his voice alone.

Although the sound on *Live Wire* seems distorted in comparison with the balance of *Six Million Dollar Band*, it quite movingly reflects Polish-American life in Buffalo, where the search for happiness has gotten more desperate. This album is also a rare point of access to the polka bash for those who can't get to the live scene, the polka equivalent of B. B. King's *Live at the Regal*, and is therefore the best polka record to buy if you are not buying more than one. It feels as if the tape recorder was simply on for two sets of Dyna-Tones' music, and you can hear the way the band pushes the party to life, building each set to a series of climaxes. The banter between Larry and Scrubby that links the tunes together, the dedications to groups from out of town, the calls and responses, the whoops and hollers, police whistles twittering, Larry's sticks clicking off

Scrubby Seweryniak, IPA Festival, Milwaukee, 1976.

the tempos, the crowd screams, the manic laughter, the chanted "go go go" and "yo yo yo" are included for the first time. One wonders again why all the other bands have avoided live albums for the past thirty years.

LARRY: OK. We're gonna send this next tune out especially to some real good friends of ours from the Albany-Cohoes area. . . . they're notorious throughout the nation . . . the one and only Huruku's Hell Raisers, and kind of a mini-subculture from that group, the Loadatones, who are in the house with us tonight, their theme song . . .

SCRUBBY (singing in a low, blurry, doltish voice): Load-da-tones, Load-da-tones, Load-da—oh, wait, excuse me I got carried away for a minute.

LARRY: . . . their theme song, here we go with one called "The Drunkard's Lament, *Lamen Piaka*."

Larry's high, clear vocal contrasts with a moaned ohhhh, ooohhhhh, ohhhhh singalong by the crowd, which is deliberately out-of-tune, maximizing its moans with controlled dissonance.

Without an introduction, the band moves next into Scrubby's famous maudlin waltz medley. This opens with "Mr. Bartender" in English, r's rolled beyond endurance and v's substituting for w's.

> Mr. Barrrtenderr, give me a drrrink.
> Mrrr. Barrtender, I vant to drrink.
> Mrrrr. Barrtenderr, I feel so bahlue,
> Mrr. Barrtenderr, the drrinks are on you.
> Drrink your trroubles avay,
> Tomorrow's anotherr day.

Between the lyrics Scrubby's bawling "la la la" blends into the sweet trumpet harmonies as a tribute to Li'l Wally's way with a waltz. Then it's on to the Polish lyrics and a wonderfully pathetic call-and-response section with the audience. Scrubby keeps his emotions barely under control in the first stanza as the crowd groans and moans its sympathy after each line. There-after, he breaks down completely and weeps into his hanky—blathering, blubbering, blowing his nose—without missing a single Polish syllable. Before people actually drown in their beer, however, a happy snappy "Where Were You Johnnie Polka" wraps up the set.

"The Drunkard's Lament" and the maudlin waltz medley might not win the approval of social climbers

Joyce Czarnecki *(center)*, Mickie's Hall, Buffalo, c. 1973.

who promote "respectable" expressions of Polish culture, but it is artistry and cultural heritage of a high order that the Dyna-Tones display nevertheless. They mock the excesses of drunkenness that could give polkas a bad name, but they are not about to give up singing, dancing, drinking, and partying for something as elusive as a "better image." On the contrary, the pursuit of polka happiness over the generations has been a continuing effort to be real, to intensify participation so that life and art fuse into each other once again. All the consumption of food and drink is meant to result in a spiritual production, in music, dance, and happiness.

Pages from a Polka Diary

Festival at Black Rock Church of the Assumption

BY ANGELIKI V. KEIL

The Assumption Community Hall is one of the most modern, spacious, and well-designed social halls in the old churches around Buffalo.[20] The entire length of the church basement has been remodeled with paneling, a vinyl floor, and ceiling tiles. It gives a scrubbed, shiny, "practical" impression; like a bigger and better version of a renovated kitchen and den in one of the homes of the polka people we have visited. As you come in the door, the very space promises a comfortable evening.

A modern steel and glass entrance at the side of the old (1889) church edifice, leads down several wide, comfortable steps to a long table arranged with the tickets and the cashboxes of fund-raising affairs. The three teenage girls staffing it are cheerful and business-like, exemplifying the cultivated feminine know-how and composure of active churchwomen. These young women are already accomplished by the age of fourteen or fifteen. All ablush with the excitement and exhaustion of long preparations, they practice that cheerful restraint which is the rule in meeting the public. We are the only ones near the ticket table right now, and their attention envelops us. We can hear the Krew Brothers playing inside, and just a few yards away we can see one end of the dance floor, polka couples going not too furiously by. On our right, four or five men in their twenties surround two young women who are tending the coat rack. They wait for us to check our coats and then resume their talk.

At least two hundred people are sitting at the long tables on the floor or polkaing around. The room is

Tony Krupski *(left)* and brother Dennis, North Tonawanda, New York, 1976.

pleasantly populated but nowhere close to being full; twenty tables with twenty chairs at each one could easily accommodate four hundred people. Just ahead is the bar, tended by a rather large group of eager and well-scrubbed young men in shirtsleeves, looking very much like young businessmen. Beer pitchers and set-ups are sold separately out of two different windows. Behind them is the kitchen. The swinging doors are closed. Nothing seems to be happening there.

As we pick our way to the bandstand, dodging whirling couples, we stop by a table exhibiting several different Polish Heritage books of the Copernicus Foundation. Business there appears nonexistent. The unabashed peddling that goes on in other benefits is absent; this table is no more than a consciousness-raising exhibit. Nevertheless, Charlie buys a copy of *Polish Heroes.*

The hall is tastefully decorated in red and white, the Polish national colors. The pillars, those irritating structural features in basement halls which are bemoaned in just about every discussion appraising a site for a polka dance, are almost unobtrusive: draped in white and red satin, they demarcate the limits of the dance floor, which is canopied in the same material, filtering the light warmly. For the first time I begin to feel a pang of sympathy with those colors. Usually, I search out the cool, strict evocation of Greece: white and blue, standing for sky, sea, rock, and the whiteness of a seering August noon. When faced with other colors, my ingrained national proclivity is to consider all of them a shabby charade, leaving me sometimes amused but almost never moved. This time I catch myself comforted by the Polish red and white. How have I kept the red and white at a distance all this time? How did I manage to disregard its ambience until now? Here, drawn to the colors, I find myself warmed. The white glows warm and golden, right next to the red. And the red—suddenly the red is special, a palpitating evocation of life itself. It begins to differentiate itself from other reds: it is lighter and warmer than the furious red of the revolution; it is not as dark and stern as the apotropaic red of village weaving; nor does it partake of the darkness of spilled blood. This is the sunny, live red of poppies in the fields, of dancing fire, of coursing blood.

My reverie on red and white floats over the dense sound of the Krew Brothers. Tony is bent over the mike, punching out with precision and emotion a Polish-lyric polka. Every Krupski is concentrating seriously on his instrument. Little Kenny on the drums gives me a welcoming wink. One Polish number succeeds another. There seem to be more Polish-lyric polkas at this dance than ever before. Maybe the Krews are reacting to some fans' grumbles: "They are good, but what's it to me? I never hear them play too many polkas." So now they are giving the fans not only polkas but Polish lyrics to boot.

Tony emcees masterfully. He keeps communication with the audience flowing—not only through the music-dance connection but through his announcements as well: "Another polka coming your way next!"

You feel personally honored by what he says. "Ladies and gentlemen, they are selling kielbasa sandwiches in the kitchen. So if you get hungry, visit the kitchen at the back of the hall. It will be open all night long. Keep it in mind." He is at once the solicitous host and the shrewd businessman. After all, we are here to raise money for the church. It is the perfect polka scene: food, money, dance, music, good works, and community all rolled into one.

The floor fills again, and two women dance by: a svelte, fortyish, blonde in a knockout red jump-suit with a hood, and a very big young woman in her twenties, weighing in at perhaps two hundred and fifty pounds and wearing pants of the same red as her partner's; they must have sewn their outfits with such occasions in mind. I am hypnotized by the life in this dancing couple. The big fat girl with the powerful behind is moving steadily to the polka beat, the blonde fleeting around her almost in double time in an awkward harmony of rhythms. The effect is exhilarating: two such different people, such different dance styles, blending into a dazzling polka couple. As this satisfying unison of disparate forms moves on, I am confronted by its contradiction: a lithe couple in their twenties, tall and slim; they look like a romantic TV commercial. She is in a long, sleek aqua dress, he in a casual beige suit. They float weightlessly in smooth motion, touching down only to push off together.

The Krews are now taking their leave by reminding everyone that there is continuous music tonight and introducing "The Dyna-Tones Orchestra." The dancers' applause as the Krews walk off the floor gives the pleasant impression that it is for both bands. The Dyna-Tones, resplendent in shirts with a bold green leaf print, are ready to go.

Scrubby, smiling in the genial manner he cultivates, takes over as master of ceremonies with a gesture that includes both polite appreciation and friendly, spirited rivalry: "How about a big hand for the Krew Brothers before we give you some polkas, Chicago style." He stresses "Chicago" slightly and then relaxes the tension with a laugh, appearing to chide the Krews for not playing Buffalo's beloved style.

He announces "Beethoven's Ninth Polka" for "Ray

and Emily and the whole gang," recognizing the large group from the Polka Boosters Club who have come all the way across town from Sloan and Cheektowaga to support both bands at Black Rock. The Dyna-Tones play a rousing symphonic polka. The instrumental is dense and funny at the same time. You can feel the energy going round and round the dance floor. More people are dancing than sitting. I watch the general movement of the crowd and then observe particular couples, enjoy their dance style, get to know them a bit, and then pick out the next couple to observe.

Here is a stately pair in their sixties holding on to each other, not passionately but closer than the rest, friendly and hardly moving. Dancing in small steps, rather intimations of steps, these two seem like a world unto themselves, revolving in their own comfortable circle amid the general trajectory of the dance.

Young Kenny Krupski comes furiously around the corner, clowning in splayed-leg fashion like a skier who has lost control, each leg revolving around crossing axes, his body all bent over. He is fulfilling the primary function of the polkaing lead: take her straight down the floor. Again and again and again. His partner, short skirt whirling around her knees, now to the right, now to the left, hovers around his drunken legs and feet, daintily, prettily, airily weaving a steady light beat of arabesque polka steps. Again, what a perfect union of opposites.

As if to clinch the hypothesis that the musicians are the funniest, most grotesque dancers in the polka scene, Hank the drummer comes along, towering in a menacing slant over his partner. She is flirting around him prettily. Both smile angelically as if to unify their felt sense of the dance.

A young man, suited and vested in blue to almost British elegance, comes around next, in perfect synchrony with his statuesque partner, dressed in white chiffon above dark hose and white, heeled sandals. Dancing fast, they turn their heads with each step in a precious ballroom manner, not a trace of smile on their faces. Is that Sonny, the trumpet with the Modernaires?

Scrubby punctuates the beginning of every number with special dedications, turning the hall into a group of "friends." We may not always know the people named, but they are intimates of the band, and we know the band, so everybody feels connected to everybody else. The band creates not only the music, not only the dance, but the very group around us. Each dedication defines the social space:

> And now ladies and gentlemen, for Ben, Jennifer, and Marlene, "The Boys and Girls Polka" . . .

> "The Cookoo Oberek" for the Polka Boosters who are out here in force tonight. And for Charlie Keil taking pictures and his lovely wife making notes. Why I wonder is she making notes? Ha, ha, ha . . .

> For our next number we'd like to feature Larry Trojak on the vocal singing "Mariana" especially for Michaeline . . .

> Let me remind you that they are selling raffle tickets for a trip to Poland and fifteen hundred in cash—oh no [laughing], that's *or* fifteen hundred in cash.

After some prompting from the band, Scrubby's mirth finds another target: "There are also raffles for the Krew Brothers' postcards. Twenty postcards for a penny, and if you do not want to pay the penny, they'll give 'em to you free." At their overflowing table the Krews look stung, but they keep smiling and kibbitzing and taking girls and women from their party around the dance floor, showing their lack of concern. The friendly rivalry between the two bands adds to the spice right now and will become part of the legend of this evening, reminisced about in the fan clubs, at the bars, in kitchen-to-kitchen phone calls.

Scrubby dedicates " 'The Mountaineers Polka' especially for the members of the Modernaires Orchestra here with us tonight." Drummer Larry Trojak leans into the microphone to project his lusty Polish syllables with crackling enunciation and snapping sticks. A short couple in their middle fifties, dancing lightly and with gusto, find themselves in front of the bandstand at the end of the song. The man steps forward, smiling and huffing, throws his arms open as if to hug them all, and says with great conviction: "You guys are great!" I am stung by a spark of love for this community, and tears come to my eyes. But for everyone else it is just a high moment in a polka dance.

Scrubby is joking again, teasing the rivals. "Soon, ladies and gentlemen, our very own Tony Krupski will sing special for Valentine's day 'Je Che, Je Che' in twenty languages." There is general mirth at the expense of Tony's sexy style of sentimental ballad. Then the band launches into a waltz with abandon, letting all the pain and powerful yearning pour out. It's a Li'l Wally tune, and they play it with his voice-over-instruments LA, LA RI LA sound. It has the same going-to-hell-or-heaven-and-I-don't-care-which feeling that panics so many polonaise people into scorning Li'l Wally.

Michaeline stops to introduce her willowy partner as her baby sister and to inform me that she cochaired the dance. She looks radiant and elegant. She attributes that to how exhausted she is and then flies off again around the dance floor.

Scrubby is advertising food once more, this time poking fun at the infamous Polish accent: "If you have worked up an appetite, there are kielbasa and *rose* beef sandwiches." This is the kind of joke that not everyone laughs at, but it serves to keep up the goofy feeling among the band members.

At this point we are ready to eat something. To my dismay, I find that I cannot order simply one glass of beer or a shot but must buy a pitcher of beer or a setup. This is probably both an encouragement to consumption and realistic packaging, since most people attend in groups. Actually, however, the large group is seldom the buying unit at these dances. More likely, two or three men pool their money and buy drinks together for themselves and the women they're with.

When I tell the bar man that I do not have money for a set-up, he immediately offers a shot for fifty cents. When I say, "Make that a double shot," thinking that I will pay a dollar, he says, "Fifty cents only." These church people are dedicated to raising money to benefit their church, yet the concept of tender care for guests, rather than the hard sell, prevails.

Behind the food stand seven or more teenagers keep moving from one part of the kitchen to another, following the patterns of outlined tasks. Two girls emerge at the same time to take our order—a kielbasa sandwich or roast beef on rye.

Five of the Krew Brothers, North Tonawanda, New York, 1976. *Left to right:* Dennis, Rickie, Kenny, Alan, and Gary Krupski.

Others are selling more raffle tickets: three young women parade along each table with a yard-long spiral of a bottle full of red booze, trying to interest every person in the hall in buying raffle tickets for it. They stand in front of each table with an engaging gaze that fastens in turn on each guest's face as they wait patiently for the preposterous nature of the bottle to work its magic. I admire their practiced expertise: they seem a little timid, they are not glib, and they persist. When an older man gives them a hard time—the usual straw-man teasing that Am-Poles seem to love—the girls keep their dignity; they do not give back as good as they got, as an older parish woman might do, but do not get ruffled either. They continue with their mission: completing one more raffle in the life of American Polonia, one more tiny component in the far-flung economic mesh underpinning this community.

From time to time, women go over to the stand to ask for announcements and engage in short business chats with Scrubby, whose job is to be not only a musician but also a facilitator, the humble auctioneer at the service of the benefit.

The dancers are doing a rhinelander now (it turns out to be the only one of the evening): the choppy three steps one direction, then a quick 180-degree turn, long tresses curling around lithe necks, short skirts flying around shapely (or monumental) thighs, high heels stamping the floor in a kind of musical hopscotch. Its mood is so different from the fluid polka that the

rhinelander seems to attract both younger and older people. A magical girl in emerald green with golden-heeled sandals catches my attention. Her face never loses its smiling radiance as she keeps lightly in touch with her partner and rushes one way and then another.

The last number of the Dyna-Tones' set is dedicated "especially for our friends here from Binghamton, New York." It adds a touch of cosmopolitan feeling to the gathering and sets me thinking: Where else do they know and care that the Church of Assumption at Black Rock is having a benefit? Scrubby, following his well-practiced path, sees Hank Mazurek and hurries to include him: "—and for the owner of the Broadway Grill." It is a typical exchange of back scratching, since the Dyna-Tones play regularly at Hank's bar. Public recognition of existing relationships is the heart of emceeing.

As the Dyna-Tones finish the set, the Krew Brothers quickly set up and are ready to go again. Tony sweetly repays the teasing of their rivals: "Sorry, ladies and gentlemen. You were promised continuous music tonight, but there has been an hour's delay. We'll do our best to set this right." There are guffaws from the floor, while those who did not understand what he said consult with their neighbors and then, as they get the message, join in the merriment. The laughter is hushed as the Krews plunge deliberately into "After the loving I'm still in love with you."

It is the valentine mood. Heterosexuality. There

Mickie's Hall, Buffalo, c. 1973.

are no two-women couples on the floor for this number. Even though some elders hold each other in the old-fashioned manner—right arm at the waist, left arms clasped and extended to the side—the mood turns mushy-tender, and most women give the impression of hanging by their thumbs from their partners' necks. The open camaraderie of the polka is gone. Men and women are now intent on each other, oblivious to the rest of the world. Some women look into the faces of their men; others rest their heads on their partners' chests, eyes closed in abandon, each couple the powerful symbol of romantic love. I'm stunned by the change of mood, of style, of the entire feeling of the dance.

But the very shift is a reminder that *both* styles are a kind of play. This is a put-on, a made-up reality, a stylized appearance: Tony's intensity in enunciating the lyrics, his well-modulated formulation of each word, his phrasing calculated to pull at all the strings of the need for heterosexual romance is magnificent. His intensity is so obvious and his "art" so practiced that I am carried away, almost forgetting that he is working very hard to evoke all this. But it is precisely this mediation that I admire so much: his ability to mold time, sound, image; to tug at fantasies, hopes, memories of romantic love; to flood us with feeling.

As the band begins "Blueberry Hill," the cou-

pling mood continues, but now a new element asserts itself; it is the mocking funkiness of tenor saxophones, "yakety-yaking" in the best tradition of making fun of romantic love. Tony continues to be as sexy-romantic as he knows how with the lyric, but the African-American element of funk continues to mock him. That makes the transition to "My Funny Valentine" truly funny. The humor of "Blueberry Hill" has broken the spell of unreality.

I start thinking about the Krews again, pondering Tony's schmaltzy singing style and the hip aversion to the polka. I think about my students and friends who groove to black rhythms and political songs and who would be put off by Tony's sexy style. Why does he move me? Why do I think he's great? Because I see in what he's doing the elements of black and pop influences, and I see him digesting all this and pushing it into form. It's obvious that the Krews are too preoccupied with craft to be just schmaltzy. Form is the critique, the connection with community, history, other traditions. Form is the crystallization of experience. Form is delicious, nourishing to the senses and to communal life.

This reverie in the theory of art is both arrested and confirmed by the clowning going on in the aisles. Emily has put a balloon under her blouse and pretends she is pregnant. People around her are laughing convulsively. How much more concretely can one amend romantic sentiment!

The band moves on to a series of rock numbers, starting with "I Saw Her Standing There." Girls kick off their clogs and rush to join the young men on the floor (the oldsters sit out these numbers). The Krews' rock is superb. They orchestrate the parts to wring the most effect out of every phrase in the song and every lick in the melody. When the Beatles burst on the scene, their message was "We are the Beatles, polite, cockney kids from the heart of industrial England, and we have discovered black American blues. And listen, blues can talk to the experience of being seventeen now." I listen to the Krews sing the simple youth hymn. The Am-Poles from Cheektowaga, great respecters and practitioners of craft that they are, mime perfectly what the British borrowed from an American music born in segregated, despised communities; they make audible and danceable every possibility in the song—like a Bach chorale, accompanied on the most subtle and rousing of organs. The masterful care of the working-class ethnic musician does not begrudge a lifetime of moonlighting to play the music right.

The rockers on the floor, for the first time separated from the entire polka community, respond to the end of the rock tunes by chanting, "More, more, more." For the first time, the kids are acting like kids, gingerly selfish but selfish nevertheless. From the other side of the hall someone interjects in a jeering tone: "Play something for the senior citizens." Faced by a split, clearly if playfully exposed, Tony solves it in true Am-

Dale Wojdyla, Erie Days, Erie, Pennsylvania, c. 1973.

Erie Days, c. 1973.

Ronnie May, Erie Days, c. 1973.

Sylvia Bracikowski, Erie Days, c. 1973.

Michaeline Wyrobek, Erie Days, c. 1973.

Pole fashion: he affirms the polka, affirms unity by not unraveling the community into special interests. Brooking no opposition, he announces, "Polka time again, ladies and gentlemen!" He starts with "Wo We Like You Polka" (the first word, "oh," is especially intoned in the Am-Pole dialect to sound like "wo"). Who can challenge this choice? The floor fills with youths, senior citizens, and everyone-in-between—and before the dancers have a chance to sit down, Tony begins his own composition, the well-loved "Judy Polka." Then he teases the Dyna-Tones by introducing "The Clarinet Polka" and assigning the rival band an impossible task: "We'll do the instrumental version, ladies and gentle-men, and the Dyna-Tones will do the vocal." The Krew Brothers end their set.

The people as well as the bands are getting looser, more juiced, and more bawdy as the night runs on, but the standards of appropriate decorum remain quite high. The clowning and bawdy posturing are limited to a few—especially the Polka Boosters' table. Still, more and more kids are kicking off their shoes; more girls are playing provocatively with red balloons; one couple semidrunkenly trails a two-yard piece of toilet paper as they polka. The dance is getting there, and even within the strict confines of a church hall, polka happiness has arrived.

Epilogue

We have described a few polka parties in the preceding chapters, from the back room at the friendly tavern to a big polka festival and back to a parish dance, but polka happiness is probably not something that will fall upon you as you read a book.[1] If none of these chapters got you up and moving to the nearest polka dance, please go now and experience some polka happiness for yourself—before it is too late.

Polkas have persisted for 150 years on all the continents and many islands too, but despite great diversification of ecological niches, the species is endangered. We need to be clear about just what it will take to maintain polka parties and polka happiness in any particular community.

Seeing the conditions of polka practice not as a single party or synchronic event but as a diachronic problem of style maintenance over time raises some big, interrelated questions that we can only comment on here. More complete answers await more extensive and intensive research.

The first necessity is to pass polka style on to a new generation of musicians, and the question is how to do so. Can polka style and techniques be transmitted today in the same way as they were in the past? For any one of the styles within the six North American polka worlds to continue, there must be musicians who not only know that style but are willing to teach it. From the 1920s into the 1960s, all the polka localities in Polonia had music stores and studios where youngsters went to learn how to play instruments and form bands. More recently, the young musicians who do start bands are getting their instrument lessons in school or privately and probably copying records to form a repertoire, just as young rock bands do. But can you learn concertina from records? Do today's experts have any apprentices coming along?

A second requirement for style maintenance, of course, is the presence of young people who find the style attractive enough to learn it. Either their parents need to be enthusiastic enough to pay for instruments, lessons, equipment, or the kids' passion for polkas has to push them past the family's loss of interest and the heavy peer pressure toward rock or toward anything-

Polka publicity.

but-polkas. Two possible avenues exist here. A revival of family values and a renewed interest in generational continuity might save the day, with children picking up this music to please mom and dad and grandpa. Or polkas might come to be seen by young people as so "far out, old and funky" that they become the "in" thing. Avant-garde composers are writing for the accordion in New York City these days. Zydeco buttonboxes are cool. Los Lobos has crossed over. Brave Combo, a "new wave" polka band from Texas, made an appearance at Buffalo's Polish Community Center in May of 1990. Maybe polkas are indeed becoming "hip" in an MTV-satiated world.

Third, the style must be kept up to date. It must change and be capable of competing with mainstream popular culture fads and fashions, or it will become archaic "folklore" and "heritage." Polkas have always evolved in response to pressure from the dancing public. But are 1960s and 1970s fusions with country-and-western enough? Are "push" and "power" polkas just the beginning of a more aggressive polka sound, or is it a mistake for polka bands to try to compete with rock in terms of "edge" and amplification? Los Lobos and

IPA Festival, Rosemont, Illinois, 1983.

Brave Combo will represent more than fads within the pop field if they actually inspire some teenage neotraditionalists to come forward as musicians and dancers in the polka localities. But do the post-punk and post-modern fans of Brave Combo and Los Lobos actually dance the polka? Or do they "pogo"? Or do they just stand there?

Fourth, even if new generations of polka musicians do develop, polka music will stagnate without opportunities for performance for bands at all levels of accomplishment: there must be a continuum, a ladder of development for bands to climb. In the present environment of shrinking performance opportunities, is there sufficient tolerance and encouragement for beginning bands?

Fifth, the Polonian audience must be large enough to permit the operation of aesthetic standards that encourage bands to improve. Without development and the operation of such standards, there is no excitement for young people to absorb, nothing to strive for in forming a band.

These five requisites are not easily separated, and none is really more important than any of the others. Although the minimum requirements for a single successful polka dance may not be so hard to meet, the continued renewal of these five interdependent condi-

Young dancers, Chicago, 1988.

tions for style maintenance seems much more difficult. The polka's ability to survive twentieth-century pressures on young people to consume the latest rock and pop fashions from their preteen years to marriage is being tested, and the recruitment of young dancers and musicians has been the most formidable challenge to polka continuity since the early 1950s. Young musicians form groups to give the polka a whirl, but where are the throngs of young dancers? If young people can break the constricting molds of cultural conformity to participate in musics that are local, diversified, rooted in tradition and community, then the polka has a bright future.

Notes,
Select Discography,
Permissions,
and Name Index

Notes

Preface

1. Angeliki V. Keil, *Markos Vamvakaris* (Athens: Papazissis, 1972, 1978). In Greek.

Introduction

1. Charles and Angeliki V. Keil wrote the Introduction jointly.

2. The following three paragraphs, including the listed features of a polka party, are adapted from Angela and Charles Keil "In Pursuit of Polka Happiness," *Cultural Correspondence* 5 (Summer–Fall 1977): 4–11, 74. It was reprinted in *Musical Traditions* 2 (1984): 6–11, and a briefer version appeared in *Popular Culture in America*, ed. Paul Buhle (Minneapolis: University of Minnesota Press, 1987), pp. 75–83.

3. The Dyna-Tones, *Live Wire*, WAM LP 4067.

4. "The Drawing-Room Polka," *Illustrated London News* 4 (May 11, 1844): 300–301.

5. Manuel H. Peña, *The Texas-Mexican Conjunto: A History of a Working-Class Music* (Austin: University of Texas Press, 1985).

6. Robert Dolgan, *The Polka King: The Life of Frankie Yankovic as Told to Robert Dolgan* (Cleveland, Ohio: Dillon/Liederbach, 1977); Charles Frank Emmons, *Economic and Political Leadership in Chicago's Polonia: Some Sources of Ethnic Persistence and Mobility* (Ann Arbor, Mich.: University Microfilms, 1971); Janice Ellen Kleeman, *The Origins and Stylistic Development of Polish-American Polka Music* (Ann Arbor, Mich.: University Microfilms International, 1982).

7. Richard K. Spottswood, "The Sajewski Story: Eighty Years of Polish Music in Chicago," in *Ethnic Recordings in America: A Neglected Heritage* (Washington, D.C.: American Folklife Center, Library of Congress, 1982).

8. Caroline Golab, *Immigrant Destinations* (Philadelphia: Temple University Press, 1977).

9. The literature on the history and culture of Polonia is large and growing. The following sources are a starting point: Stanislaus A. Blejwas and Mieczyslaw B. Biskupski, eds., *Pastor of the Poles: Polish American Essays Presented to Right Reverend Monsignor John P. Wodarski in Honor of the Fiftieth Anniversary of His Ordination*, Polish Studies Program Monograph (New Britain, Conn.: Central Connecticut State College, 1982); John J. Bukowczyk, *And My Children Did Not Know Me: A History of the Polish-Americans* (Bloomington: Indiana University Press, 1987); Stefan Kieniewicz, *The Emancipation of the Polish Peasantry* (Chicago: University of Chicago Press, 1969); Helena Znaniecki Lopata, *Polish Americans: Status Competition in an Ethnic Community* (Englewood Cliffs, N.J.: Prentice-Hall, 1976); Frank Renkiewicz, ed., *The Polish Presence in Canada and America* (Toronto: Multicultural History Society of Ontario, 1982); William I. Thomas and Florian Znaniecki, *The Polish Peasant in Europe and America*, 5 vols. (Boston: Richard G. Badger, 1918–20; rpt. New York: Dover, 1958); Paul Wrobel, *Our Way: Family, Parish, and Neighborhood in a Polish-American Community* (Notre Dame, Ind.: University of Notre Dame Press, 1979).

10. In Buffalo's Polonia the following people immediately come to mind:

Bill Falkowski has organized cultural activities with special flair and was a co-founder of the *Polish American Voice* (February 1983–December 1984), which fused with the pre-existing *Polish American Journal: Polonia's Voice* (Buffalo, N.Y.). He is at the center of a "companionate circle" that has nurtured a number of young activist-intellectuals. His doctoral dissertation is focused on the history of the Buffalo Polonia: "Accommodation and Conflicts: Patterns of Polish Immigrant Adaptation to Industrial Capitalism and American Political Pluralism in Buffalo, New York, 1873–1901" (Ph.D. diss., State University of New York, Buffalo, 1990).

Zoe Zacharek is a university instructor, a graduate student, a union organizer, and a cultural anthropologist specializing in women's labor issues.

Mike Basinski is best known as a poet, but he also teaches writing and courses on the Polish-American experience. He has been influential in the local cultural scene through his involvement with Niagara-Erie Writers and Western New York Literary Center. He has published a poetry collection: *The Women Are Called Girls* (Clarence Center, N.Y.: Textile Bridge Press, 1983).

Kate Koperski, a talented teacher in the Buffalo parochial schools, also writes short stories; she is a folklorist with a special interest in Polish-American "folk" Catholicism. See "The Message of an Angel: Children's Guardian Angel Stories in Buffalo's Polonia," in *New York Folklore* 10, nos. 3–4 (Summer–Fall 1984), and *The Iconography of Rebirth: Aspects of the Polish-American Easter Celebration* (Niagara University, N.Y.: Buscaglia-Castellani Art Gallery, 1988).

Stan Sluberski is a connoisseur of American music and an indefatigable student of matters Polonian. His *Polka Sunday with Friends*, a successful polka program broadcast by the State University of New York's public radio station, WBFO, serves western New York and southern Ontario; informed not only by his humor but also by a sense of community typically Polonian, it is a rare example of public media dedicated to serving Polonia.

Sophie Knab is a writer of short stories, a folklorist, and a mental health counselor; see her "Polish Americans and Mental Health Services," *Journal of Psychosocial Nursing* 24, no. 1 (January 1985): 31–34.

Every Polonia has its own young intellectuals, who can be excellent guides to those who want to learn more about the Polonia closest to them.

Chapter 1

1. This chapter was written by Charles Keil.

2. See Kleeman, *Origins and Stylistic Development*, p. 2. Since Kleeman's thesis is unpublished we include her description of the Kolberg collection (pp. 1–2): "Crucial to my research on the original folk style polka in Poland is the primary source material contained in the collections of the 19th-century Polish folklorist, H. Oskar Kolberg (1814–1890). Kolberg's lifelong work with Polish folk music and folklore was inspired by the ideals of the Polish Enlightenment, a Romantic movement which sought to find a national consciousness in the traditions of Poland's common people. A professional musician, pianist, and composer . . . Kolberg early in his career set about gathering and transcribing folk music from all areas of Poland. Eventually he expanded his effort to include the entire spectrum of folklore: customs, legends, proverbs, ceremonies, plays, dances, etc. His major undertaking was the geographically arranged folklore collection *Lud* (The folk), of which 33 volumes, containing over 10,000 melodies, were issued during his lifetime (1857–1889). In addition, Kolberg produced many ethnographies of regions of Poland not included in *Lud*, and upon his death he left thousands of pages of unedited manuscripts. These manuscripts, along with all of Kolberg's published works, were compiled and published by the Polish Folklore Society between 1961 and 1979. *Dzieła Wyszystkie* (Complete works) contains 66 volumes."

3. Spottswood, "The Sajewski Story."

4. " '*Górale*' (after *góra* = hill) technically refers to anyone living in Highland areas. It can be used, therefore, to refer to those living in any of the Highland areas of Poland—that is, not only those in the vicinity of the Tatra mountains but also the Sudetes, Gorce and Beskides, region of Pieniny, and so on. . . . '*Górale*' is the plural form (*Góral* = Highlander man; *Góralka* = Highlander woman). I adopt

the plural '*Górale*' to use as both noun and adjective in an effort to adopt a gender-neutral designation": Louise Wrazen "Traditional Music Performance among *Górale* in Canada," *Ethnomusicology* 35, no. 2 (1991): 175. In polka circles the male form *goral* is used as an adjective irrespective of gender, but we follow Wrazen's example and use the plural *gorale* as a gender-neutral adjective.

5. "Society music" is a major musical style as neglected in scholarship as the polka. Are Lester Lanin and Meyer Davis still alive? Do their bands and "sound" continue to serve the rich? Has anyone interviewed Duchin the Younger in New York City and counterparts in other cities; collected revelations and gossip from the sidemen; discussed with jet setters the selection of music for every occasion? What is the secret of the beat that makes the elite tap their feet? Is "society music" a restricted code? Why does it often sound like a Muzaked early Duke Ellington? What do "polka" and "society" have in common beyond the two-beat bounce? Have "rock" and "Latin" been successfully socialized by the society bands?

6. Kleeman, *Origins and Stylistic Development*, p. 122.

7. Ibid., pp. 122–23.

8. Ibid., p. 121. Richard K. Spottswood (personal communication, August 13, 1986) states that Leon's presence is noted in Victor's recording logs through 1928, so there is some question as to whether he died as early as 1923.

9. Spottswood, "The Sajewski Story," p. 157.

10. Chet Schafer Productions/Chicago Polkas SLP 2700.

11. Charles Keil interview with Alvin Sajewski, March 28, 1975, at Sajewski's Music Store in Chicago.

12. Kleeman, *Origins and Stylistic Development*, p. 114.

13. Ibid. p. 116. Kleeman uses the concepts "pitch" and "talent" in somewhat ethnocentric ways. The people of mountainous Epirus in northern Greece would almost certainly hear the *gorale* fiddlers as right on pitch, perfectly in tune; the music from the valleys of the world might sound out of pitch to them. It may take just as much talent, whatever that is (see Henry Kingsbury, *Music, Talent, and Performance: A Conservatory Cultural System* [Philadelphia: Temple University Press, 1988]), to sing without a vibrato as with one. Spottswood (personal communication, August 13, 1986) believes that Zielinski was "added to Dukla's records by Victor. His singing seems to be out of synch with the music."

14. Spottswood, "The Sajewski Story," pp. 141–42. The break-even point rose so swiftly after the war that by the early 1950s the major labels had abandoned the ethnic markets as unprofitable, even though thousands of records were being sold. Today you would probably have to persuade the

Columbia executive that the group could sell 50,000 albums (not singles) just to get a foot in the studio door.

15. Spottswood, "The Sajewski Story," pp. 143–44.

16. Listen to Folklyric Records 9026, *Polish-American Dance Music—The Early Recordings: 1927–33*, for examples of these predecessors.

17. Keil and Keil, "In Pursuit of Polka Happiness."

18. Folklyric Records 9026.

19. The oberek is a dance in 3/4 time, slightly faster than a waltz (a clever *Village Voice* writer once called it an "industrial-strength waltz"), and a small but important part of every Polish-American polka band's repertoire of "polkas, waltzes and obereks."

20. Spottswood, "The Sajewski Story," pp. 159–60.

21. Kleeman, *Origins and Stylistic Development*, pp. 123–25.

22. Milton Gordon, in *Assimilation in American Life: The Role of Race, Religion, and National Origins* (New York: Oxford University Press, 1964), 51–54, coined the term "eth-class" to emphasize that U.S. working-class experience and identity are always clothed in the cultural garb of a specific ethnicity. Our book is a study of how polka styles reflect this fusion of class and ethnic identities.

23. Charlie Keil interviewed Ed Krolikowski on October 14, 1975.

24. Spottswood (personal communication August 13, 1986) confirms Krolikowski's general chronology—Victor, 1929; Columbia, 1934–35—but notes that the big hit versions of "Dziadunio," "Baruska" and "Helena" came from Ed's April 5, 1940, recording session in New York.

25. Joe Lazarz was interviewed by Johny Prytko, February 11, 1971.

26. Max Ciesielski was interviewed by Charlie Keil on June 19, 1975, at his home on Sweet Ave. on Buffalo's East Side.

Chapter 2

1. This chapter was written by Charles Keil in 1976 and partially revised in 1986.

2. Walt Solek was interviewed several times by Charlie Keil in the mid-1970s. The extracts in this chapter are from October 16, 1975.

3. *Polak* means Polish man in Polish; "polack" is a racial slur. See note 5, Chapter 3.

4. Somewhere in the 1960s these terms for the style probably became interchangeable. The word "honky"—applied to the wilder, village style of polkas—may resonate differently for different people. It almost certainly comes originally from "hunky," short for Hungarian and, by extension, a slang slur for all Eastern European immigrants. But did this term come to describe the music before blacks started calling whites "honkies," or after? If after, then there is an ironic and defiant self-reference in the usage: "Yeah, we're honkies, and we have a soul music too." One Buffalo musician remembers his father saying of a wedding in Pennsylvania in the 1960s (probably before the black usage became common) that "they'll probably have one of those honky bands," meaning a little combo of three or four instruments. It is also possible that "honky" is short for "honky-tonk," the little "down and dirty" nightclubs referred to in the lyrics of both country-and-western and rhythm-and-blues songs. Or it may be onomatopoeic, as in honking trumpets, saxophones, clarinets—honking a horn of any kind. Whatever its etymology, today in the polka world "honky" refers to the very specific Li'l Wally instrumentation and beat of the early 1950s: heavy on the snare drum, concertina prominent, improvising trumpet and clarinet playing "by ear," and Polish lyrics sung "from the heart."

5. Like much of Wally's creative work, our interview taping in Florida (May 11–12, 1976) was done in a big burst of energy. I (Charlie Keil) took a lot of notes before, during, and after dinner with Jeanette and Wally. Themes for further development kept popping up in our conversation. Later at my hotel, Wally talked all through the night. We sipped at a bottle of scotch, smoked cigarettes, and popped cassettes in and out of the recorder until Wally left after dawn. Noticing that I looked a little tired, he said he would call Jeanette to pick him up and see me later in the afternoon. I hadn't yet fallen asleep when he phoned from the lobby to say he was ready to continue. So we went on through the morning with a little breakfast sent up, went down for lunch, back up for more taping and finally broke it off in midafternoon—around 4:00 P.M., as I recall. It was close to a thirty-hour interview (if you count the few tapes in preparation before dinner the day before)—a record, at least in my experience!

6. Wally and others usually speak of "the Lucky Stop." The sign over the door may have read "Lucky's Stop Inn," but that name is rarely used in conversation.

7. Charlie Keil interviewed Stas Przasnyski of the Connecticut Twins in July 1974.

8. See Charles Keil, "Participatory Discrepancies and the Power of Music," *Cultural Anthropology* 2, no. 3 (August 1987): 275–83.

9. Charlie Keil interviewed Happy Louie Dusseault on August 22, 1977.

10. Charlie Keil interviewed Bill Mahoney on August 22, 1977.

11. *Polka Concert*, Bel-Aire LP 3023.

Chapter 3

1. This chapter was written by Angeliki V. Keil in 1977 and revised in 1986 (the revision did not include bringing the story of the IPA up to date). Unless otherwise noted, the interviews for this chapter and Chapter 4 were obtained during the August 6–8, 1976, convention of the International Polka Association at the Red Carpet Inn, Milwaukee, Wisconsin.

2. The Polka Music Hall of Fame was established in 1968 and had its first inductees in 1969. The building at 4145 South Kedzie Avenue, Chicago, Illinois 60632, which houses the Polka Music Hall of Fame and Museum and the IPA offices, was dedicated in 1982. IPA publications can be obtained by writing to this address.

3. For a discussion of Polonian organizational activity, see Lopata, *Polish Americans*.

4. Emmons pioneered polka studies in *Economic and Political Leadership in Chicago's Polonia*. He apparently studied the International Polka Association (calling it the "Polka Federation" in the fashion of field researchers) and compared its members, as economic leaders, with a more traditional leaders' group (which he called the "Polish Association"). He notes (p. 2) that "the largest single Polish ethnic industry is the polka business and the Polka Federation has been promoting the economic and prestige mobility of the polka industry by patterning its activities after higher-status Polish associations and mainstream music cultures." His dissertation, an excellent study of the IPA as a Polonian organization, provides an introduction to the polka world as community and business (pp. 172–204).

5. We use quotation marks to emphasize once more that in reality there is nothing necessarily embarrassing or shameful about being called a *Polak*, which simply means "Polish male," just as *Polka* means Polish female. The term "polack," however (though pronounced exactly like the Polish self-reference), has been used by non-Poles as a racial slur: cf. "nigger," "dago," etc.

6. We remind readers (see Chapter 2, note 4) that the use of the ethnic slur "honky" as a self-reference of ethnic pride for hyphenated Americans of central European origin may have emerged from the process of ethnic affirmation that was initiated by the "black is beautiful" campaign of the 1960s, a model for the "New Ethnicity" movement of the 1970s.

7. *Polka Guide* 7, no. 4 (July–August 1965).

8. Samples of these publications may be obtained from the IPA (see note 2).

9. For example, Leon Kozicki appears as editor-publisher of the *Polka Guide* 6, no. 4 (July–August 1964): 2. On page 12 there is a listing for his Saturday WOPA *Parade of Polka Hits*, and Leon Kozicki and his Diamontones are listed as a Chicago polka band on page 20. Similarly, Eddie Blazonczyk, Dick Pillar, Chet Schafer, Johnny Hyzny, Chet Gulinski, Jimmy Sturr, to mention just a few, keep appearing on different pages in their multiple polka world capacities.

10. In *Polka Guide* 6, no. 4 (July–August 1964) and 7, no. 4 (July–August 1965), Dick Pillar from Connecticut writes the "New England Polka Brief Case" column; Jimmy Sturr reports from Florida, New York; Stan Skawinski offers "New Jersey Music Notes" and news from Meriden, Connecticut. In both issues, in addition to news from the Buffalo, New York, convention, there are small items from Pawtucket, Rhode Island; Muskegon, Michigan; South Boston, Massachusetts; Cleveland, Ohio; Philadelphia and Shenandoah, Pennsylvania; Binghamton, New York.

11. Polka programs on seven Chicago radio stations—WOPA, WTAQ, WSBC, WEDC, WJOB, WLOI, WIMS—and twenty-five polka disc jockeys are listed (among them, Johnny Hyzny, Chet Schafer, Li'l Wally, Joe and Jean Salomon, Leon Kozicki, Chet Gulinski). Most bands give just their name, leader, and phone number, but Eddie Blazonczyk and His Versatones, Johnny Hyzny and His Music Makers, the Casinos and Don Ptak, Sally Szymarek and His Polka Masters, Joe Pat and His Orchestra, Li'l Richard and His Shytones, Ted Bonk and the Polka Tops, Marion Lush and the Musical Stars provide dates and places where they are scheduled to appear during the two months between issues of the *Polka Guide*. Most of these gigs are weekend engagements for the polka spots in Chicago and nearby locations such as the State Line Tavern, and South Bend or Michigan City, Indiana. Blazonczyk's is the only band that lists more distant appearances: Twin Lakes, Wisconsin; Pittsburgh and Mount Pleasant, Pennsylvania; the polka convention in Buffalo, New York.

12. John Lewandowski, "The Aspirations of the Polka Guide," *Polka Guide* 7, no. 4 (July–August 1965): 2.

13. Ibid.

14. Leon Kozicki, "How the International Polka Association Began," souvenir program of the 1976 International Polka Convention and Festival, p. 6.

15. The traditional moonlight dance was incorporated

on Friday evening, and "to make the eastern polka fans feel at home, the committee is presenting the musical rage of Connecticut—Dick Pillar and his Orchestra. . . . The Saturday afternoon segment will consist of the convention meeting of the delegates. Admission to the meeting is restricted to polka DJs, musicians, proprietors of lounges and ballrooms, record company representatives, and other people affiliated with the polka music industry" ("Enthusiasm 'Greatest Ever' for Polka Convention," *Polka Guide* 6, no. 4 [July–August 1964]: 2).

16. Souvenir program, 1976 International Polka Convention and Festival, p. 6.

17. These are 1976 figures and may be a piece of folklore, since others do not recall these contributions.

18. Lopata, *Polish Americans*, pp. 8–11.

19. Kate Koperski's studies of Polish-American folk Catholicism demonstrate an "egalitarian thrust in a hierarchical world," as she puts it, that characterizes Polonian everyday behavior ("Easter People in a Christmas World," unpublished manuscript, 1987).

20. With a few exceptions such as Eddie Blazonczyk, whose interrelated enterprises make him one of the most successful, the polka professionals discussed here make their living through other full-time work. Income from polka activities is a welcome adjunct, but the limited economic impact of such activities on their overall livelihood helps allay fears that they will make decisions for the love of economic profit rather than on the basis of aesthetic, recreational, and community values.

21. There is no question that the IPA is de facto a Polish-American organization asserting and providing leadership to a polka world that in practice includes the American traditions of many central European ethnics. The strongest American polka tradition, however, is probably the Texas-Mexican one. It is well represented in Chicago, where a great many Chicanos live, often in the old Polonian neighborhoods that were partially abandoned by Poles leaving for the suburbs. The Polka Hall of Fame and the bands playing at IPA dances show a sprinkling of Slovenian, German, and Czech-Bohemian names. No Mexican name has come to our attention, although the Polka Family, a Polish/Mexican band that is the result of a Polish/Mexican marriage, has now emerged as a major new force in the polka scene. This must be attributed to the cumulative effects of racism that keep groups divided by race socially distant, even though they may be united by class, religion, spatial proximity, and the polka. As a marker of ethnic identity, the polka requires the specificity and well-demarcated boundaries of an ethnic com-

munity in order to be confirmed ritually again and again. Yet it is a symbol of ethnic conviviality, and so these boundaries can be stretched to include people from the culture areas of central and eastern Europe. So far, the symbolic realm of the IPA's polka world has not moved beyond the major divisions that plague the wider society.

22. Reprinted in *IPA News* 5, no. 7 (July 1975).

Chapter 4

1. This chapter, written by Angeliki V. Keil, describes the 1976 IPA convention in Milwaukee. Since 1983 the convention and festival have been held in Chicago.

2. "Why? Because I Love You Polka," from *More Country Flavored Polkas*, vol. 2, Bel-Aire Records LP 3021.

3. In a polka Mass the traditional singing is replaced by polka and oberek tunes while keeping the texts of the liturgy. Improvised polka Masses popped up in many locales in the late 1960s and early 1970s. Around Chicago, Father Perkovic—a Slovenian priest in a Slovenian-Croatian parish in Evelet, Minnesota—was considered the originator. Chet Schafer said: "Father Wally Szczypula, the chaplain of the IPA, heard about it and brought it to the attention of the IPA and said that here in the convention we have all the people who come from all around, and if we had a polka Mass it would fulfil their Sunday Mass obligation. This was 1972 when the convention was in the Red Carpet Inn in Milwaukee. So Szczypula got after Joe Pat Paterek and Joe Pat got after me and I talked to my daughter who was in the music school in De Paul University. How can we take the liturgy and put polka tunes to it? So we started having skull sessions every second Wednesday in my home. What songs shall we use here and there? And by October we had a Mass" (personal communication, March 13, 1992).

4. A "lawn fete" is a weekend fund-raising mini-carnival. Most of the Polish-American Catholic parishes in the Buffalo area sponsor one each summer, and it is a great place for beginning polka bands to gain experience.

5. "Opening Theme Polka," from *Polka Concert*, Bel-Aire LP 3023, 1975.

6. "Sweet Bippy Polka," from *Polka Spotlight*, Bel-Aire LP 3025, 1976.

7. "Judy Polka," from *Polka Spotlight*.

8. "I Love Everybody Waltz," from *Polka Spotlight*.

9. "My Mary Lou Polka," from *Polka Concert*.

10. In more recent years all-girl bands such as the Polish Peaches (out of Ohio) and Renata and Girls (featured in the

Les Blank film *In Heaven There Is No Beer*) have gained a lot of popularity. The Irene Olszewski Orchestra, a woman leading four men, is the subject of an unpublished master's thesis by Mary Spalding, "The Irene Olszewski Orchestra: A Connecticut Band" (Wesleyan University, 1986). The few women who have emerged as regular singers and instrumentalists in otherwise male bands appear to be accepted on their merits as musicians, but their numbers are still too small to suggest a trend.

11. See Jane Ellen Harrison, *Themis: A Study of the Social Origins of Greek Religion* (Cleveland: World, 1962), p. xv.

Chapter 5

1. Parts of this chapter, written by Charles Keil, are adapted from "Slovenian Style in Milwaukee," in *Folk Music and the Modern Sound*, ed. William Ferris and Mary L. Hart (Jackson: University Press of Mississippi, 1982), pp. 32–59. All the interviews with Jimmy Maupin, the old-timer, D. P. Winkler, and Louie Bashell took place during June 20–23, 1976.

2. Quoted in Norbert Blei, "The Long, Lusty Reign of Franky the First," *Chicago Tribune Magazine*, April 13, 1971, p. 42.

3. See Keil and Keil, "In Pursuit of Polka Happiness."

4. See Charles Keil, *Tiv Song* (Chicago: University of Chicago Press, 1979), pp. 6–7.

5. We have kept the German terms for these areas, Steiermark and Kreinmark, because they were under Austro-Hungarian control during the period when most of the Slovenes who came to Milwaukee were emigrating, bringing their sectional rivalries with them. Today these areas are called Stajerska and Krajnska.

6. See Mary Douglas's insightful summary of Basil Bernstein's early work in her *Natural Symbols: Explorations in Cosmology* (New York: Pantheon, 1970).

7. These recollections are adapted from Richard Blau, "Polka Soul," *Insight* (now *Wisconsin*, the *Milwaukee Journal* magazine), December 18, 1977.

8. "Let the Sun Shine In" from *The Golden Brass*. Steljo 718.

Chapter 6

1. This chapter, written largely by Charles Keil, incorporates a Larry Trojak interview by Bill Falkowski.

2. The following paragraphs are adapted from Charles Keil, "The Whole Buffalo Polka Band Catalogue," *Courier Express Magazine*, July 25, 1976, pp. 4 7, 9.

3. Cheektowaga, a suburb adjacent to the East Side of Buffalo, has a high concentration of Polish-American residents. The International Polka Convention took place there in 1965 as the IPA was getting established (see Chapters 3 and 4).

4. Edwin's Music Store, 1515 Broadway in Buffalo, continues to make available instruments, published music, an efficient repair service, and music lessons by accomplished professionals—in the best Polish-American music store tradition.

5. "Chopin's" (at 18 Kosciusko Street) refers to the club rooms of Chopin's Singing Society, a venerable mixed chorus of the Buffalo Polonia.

6. *Golabki* (plural) means literally "little pigeons" and refers to the stuffed cabbage rolls characteristic of Polish cuisine. *Kielbasa* is Polish sausage. Most of us not fortunate enough to have a live connection with Polish culture know it in its standardized supermarket form; Polish-American families honor their own heirloom recipes, and holiday kielbasa with special spices is at the center of traditional feasting.

7. On Christmas eve when the first star appears, Polish-American families sit at a traditional meatless meal with an uneven number of dishes—the *Wigilia*. Most families have twelve dishes for the twelve apostles and one for the unknown visitor, who might come through the door that is left invitingly ajar for that purpose. Families take care to invite those who may be alone that night. First the celebrants share the *oplatek*, a ritual wafer in the shape and size of a postcard, stamped with the nativity scene. Pink *oplatek* were shared with the farm animals, and *oplatek* were sent through the mails between Poland and the United States, keeping divided families ritually intact. Kate Koperski (*Ritual Renewal: Polish-American Easter Traditions*, exhibition catalogue, Niagara University, Niagara Falls, N.Y., 1989) remembers her grandfather telling her on Christmas eve when she was a little girl that "Poles all over the world are sharing *oplatek* when they see the first star tonight" and her awe as her imagination stretched in communion with all the Polish souls around the globe. The *Wigilia* ends as the family prepares to attend the Midnight Mass of the Nativity. A festive meal with meat is served at a Christmas party after Mass.

8. Manny Fried, *Elegy for Stanley Gorski* (Buffalo: Textile Bridge Press/Labor Arts Books, 1970).

9. According to Kate Koperski, *Ritual Renewal*, pp. 6–7: "The word *dyngus* is probably derived from the German

dingen: 'to buy back or redeem.' . . . The playful switching of young women evolved from the ancient belief that touching a woman with new growth imparted the budding branch's fertility to her. In Poland, pussywillow branches were favored for this rite. In a related custom, young women were doused with water on Easter Monday in some parts of the country." The custom was brought over to the New World. Koperski quotes an old Polish-American man's description of the celebration at the turn of the century in Buffalo's Polonia: "All the aunts and uncles in our families would try to induce us to come over on *Dyngus Day* and whip their daughters' lower legs with the twig. We'd start out real early in the morning so we could make as many stops as possible, because for each house we visited we'd get five cents or so to share for 'dyngusing' the girls. The girls would sort of go along with it. Of course, they were screaming and running around, so we tried not to hit them too hard." In Buffalo the custom had almost died out when it was "revived" in the early 1970s by the Chopin Singing Society and the merchants on the East Side. Contemporary Dyngus celebrants, starting at noon, engage in major drinking and bar-hopping in the old neighborhood. Polka music has become central to the Dyngus Day revival.

10. This and the next two sections are adapted from Charles Keil, "The Dyna-Tones: A Buffalo Polka Band in Performance, in Rehearsal, and on Record," *New York Folklore* 10, nos. 3–4 (Summer–Fall 1984): 336–49.

11. In 1976–77 the Dyna-Tones were Dave "Scrubby" Seweryniak, concertina and vocals; Bill Barnas, bass; Roger Nowaczyk, sax, clarinet, and vocals; John Kilian, trumpet; Bob Wroblewski, trumpet; Stas Malkiewicz, violin; Larry

Trojak, drums and vocals. The Grill came to an end in a fire in December 1990, but polka music had not been featured there for several years before that.

12. Charles Keil, *Urban Blues* (Chicago: University of Chicago Press, 1966, 1991), p. 93.

13. WAM Records 4039.

14. WAM Records 4032.

15. WAM Records 4050.

16. Kate Koperski's short story "Passion Play," *Echology*, no. 2 (1988): 86–88, explores these themes in children's lives.

17. WAM Records 4067. The other Dyna-Tones on this album are Al Piatkowski, accordion, concertina; Chris Gawlak, trumpet; Mike Evan, trumpet; Dave "Nigel" Kurdziel, Rickenbacker bass.

18. See Friedrich Nietzsche, *The Birth of Tragedy from the Spirit of Music*, in *The Philosophy of Nietzsche* (New York: Modern Library, 1954). See also Charles Keil, "Applied Ethnomusicology and a Rebirth of Music from the Spirit of Tragedy," *Ethnomusicology* 26, no. 3 (September 1982): 407–11.

19. See Charles Keil, "People's Music Comparatively: Style and Stereotype, Class and Hegemony," *Dialectical Anthropology* 10 (1985): 119–30.

20. These recollections were written by Angeliki V. Keil in 1975.

Epilogue

1. The Epilogue was written by Angeliki V. Keil.

Chicago, 1988.

Select Discography

This select yet varied list of records, compiled in consultation with local experts, is intended as a sampler for anyone who wants to hear what has been going on in Polish-American polka music from the 1920s to 1990. You might think of these records as the core set that a disc jockey needs in order to handle requests and dedications from discerning fans in Buffalo. The "Roots" group is probably too old for airplay these days, but it is surprising how much historical depth and geographic breadth there is in the programming of contemporary Buffalo disc jockeys.

This list attempts the impossible: presenting a rough chronological order while illustrating styles and highlighting the differences in local "echologies." The truth is that every band whose members play together for a few years represents a unique polka style that has co-evolved to fit its ecological niche. It is also true that every band since the 1920s, having a wealth of polka records to learn and borrow from, has transformed every borrowing to fit the band's style and local tastes. So, for example, this discography compiled in Buffalo does not contain classic records by Chicago greats Steve Adamczyk and Johnny Bomba, perhaps because their styles sound more "Eastern" than "Chicago" to our ears, whereas bands in the East that adapted mainstream developments in Chicago—Zima to Wally to Lush to Blazonczyk— do rate a heading of their own. In other words, if a scholar, a disc jockey, and a band leader in Cleveland or Hartford got together to compile a discography, it would be a very different list.

Roots

Polish-American Dance Music—The Early Recordings: 1927–33. Folklyric Records 9026.

Starokrajskie Wesele: John Zurawski and the Old Country Village Musicians. Chet Schafer Productions/Chicago Polkas SLP 2700.

Marisha Data. *Polish Song Favorites*. Sajewski LP 8882.

Eddie Blazonczyk, Chet Kowalkowski, and the Polish Mountaineers. *Po Staru Krajsku*, vols. 1 and 2. Bel-Aire 3004 and 3007.

47th St. Concertina Club. *Pod Nogi Favorites*. Chicago Polkas 7603.

Eastern Style

Frank Wojnarowski. *Jedzie Boat*. Dana 1220.
———. *Matka*. Dana 1202.
Bernie Witkowski. *World's Greatest Polka Band*. Stella 900.
Ray Henry. *Ray Henry*. REX 816.
Walt Solek. *The Clown Prince of Polka*. Dana D598-12.
Gene Wisniewski. *Polskie Dziewczklynki*. Dana DLP 1272.
Connecticut Twins. *Holiday in Poland*. Stella SLP 926.
———. *My Girl Duda*. Stella 917.
Ray Budzilek. *Polish Songs Mama Never Taught Me*. Roulette 25266.
Bud Hudenski and the Corsairs. *Power Packed Polkas*. WAM 4071.
Jimmy Sturr. *I Remember Warsaw*. Starr 561.
———. *Million Dollar Polkas* (with Walt Solek and Gene Wisniewski). Bruno Dean Enterprises. BD 516/517.

Chicago and Honky Style

Eddie Zima. *Zima Favorites*. Jay Jay 5033.
———. *Circus Polka*. Dana 1207.
Li'l Wally. *Sings No Beer in Heaven*. Jay Jay 5079.
———. *Polka Party with Little Wally*. Jay Jay 5147.
———. *Beautiful Polka Music*. Jay Jay 5023.
Ampol-Aires. *Polish Picnic*. Ampol Records 5006.
Marion Lush. *Na Zdrowie*. Dyno DLP 1606.
———. *An Evening with Marion Lush*. Dyno LP 1632.
———. *Polka Time*. Dyno DSLP 1611.
Eddie Blazonczyk. *Polkas a Plenty*. Bel-Aire LP 3013.
———. *Honky Style*, vol. 1. Bel-Aire LP 3017.
———. *Country Flavored Polkas*. Bel-Aire LP 3018.

Buffalo

Walt Jaworski and Eddie Olinski. *Two Guys from Buffalo*. Dala Records 336.
New Yorkers. *Hello Dolly and 11 Other Favorites*. PAN 2100.
Krew Brothers. *A Lively Polka Session*. Steljo SLP 715.
———. *Yes, We Are All Brothers*. WAM 4037.
G-Notes. *At Last*. WAM 4029.

Dyna-Tones. *Six Million Dollar Band*. WAM 4032.
———. *Down at the Friendly Tavern*. WRS 20039.
———. *Chapter VII*. WAM 4050.
———. *Live Wire*. WAM 4067.
Wanda and Stephanie. *Entertainment Just for You*. Bel-Aire 4048.
Modernaires. *The Modernaires*. WAM 4028.
Sunshine. *Polka Life*. Sunshine SN103.
Happy Richie. *Strike It Happy . . . Strike It Rich*. Jen J100.
Steel City Brass. *Through the Looking Glass*. Bel-Aire 4067.
Two recent albums by the PFC Players, *Polkas for Children* (Sunshine LP 104, 1987) and *A Kolberg Sampler* (PCCB 1081, 1990), deserve special mention because they are well-documented efforts to create new polkas from traditional resources as part of a cultural program. They are available from the Polish Community Center, 1081 Broadway, Buffalo, NY 14212.

Chicago

Stas Galonka and the Chicago Masters. *Hooked on Honky*. WRS 20082.
Eddie Blazonczyk. *Polka Hits*. Bel-Aire 3020.
———. *Polka Spotlight*. Bel-Aire 3025.
Lenny Gomulka and the Chicago Push. *A Twelve Pack of Polkas*. Bel-Aire 4059.
Ampol Aires. *One More Time*. Ampol 5031.
Windy City Brass. *Windy City Brass IV*. Starr 559.
Little Richard. *To All the Polka Fans*. Aleatoric A4016.
Casey Siewierski. *Let's Dance to . . .* Chicago Polkas LP7201.
The Naturals. *Polka Sound of the 70s*. Chicago Polkas LP4000.
The Tones. *Polkas from the Heart of Chicago*. Ampol 5009.

Cleveland

Joe Oberaitis. *Mr. Polka Dynamite*. Delta International 7037.
———. *Past, Present, Future*. Kerebo 20004.
The Brass Connection. *Got No Reason*. LeMans 119.

Detroit

Dynasticks. *Take Another Look*. Ampol 5029.
Dyna Dukes. *Not Your Average Polka Band*. DJRC 1002.

Minnesota

Bill Czerniak and Polka Soul. *On and On*. Aleatoric A 2006.
Mrozinski Brothers. *In Session*. Aleatoric A 1003.

Canada

Canadian Fiddlestix. *Half Na Pol*. WAM 4040.
The Polish-Canadians. *Days of Wine and Polkas*. Ray RRSLP 2006.

Pittsburgh

Henny and the Versa Jays. *Home Style Polkas*. WAM 5061.
Ray Jay and the Carousels. *Here's to You*. WAM 4069.
Trel Tones. *Celebrating 25 Years*. WAM 4055.
The Sounds. *Open Up Your Heart*. WAM 4052.

Pennsylvania/Ohio

Touch of Brass. *A Touch of Brass*. Peppermint Presents PP 1432.
Pennsylvania Merrymakers. *Let's Have a Polka Picnic*. Starr LP 537.
Polish Friends. *Just between Friends*. WAM 4054.
Polka Happiness. *Here's to You*. WAM 4064.
Stanky and the Coalminers. *Polkas Good to the Last Drop*. Stan-Dot DK410.

Geographically Eastern but Chicago Style

Happy Louie. *Best of Happy Louie*. Rex RLP 724.
———. *Fantasy Time*. Halo 5011.
———. *Red Hot Polkas*. Dyno 5002.
Dick Pillar. *Polkabration 25*. Steljo 729.

New Brass. *Roll Out the Barrel*. WAM 4035.

Jersey Polka Richie. *Presents Concertina Happiness*. Star Note SNR1631.

Bay State IV. *Our First One*. Polka Train 8201.

The Boys from Baltimore. *The Boys Are Back*. LeMans LPC 88.

Magitones. *Made in New York*. WAM 4063.

Recent "Push" Style

The Dynasticks. *Back on Track*. WRS 20100.

Eddie Blazonczyk. *Polka Music Is Here to Stay*. Bel-Aire 3034.

Lenny Gomulka and the Chicago Push. *Join the Polka Generation*. WRS 20092.

Bay State IV. *Salute to the Polka Stars*. Polka Train 8401.

Dyna-Tones. *Live Wire II*. WRS 20086.

Record Companies

Some of the albums listed above are out of print; indeed Stella and Dana LPs are becoming collector's items. Here are the available current addresses for the record companies listed.

Aleatoric, 725 Harriet Ave., St. Paul, MN 55112.

Ampol, c/o Bel-Aire, 7208 S. Harlem Ave., Bridgeview, IL 60455.

Bel-Aire, 7208 S. Harlem Ave., Bridgeview, IL 60455.

Bruno Dean Enterprises, P.O. Box 471, Rye, NY 10580.

Chicago Polkas, Box 7901, Chicago, IL 60680.

Dyno, c/o World Renowned Sounds, Box 91906. Cleveland, OH 44101.

Ha-Lo, 154 River St., Palmer, MA 01069.

Jay Jay, Box 4155, Normandy Branch, Miami Beach, FL 33141.

LeMans, Box 24, Belle Mead, NJ 08502.

Peppermint, 803 E. Indianola Ave., Youngstown, OH 44502.

Polish Community Center, 1081 Broadway, Buffalo, NY 14212.

Polka Train, Box 934, N. Elizabeth Station, Elizabeth, NJ 07208.

Ray, Box 128, Columbus, NE 68601.

Rex, 34 Martin St., Holyoke, MA 01040.

Stan-Dot, 410 Espy St., Nanticoke, PA 18634.

Star Note, 163 Starmond Ave., Clifton, NJ 07013.

Starr, Box 1, Florida, NY 10921.

Steljo, Box 305, Uncasville, CN 06382.

Stella, Box 84, Hillside, NJ 07205.

Sunshine, 22 Freund St., Buffalo, NY 14211

WAM, c/o World Renowned Sounds, Box 91906, Cleveland, OH 44101.

WRS (World Renowned Sounds), Box 91906, Cleveland, OH 44101.

Permissions

Text

Chapter 1: Portions of Charles Keil and Angeliki Keil, "In Pursuit of Polka Happiness," *Cultural Correspondence* 5 (Summer–Fall 1977), are used with the kind permission of the publisher.

Chapter 2: The quotes of Li'l Wally from his interviews with Charlie Keil are used with the permission of Walter E. Jagiello.

Chapter 4: Lyrics to the song "Why? Because I Love You" by Buddy Alan, copyright © 1973 Tree Publishing Co., Inc. (all rights administered by Sony Music Publishing, 8 Music Square, West, Nashville, TN 37203), are used with the permission of Sony Music Publishing. Lyrics to the song "Opening Theme Polka" by Lenny Gomulka are used with the kind permission of Pulaski Publishers. Lyrics to the song "Sweet Bippy Polka," Chicago Polka Music Publishing Co., a division of Chet Schafer Productions, are used with the kind permission of the publisher. Lyrics to the song "Judy Polka" by Tony Krupski are used with the kind permission of the author. Lyrics to "My Mary Lou Polka" by Eddie Blazonczyk are used with the kind permission of Pulaski Publishers.

Chapter 5: A revised version of Charles Keil, "Slovenian Style in Milwaukee," in *Folk Song and Modern Sound*, William Ferris and Mary L. Hart, eds., is used with the kind permission of the University Press of Mississippi. Lyrics to the song "Let the Sunshine In," written by B. Czupta, 1971, Jaybil Publishers, BMI (members of the Golden Brass band: Michael "Mitch" Biskup, Bill Czupta, Roger Lichwala, Carl Haynoski, Steve Dudas, Tom Kostek), are used with the kind permission of Michael S. Biskup. A revised version of Richard Blau, "Polka Soul," *Insight*, December 18, 1977, is used with the kind permission of the *Milwaukee Journal*.

Chapter 6: A revised version of Charles Keil, "The Dyna-Tones: A Buffalo Polka Band in Performance, in Rehearsal, and on Record," *New York Folklore* 10, nos. 3–4 (Summer–Fall 1984), is used with the kind permission of the New York Folklore Society, Inc. The text of an interview with Larry Trojak by Bill Falkowski is used with the kind permission of Bill Falkowski. Lyrics to the song "We're But a Moment," as recorded by the Dyna-Tones, are used with the kind permission of the author, Larry Trojak. Lyrics to the songs contained on the album *Chapter VII*, as recorded by the Dyna-Tones, are used with the kind permission of the author, Larry Trojak. Lyrics to the song "Mr. Bartender" by Walter E. Jagiello are used with the kind permission of the author and Jay Jay BMI.

Photographs

Photographs not listed below are by Dick Blau.

Photographs by Charles Keil are on pages 39, 40, 44, 45, 59, 65, 67, 164, 165, 177, 191, and 194.

Page 9: Cartoon from *Punch* 7 (1844): 172. Reproduced by permission of *Punch*.

Page 11: Lithograph from *A History of Dancing*, Vuillier, Paris, p. 312.

Page 11: *Punch* cartoon from *Punch* 8 (1845): 86. Reproduced by permission of *Punch*.

Page 12: Dessin de M. Morin, grave par M. Moller. From *Paris Guide* vol. 2, Librairie Internationale, Paris, 1867, facing p. 992.

Page 13: *(left)*: From *Illustrated London News*, April 27, 1844, p. 280.

Page 13: *(right)*: Vuillier, p. 296.

Page 15: Courtesy of Jim Griffith.

Page 18: From the Roman Kwasniewski Collection, Milwaukee Urban Archives, Golda Meir Library, University of Wisconsin, Milwaukee.

Page 20: In Kazimierz Saysse-Tobiczyk: *Pod wierchami Tatr*, Warsaw, 1956, p. 157. Courtesy of Urszula Czartoryska, Muzeum Sztuki w Lodzi.

Page 22: Courtesy of Chet Schafer.

Page 25: Courtesy of General Electric Company and Sandra Zych.

Page 28: Courtesy of Gloria K. Furney.

Page 31: Sicienski Studio, Wilkes Barre, Pennsylvania. Courtesy of Chet Schafer and Lucian Kryger.

Page 33: Courtesy of Max Ciesielski.

Page 35: Courtesy of Doc Penkson.

Page 37: Courtesy of Chet Schafer.

Page 38 *(bottom)*: Courtesy of John Stanky.

Page 41: Courtesy of Walt Solek.

Page 43 *(left)*: James J. Kriegsmann. Courtesy of Chet Schafer.

Page 43 *(right)*: Courtesy of the International Polka Association.

Page 46 *(left)*: Courtesy of the International Polka Association.

Page 46 *(right)*: Courtesy of Li'l Wally.

Page 50: Joseph F. Koperski. Courtesy of Kate Koperski.

Page 51: Courtesy of Alvin Sajewski and Sandra Zych.

Page 57: Courtesy of Li'l Wally.

Page 68: Courtesy of Eddie Blazonczyk.

Page 69: Courtesy of Eddie Blazonczyk.

Page 87: Courtesy of Chet Schafer.

Page 130: Courtesy of Jimmy Maupin.

Page 142 *(right)*: Courtesy of Louie Bashell.

Page 168 *(right)*: Courtesy of Bel-Aire Records.

Page 181: Courtesy of WAM Records.

Name Index

219